The Lineages and Composition
of Gurkha Regiments
in British Service

FIRESTEP
Books

www.firesteppublishing.com

The Lineages and Composition
of Gurkha Regiments
in British Service

FireStep Books
An imprint of FireStep Publishing

Gemini House
136-140 Old Shoreham Road
Brighton
BN3 7BD

www.firesteppublishing.com

© 2013 The Gurkha Museum

First published in this format by FireStep Books,
an imprint of FireStep Publishing, in association with
The Gurkha Museum, 2013

A CIP catalogue reference for this book is
available in the British Library.

ISBN 978-1-908487-41-4

Cover design FireStep Publishing
Typeset by FireStep Publishing

Printed and bound in Great Britain

The Lineages and Composition of Gurkha Regiments in British Service

The following notes contain a description of all units in British Service which have enlisted Gurkhas at some period. The origins and class composition of these units is given where known, and in the lineage lists the authorities for changes of title are quoted where they can be found.

Help was received from many people in researching the data for this work, in particular

Captain A P Coleman	1 GR
Colonel D R Wood MBE	2 GR
Lieutenant Colonel A A Mains	9 GR
Major General D K Palit VrC	9 GR
D F Harding, Esq, MA	10 GR
Lieutenant Colonel M C Barrett OBE	QG Sigs
Lieutenant Colonel A L Bridger OBE	QOGLR
Colonel J R Cawthorne	QOGLR
Brian Stevens, Esq	
Tony McClenaghan, Esq, BEM, JP	
Richard Head, Esq	
Captain Ashok Nath	
Gavin Edgerley-Harris, Esq	

The many revisions and amendments to the text could not have been completed without the patience and commitment of Arminel Tottle at the Gurkha Museum.

John Chapple

J L CHAPPLE

March 1978
Revised May 1982, September 1984 and May 1997
Second Edition March 2010
Revised May 2012

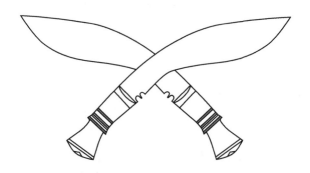

CONTENTS

PART 1 - LINEAGES, COMPOSITION AND TOTALS

PART 2 - LINEAGE LISTS OF GURKHA REGIMENTS AND UNITS

LINEAGE LISTS OF GURKHA REGIMENTS (Continued)

LINEAGE LISTS OF GURKHA REGIMENTS (Continued)

THE LINEAGES - EXPLANATORY NOTES

THE AUTHORITIES

The titles of Gurkha Regiments in British Service have been subject to frequent changes and those given in the lineage lists which follow are based on the best authorities that can still be found.

The various series of orders in use during the 19th Century reflect the administration of military affairs, with its insistence that final control lay with the civil authority. The Commander-in-Chief who sat as a member of the Governor-General's Council, was essentially the head of the military executive and his orders (GOCC) are mainly concerned with training, discipline, promotion, etc. Policy decisions lay with the Governor-General (later the Viceroy) and his orders (GGO or GOGG) are normally on less mundane topics. In practice, though, there was much overlapping. The system was rationalized in the 1880s to a single run of General Orders (GO) retitled Indian Army Orders (IAO) after the amalgamation of the three Presidency Armies in 1901.

There are also Gazette of India (G of I) notifications, and after 1948 there are London Gazette (LG) notifications and Army Orders (AO) and later Defence Council Instructions (DCI). In some cases there will be letters and establishments issued by Headquarters Far East Land Forces (HQ FARELF or FE); or by HQ British Forces Hong Kong (HQLF or HQBF); or by the relevant branch of the Ministry of Defence, such as Headquarters Director of Infantry (HQ D INF) or Army Staff Duties (ASD) or the Adjutant General's Branch (AG or PS).

All the above constitute, in one form or another, a proper authority. However there are numerous other official documents which reflect changes of title and which should be correct. The most common of these are the Army Lists, published at frequent intervals, and which give an indication of the current title at the time of publication, although they are not properly speaking an authority for this title.

THE SPELLING

The spelling of the titles is first of many difficulties. In the early days there was little general agreement about the correct transliteration of Devnagri script. There was also considerable inconsistency in the staff work. There are cases of the same word being spelt differently in the same document.

The word 'Gurkha' is the best example of this. In its earliest romanised form it seems to have been spelt as 'Gorka', then for a period it became 'Goorkah' or 'Goorka', followed by 'Goorkha', which is the form found throughout most of the 19th Century. In 1891 there was an official revision of all romanised transliterations, and from that date the official spelling in use in British Service has been 'Gurkha'. The Indian Army, shortly after Independence, changed their official spelling to 'Gorkha' to conform to that used in Nepal. There are other spellings such as 'Ghurka', which are sometimes found, but these are often printer's errors. Between 1902 and 1915 the Army Lists show an acute accent on the 'u' of Gurkha. In the lineage lists, the spelling which was contemporary with the authority has been used. There is even confusion over this because subsequent publications such as Army Lists always use the spelling at the date of publication, and they alter all the previous spellings to conform.

THE TITLES

Apart from the published authorities, there are a number of other sources which give the titles of units at certain times and these in some cases do not conform to those given by the contemporary authorities. Thus on two sets of old Colours of the Sirmoor Battalion (later 2nd Gurkha Rifles) the words 'Sirmoor Light Infantry' appear. This was never the official title of the regiment at any time. The only explanation is that all local infantry were thought of as light infantry, being dressed and equipped accordingly. Again there is an early belt plate of about 1815 with the words 'Sirmur Battalion', although this may not be genuine. At no time does the spelling 'Sirmur' seem to have been authorised, although incidentally it should have changed to this spelling in 1891 to conform to the revised romanised script. Why it did not do so is a mystery. It is still officially spelt with the double 'oo'. The Indian State of Sirmoor did change its spelling to Sirmur in the early 1900s.

The next problem is to decide whether to include the definite article as part of the regiment's title or not. The authorities use it haphazardly, sometimes with and sometimes without an initial capital letter. The current British Army official usage is to include the definite article as part of the title of the regiment when the title is a name only (e.g. The Queen's Gurkha Engineers), but not when the title is preceded by a number (e.g. '10th Princess Mary's Own Gurkha Rifles'). This does not always follow consistently however, thus The Queen's Own Gurkha Engineers has the word 'The' as part of their official title, whereas the Queen's Gurkha Signals does not.

A small point which occurs at different times is where the apostrophe after the title 'Prince of Wales' should be placed. This affects three Gurkha regiments at different times. There is no consistency in the documents and the spelling used in the lineage lists has been taken as it appears in the authorities.

The last major difficulty is to decide what properly forms part of the regiment's title. In two instances there is some confusion. First, from 1823 until 1850, all local battalions were numbered consecutively as local units, and this numbering does not really form part of the regiment's title. Thus the '1st Nusseri Battalion' (later to become 1st Gurkha Rifles) became in 1823 the 6th Local Battalion, and was shown as the '6th, 1st Nusseri Battalion' in various documents. For the purpose of lineages given here this is the usage included. Secondly, any regular (as opposed to local or irregular) regiment in the old East India Company's armies was correctly titled by a number followed by the words 'Regiment, Native Infantry'; thus '66th Regiment, Native Infantry'. However, to distinguish between the Armies of the three Presidencies, the more commonly used titles in historical documents would include the name of the Presidency, thus '66th Regiment of Bengal Native Infantry'. This is generally abbreviated to '66 BNI'. It is probably true to say that inside the Presidency, the name of that Presidency was not used, but elsewhere in India it was invariably added. Since the authorised title was normally given in Presidency Lists, the official gazettes omit the name of the Presidency. Separate Presidency Armies were abolished in 1901. The word 'Native' in regimental titles was discontinued officially in January 1885.

PRECEDENCE

In the Indian Army, precedence was always taken from the date that a regiment became a regular unit. There were many reorganisations of the Indian Army up to 1947 and the numbers subsequently allotted to regiments do not necessarily reflect their order of seniority or precedence. Thus the 9th Gurkha Rifles was the senior Gurkha Regiment although not the earliest raised and not a Gurkha regiment at all until sometime after it was raised. In some old Indian Army regiments there was even a different precedence between battalions, but this principle does not seem to have been applied to Gurkha regiments who took their precedence as a whole from that granted to the senior element of the regiment. Thus the 2nd Battalion 8th Gurkha Rifles, although the oldest 2nd Battalion by direct descent is not accorded precedence above other 2nd Battalions. Similarly the 2nd Battalion, 7th Gurkha Rifles, although raised from 2nd Battalion, 10th Gurkha Rifles was accorded precedence above it. There are probably two reasons why Gurkha regiments did not follow the practice of other Indian infantry regiments in this respect. First, the earliest 2nd Battalions were raised in 1886, well before the 1903 and 1922 reorganisations of the rest of the Indian Army (and from which the custom of battalion precedence stemmed). Secondly, the majority of Gurkha regiments (all except the 8th and 7th Gurkha Rifles) raised their 2nd Battalions from their 1st Battalions, unlike the remainder of the post 1922 Indian Infantry, each of whose battalion perpetuated a completely distinct regiment.

DIRECT AND INDIRECT DESCENT

In direct descent are those units which continued their corporate existence despite changes of title, status and composition. However, it was often the case that a new corps was raised, or an irregular or local regiment transferred in, to replace a disbanded regular regiment. Sometimes this new corps inherited the place in the line of the old corps, and in some cases they also took, or could have assumed, the honours and precedence of the disbanded unit. These do not constitute regiments in direct descent although in the lineage lists there are notes to show the history of units whose place was taken by a Gurkha regiment.

THE GURKHAS OR GORKHALIS

In 1769, the Army of Prithwi Narayan Shah from the kingdom of Gorkha (in West Central Nepal) overran the Valley of Nepal and gradually gained control of the whole country.

Their dominions increased considerably over the following decades until they covered large areas of Garhwal and Kumaon and came up against the expanding empire of the Honourable East India Company. This clash led eventually to the Nepal War of 1814-1815, and it is from this date that the enlistment of Gurkhas in British Service began, although there is some evidence that men who would later be described as Gurkhas may well have been enlisted in local battalions from 1813.

The Army of Nepal was generally called the Gurkha Army, taking its name from the original kingdom of Gorkha. In time the term came to be applied to all the martial races of Nepal, and in the early days it also covered any other people who were enlisted or impressed into the forces of Nepal. The term Gurkha still has a military connotation, particularly in British usage.

ORGANISATION OF MILITARY FORCES

In British India in the early 19th Century, there were a few King's Regiments of the British Army, and three separate Presidency Armies in each of the East India Company's Presidencies of Madras, Bengal and Bombay. The Bengal Presidency was already assuming a dominant role with the largest area and greatest forces.

The Company's Armies had both regular European and Native Regiments. They also had many other military forces, including irregulars, local forces, and levies. These were often raised for specific tasks such as defence of a particular district, or for a particular campaign. Many such regiments had only an erratic existence, but those which survived were usually incorporated into the Regular Army sooner or later.

BRITISH SERVICE

This is taken to be service in the armies of the Honourable East India Company, the Army of India up to 1947, and the British Army since 1st January 1948.

THE REGIMENTS AND THEIR COMPOSITION

CLASS COMPOSITION

Many regiments which subsequently enlisted Gurkhas did not necessarily do so when they were raised. Even those which were classed as Gurkha units included a proportion of soldiers who would no longer be enlisted under that name.

THE PERIOD BEFORE 1815

There are references in 1785 to local Corps being raised in the Ramgarh Frontier, and in Sylhet. These areas were later where the antecedent units of Gurkha Regiments were raised or served. There is however no known direct linkage with the later units. The Fort William India House Correspondence of 1782–1786 has a letter dated 31 January 1785 which has the following extracts:-

"We have resolved to disband all the Sibandi Corps within the Provinces, and in order to secure the Collection of the Revenues and maintain the Peace, four Regular Corps are to be stationed at Bogga, Rungpore, Dacca, and Midnapore, these Regiments will be kept in constant movement, but never Divided into Parties of less than the Command of a European officer. They are to be relieved twice in the year from their respective Brigades. In the months of April and November, to be kept in the Field during the above period and to form a Continual Interchange of reliefs between their respective Posts".

"The nature of the Ramgarh Frontier, and the remoteness of Chittagong from any Brigade Station, have induced us to continue the Regiment of Ramgarh Light Infantry and the Independent Regiment at Chittagong on their present footing for the protection of those Provinces and the Latter consideration has also influenced us in resolving that an additional Battalion of 300 Light Infantry should be formed from the disbanded Corps of the Army for the Protection of the Province of Sylhet".

and a later letter dated 22 February 1785 which included:-

"Having understood that the Resolution which we passed on the 27th Ult, for raising an additional Battalion of 300 Light Infantry from the different Corps of the Army for the Protection of the Province of Sylhet would entail on the Company a considerable expence and be productive of no substantial service we have agreed to rescind it".

As early as August 1813 there are records that the Governor-General in Council was considering raising a corps of infantry for the defence of the "north eastern frontier of the Honorable Company's Provinces against eventual encroachment of the Nepalese and for other local duties". (Bengal Political Consultations of 20 August 1813 No 25). This is repeated in the Military Consultations dated 4 September 1813. (Extract from Political Department No 8). One corps was to cover the districts of Saran, Tirhut, Butwal and Shiraj. The other was to cover Purnea, Dinajpore, Rungpore, Cooch Behar, and Rangamatty. Significantly, this memorandum states that "The privates or the great majority of them in both Corps ought to be, as far as may be found practicable and advisable on experience of their qualification, composed of Natives of the districts, of the Northern parts in particular, in which the Corps are destined to serve....". It goes on to say that "the greater part of the Native Commissioned and Non-Commissioned Officers should for some time at least be Natives of Hindustan." This meant that the men were to be locally domiciled or locally enlisted but the senior ranks were to come from the regular regiments of the Bengal line. The districts mentioned bordered the country ruled by Nepal.

Under GOCC dated 17 September 1813, the two corps were to be designated:

> Western or Bettiah Corps
> Eastern or Rungpore Battalion.

Drafts of native officers and non-commissioned officers were sent from eight different Bengal regiments to each of these new corps. Enlistment of soldiers was "generally to give the preference to men being natives of the Districts adjoining the Frontier".

The Commanding Officer of one of these units was asked, on 10 December 1813, to raise an additional company composed of a "class of men resident in the territories of the Bettiah Raja....useful....in the mountainous part of that frontier".

This submission by Captain Hay contains the earliest specific request to enlist hillmen or 'purbuttees'. It appears to be a response to an inquiry "whether any of the military tribes inhabiting the lowlands bordering on the State of Nepal who from habit and local knowledge might be better calculated from the species of the warfare adapted to an enclosed and mountainous country than the ordinary description of People of which our regular Battalions are composed could be induced into the Company's Service". Captain Hay replied that "I deem it my duty to state that there is a class of men now settled in that part of the Terai.. who I conceive to be particularly well fitted for the duties of Light Infantry and who voluntarily offer to be entertained, to wear our uniform, carry the musquet and submit to all the necessary restraints of discipline. They are Rajputs originally the subjects of the Nepal Government and who have fled from its oppressions and established themselves in the Terai. They are not scrupulous in respect of diet, eating animal food and subsisting on their excursions in the forest and mountains upon the game they kill with their Matchlocks with which they are expert Marksmen. They are of low stature but robust frame and their limbs are unusually strong and active. Their countenance is Nepalese having a strong resemblance to the Chinese but full of vivacity and intelligence. They are represented to be excellent Soldiers and bear the character of fidelity to their Employer. Their own native arms are the same as the Mountaineers of Nepal, and consist of Matchlocks, the bow and arrow in the practice of which they are dextrous, and Swords of a peculiar construction called 'khorah' and they carry continuously at their side a case of knives the longest of which is called 'kookeree' they use both as an offensive weapon and to clear their way through the intricacies of the forest by cutting away the branches of trees which obstruct their passage, this case likewise contains a flint and steel for procuring fire. Near thirty of these 'Purbuttees' or mountaineers, the appelation by which they are known, have presented themselves manifesting an earnest desire to be enlisted, but being a description of people prescribed for Light Infantry, and the Corps already completed to the ordered strength of 8 Companies of 90 Privates each. I have told them that I am not at liberty to accept their proposed Services without special authority; that I would venture however to submit the subject to the consideration of His Excellency the Commander-in-Chief and inform them of the result."

By early January 1814 (GOGG 8 January 1814) authority had been given to raise three additional companies for the Bettiah Local Battalion and four additional companies for the Rungpore Battalion, with a note "leaving it to Captain Hay....to recruit mountaineers". By 1 July 1814 the Adjutant General is asking for a "report on how well the company of mountaineers has been found to answer the expectations that were formed of its utility, and should the result prove encouraging, the Commander-in-Chief would recommend that the additional three companies be composed of the same description of men...."

On 26 August 1814 (AG letter No 115 of 22 August 1814) the Bettiah Local Battalion was converted to a corps of Light Infantry and designated The Champarun Light Infantry.

The previously mentioned Sibundy Corps raised for the protection of Sylhet was still in existence in 1814. There are references in the Bengal Criminal and Judicial Consultations of 26 September 1814 which refer to the issue of new weapons to this Corps. (India Office Records p 131.48). It is possible that this Corps which was maintained for the protection of the Frontier of Sylhet is the direct descendant of the 1785 Corps and could be the original unit which was amalgamated with the Cuttack Legion in 1823. If so it relates to the unit called the Sylhet Frontier Corps which next appears in 1817 (see below).

There is correspondence dated 21 September 1814, 4 October 1814 and 5 November 1814 in the Bengal Military Consultations, which refer to the "very great benefit" that would occur to the Corps stationed at Sylhet if it was placed under command of a European Commissioned Officer acquainted with the language etc. This resulted in Lieutenant Hugh Davidson being appointed to command with effect from 1st November 1814.

THE PERIOD 1815–1850

The official date for the raising of the first four Gurkha regiments is given as 24 April 1815, but as already noted local hillmen had been enlisted sometime before that date.

In addition, as early as 14 October 1814, which was before hostilities had begun, the idea was put forward to raise a levy, not exceeding 1500 men. Mention was made of utilizing deserters from the Gurkha Army who themselves had many such locally raised levies. William Fraser, the Political Agent in the Doon and Sirmoor, had raised a force of irregulars of over 4000 which was commanded by Lieutenant Frederick Young. Less than half of this force was composed of hillmen. Nevertheless, they had some success in operations in Sirmoor, particularly before the strong position at Jaitak. They were, however, routed in an engagement on 21 February 1815. The first recruits to William Fraser's irregular corps were two native officers, ten sepoys and two non-combatants on 26 October 1814. There were no Goorkhas among the 'mountaineers' in Fraser's irregular corps. A suggestion was made that the 500 or so prisoners and deserters in the British Camp should be embodied, to make up the number of irregulars required (who by that time numbered just over 6000). This suggestion was agreed and from the force so formed is descended the 2nd Gurkha Rifles. Lieutenant Young writing in 1829 (letter Bengal Military Consultations No 35 dated 29 December 1829) stated that "this Corps was originally raised from the remains of the Goorkha Army which so nobly defended itself against the British Force opposed to it at the Siege of Kalunga and Jaitak". The soldiers who came over from the Nepalese Army were gathered into a separate 'corps of Goorkhas' (under Young). The first of these to arrive was a Subedar and two sepoys on 18 March 1815.

On 24 January 1815, Major General Ochterlony entered into an agreement with Jeykishen, a Brahmin Subah of Kumaon, to 'bring over' soldiers of the Nepalese Army. After a slow start, Ochterlony had recruited 324 by early April 1815, when he wrote for covering approval from the Governor General. He resolved to form them into a separate battalion of three companies. He wrote "I shall with the sanction and approbation of His Excellency call it the 'Nasiri Paltan' and consider myself their commandant and patron". This body formed the nucleus of the 1st Gurkha Rifles. 300 of these Nasiris were in action at Malaun from 14 April 1815. These "Nusseree Goorkha Companies" were well reported on 16 April 1815 by Lieutenant P. Lawtie who commanded them (Extract Bengal Secret Consultations Folios 276, 277, 278 of 23 May 1815). His report was submitted via Major General Ochterlony to the Adjutant General on 30 April 1815.

There is another letter dated 16 April 1815 from the Governor Regeneral (Extract Military Letter to Bengal Folio 294 para 37), which states "we are also willing to admit the propriety of establishing some Local Corps in the Hilly Districts lately acquired from Nepaul, but with these exceptions, we cannot consent to authorize any further permanent Extra Establishments".

In Kumaon, the Gurkha General Brahma Shah, when he agreed to withdraw from Almora, took most of his Army with him but a number of Kumaoni irregular soldiers (not more than 300) had by this time taken service with the British. From them are descended the 3rd Gurkha Rifles. The Army List states that the Kemaoon Battalion was raised both from Gurkha soldiers who took service with the British after the fall of Malaun and conquest of Kemaoon, supplemented by transfers from the Ghoruckpore Hill Rangers. All the above indicates that some Gurkhas were certainly in British Service before the official date of the raising of the original regiments, which is given as 24 April 1815. There is moreover no record of why this particular date was selected.

On 8 May 1815 the Secretary to the Government wrote to Mr W. Fraser to acknowledge his letter of 27 April 1815 in the following terms (Extract Bengal Secret Consultations Folios 279, and 280, of 6 June 1815). " Your suggestion for embodying and arming the Gorkah Deserters, collected at Nahan, and uniting them with the Corps already formed by you under the Command of the two Officers mentioned in the 6th paragraph of your letter, is considered by the Governor General to be entirely judicious, a Corps of this description formed by the Major General Ochterlony has been found to be of the highest utility and that Officer's experience has shewn, that the utmost reliance may be placed in their fidelity, while regularly paid and well treated. Of their value in all the essential qualities of Soldiers there can be no doubt, and His Lordship has no hesitation in sanctioning the arrangement proposed by you and including in it, such other of the Enemy's Troops as may come over and be disposed to enter our Service. Assurances of permanent employment may be held out to them as after the conclusion of the War, their Services will still be useful either within the portion of the Hills to be retained by the Honorable Company or in the employ of the restored Rajahs, or eventually in the Northern and North Western parts of the Honorable Company's Territories in the plains, as suggested by you. Orders have been transmitted by His Excellency the Comander in Chief for appropriating the spare Arms of the Battalion service before Jytuck [Jaitak] for the levies adverted to in your dispatch, and the necessary orders founded on the extension of the arrangement will be issued by the same authority. The Corps when embodied are to be placed under the Command of Lieutenant Young subject to your general control, and Superintendence on the same footing as the other Irregulars".

The actual agreement to allow Gurkhas to enter service is contained in Article 5 of the Convention between General Amar Singh Thapa and Major General Ochterlony dated 15 May 1815. This states that "All Troops in the service in Nepaul, with the exception of those granted to the personal honour of the Kajees, Ummer Sing and Runjore Sing, will be at liberty to enter into the service of the British Government, if it is agreeable to themselves and the British Government choose to accept their services....".

Under Article 7 of the Convention, the garrison of Jaitak was required to surrender. At Ochterlony's suggestion (agreed by Jasper Nicholls) Jeykishen marched on 29 May 1815 with 749 of Ochterlony's Kumaonis to Almora to form the main body of the Kemaoon Provincial Battalion.

In GOCC of 27 July 1815, Major General Ochterlony "Will be pleased to form the whole of the Goorkhas who came during the late Campaign ..... into three battalions ......".

In Military Consultations No 40 and 41 of 1815, dated 3 August and 9 August 1815, the Governor General approves the arrangements made by the Commander-in-Chief to form "the two Nusseeree, the Sirmoor and the Kemaoon Battalions and of the Supplementary Putties". This correspondence also contains the proposals, subsequently agreed, to move the Nusseeree Battalions and the Sirmoor Battalion to the conquered territories west of the Jumna, which led to their stationing in Garhwal and Dehra Dun. The correspondence on 25 August 1815 gave the establishments of the new units (GO No 43 dated 26 August 1815) and re-published the original orders for their raising, stating that:-

"The Right Honorable the Governor General having determined to embody and form into Battalions for the Service of the conquered Territories in the Hills, the Goorkah Troops who came over to the British Arms during the course of the Western Campaign and having issued the necessary orders to that effect to His Excellency the Commander in Chief resolved that the following Establishment of these Corps as approved by the Governor General be published in General Orders together with the Regulations for their formation and organization. His Excellency the Governor General also determined and ordered that a Local Corps should be raised and formed for the Service of the Province of Kemaon. Resolved that the Establishment of the Corps as approved by His Excellency be published in General Orders. That the Nussuree Goorkahs and those serving under Lieutenant Young at Nahun be formed into three Battalions of Eight Companies and each Company of the strength hereafter detailed, the Battalions to be numbered and named as follows:-

"The Nussuree Goorkahs to be formed into two Battalions and to be denominated the 1st and 2nd Nussuree Battalions, the Goorkahs under Lieutenant Young to form a third Battalion and be denominated the Sirmoor Battalion. The Establishment of the Kemaon Battalion to consist also of 8 companies each of the same strength and Establishment in every respect as that hereafter fixed for the Nussuree and Sirmoor Battalions and to be composed of the Goorkah Corps late under the Command of Soobah Iye Kishin of Natives of Kemaon and other classes of Hill Men".

Later in the same General Order it states that "Any number of Goorkahs, Nussurees or those under Lieutenant Young that may remain in excess to the before-mentioned establishment were ordered to be formed into supplementary Puttees of the following strength: one Jemadar, 2 Havildars, 2 Naiks and 25 Sepoys, from which casualties and vacancies are to be filled up to complete the regular companies".

The first four corps enlisting Gurkhas were:

1st Nusseree	(later 1st Gurkha Rifles)
2nd Nusseree	(broken up in 1830)
Sirmoor	(later 2nd Gurkha Rifles)
Kemaoon	(later 3rd Gurkha Rifles)

In the Military Letters from Bengal one is dated 23 June 1815 submitting a proposal to raising a 9th Company of Pioneers "with an augmentation of Privates to be composed of Goorkhas or Kumaoneeahs and allotted for the service of the Province of Kumaon where it should be formed from the Gurkhas and Kumaonis supernumerary to what may be required for the Kumaon Local Corps." The date of raising appears to be 14 July 1815 when a "Regular Company of Pioneers" is established which has authorization for the officers, non-commissioned officers and various tradesmen plus 100 Privates. This is a larger unit than normal because the strength of a Pioneer Company was usually 80 Privates. The order notifying this states "an additional Company of Pioneers with an augmentation of Privates, to be composed of Ghorkhas, and Kumaoonies …".

The original detailed class composition of these regiments with the supplementary sub-units is not known exactly. The first three were always spoken of as being exclusively Gurkhas, whereas the Kumaon Battalion was composed largely of Kumaonis and other Hillmen. The problem is that the Gurkha Army was itself made up of many names or jats which would not be recognised as either Nepali or Gurkha, including Kumaonis and Garhwalis. There was also a fair number of low caste jats.

The Marquess of Hastings writing on 2 October 1815 (Papers respecting the Nepaul War) reported on these events in the following terms (Extract Bengal Secret Consultations Folios 292, and 293, Paragraphs 316, 317, 318):-

"I have stated above that detachments of British Troops are stationed in Malown and Subathoo, and at Nahun and in the Deyra Doon. I should not think it prudent to leave these newly acquired territories entirely without regular troops, and indeed, I am not disposed to think it advisable altogether to disuse the Native Troops from the Service in the Hills, but I do not contemplate the necessity of retaining them there long in any force: and I conceive that the Goorka Troops, on whose fidelity perfect reliance may, I think, be placed, with the addition of a very few regulars, will be found fully adequate to Garrision these countries. I have stated the great defection of the Gorkha Troops, forming the Garrisons of Malown and Jyetuck and the other forts from the service of that State. The whole numbers did not fall much short of five thousand men of all classes, and I have deemed it expedient to sanction the formation of three Battalions of the strength and composition stated in the document recorded on the proceedings. A certain number of these deserters, chiefly Kumaonees were transferred to the local Corps which I ordered to be raised for the service of that province, and I have authorised the addition of two Companies of Pioneers to be composed of men who have come over from the enemy. Your Honorable Committee will be pleased to observe, that the present extent of this Establishment is only temporary. It would neither have been prudent nor consistent with good faith, to discharge from the Service of the British Government any portion of the troops who came over from the enemy. Severed from their own country, they could not be practised upon to any purpose by their former Commanders, therefore for the moment they are efficient for us. But were they cast adrift, they having not either habits or means of industry, must through necessity repair to their old standards, and range themselves in arms against us, or must betake themselves to predatory associations for subsistence. As they fall off, it is not proposed to supply vacancies, until the Corps shall be reduced to the number which may be deemed fit for the permanent establishment. What then will be I am not prepared to state, but certainly it will be very considerably within the numbers actually in our pay. Your Honorable Committee is apprised of my opinion of the Military qualities possesed by the Goorkas. My persuasion of their fidelity to us is founded on the fact of the active, zealous and meritorious services performed by those who were embodied by Major General Ochterlony in the progress of the Campaign. Major General Ochterlony's despatches, especially one enclosing a report from the late Lieutenant Lawtie, will shew your Honorable Committee the sense entertained of their value by those officers".

With regard to the other local Corps, a General Order of 16 April 1815 authorised "the Body of Hillmen collected on the Gorrockpore Frontier by the Rajah of Bootwal to be formed into a Corps of Irregulars". This was designated the Gorakhpore Hill Corps, shortly thereafter re-named the Gorakhpore Hill Rangers. Under Bengal Military Consultations dated 3 April 1816, they were ordered to be reduced.

The note stated that "such officers and men composing it as may be natives of the Hills will in conformity with the promise made to them on their enlisting be entitled on their discharge from the Company's Service to permanent provisions in land. Government will retain in the Service a portion of the Men of that Corps the Governor General in Council is pleased to determine that two Companies of it will be added to the Gorakhpore Provincial Battalion, that a Company of it be composed of picked men be added to the Champarun Light Infantry in addition to the Hill Company already attached to that Corps, and two Companies....to the Rungpore Battalion, and that a corresponding number of Companies of the Gorakpore Local Battalion and of the Rungpore Corps composed of natives of the Plains be reduced....".

Under GOCC of 14 June 1816, it was ordered that "only one Mountaineer Company shall be attached to the Rungpore Local Battalion, instead of two, as formerly ordered".

Thus between 1813 and about 1826, there were amongst many other local corps or irregular battalions, various corps which may have contained some hillmen including Gurkhas. In addition to the four Gurkha Corps raised as a direct result of the Nepal War, these were:

The Champarun Light Infantry, originally the Bettiah Corps.

The Rungpore Battalion (Rungpore Local Battalion), which became the Dinagepore Local Battalion;
  also called the Dinajpore Battalion.

The Gorakhpore (Ghoruckpore) Hill Rangers - disbanded April 1816.

The Ghoruckpore Light Infantry (Ghoruckpore Local Battalion).

The Corps of Hill Rangers.

The Rungpore Battalion was an earlier creation than the one which later became the 6th Gurkha Rifles.

The Kemaoon Battalion remained under the Civil Department from 1816 until February 1839.

The next local corps which had Gurkha connections was the Cuttack Legion raised in May 1817. This later became the 6th Gurkha Rifles. In May 1817 (Bengal Military Consultations No 50 of 16 May 1817) reference is made to "raising a Corps of the description and strength mentioned within, for the service of Cuttack, and to [be] composed of Light Cavalry and Infantry.... and appointing Captain S Fraser...to the command of the Cuttack Legion".

Under GOCC dated 23 May 1817, orders were issued to send drafts of about 50 all ranks to the new unit from each of the Ramgarh Battalion, the Champarun Light Infantry and the Rungpore Frontier Battalion. Some of these drafts were clearly unsuitable because under GOCC of 22 January 1818 unfit men were returned to their original unit and were to be replaced by new men.

Yet another unit appears in 1817 called the Sylhet Frontier Corps. This may have descended from the Sibundy Corps raised for the protection of Sylhet which has previously been mentioned. If so, this unit was in existence in 1814 and possibly much earlier. Under GOCC of 14 August 1817, orders were given to augment this corps to form into six companies. This was not the unit which later became the 8th Gurkha Rifles. It is not known whether this earlier Sylhet Corps enlisted any Gurkhas. In 1819 it is described as the Sylhet Sibandy Corps. It was reduced to four companies in April 1819 (Bengal Military Consultations of 3 April 1819), and was dissolved on 31 March 1823, being absorbed into the Rungpoor Local Battalion (GOCC of 17 February 1823).

The Cuttack Legion was authorised to raise another company with effect from 13 June 1819. (Bengal Military Consultations No 14 of 7 August 1819). It was composed of Paiks. There were probably no Gurkhas enlisted at the beginning. This Corps moved in late 1822 to Rangpur where it became the Rungpoor or Rungpore Local Battalion, with effect from September 1822, replacing an earlier unit of that name which in turn took the name of the Dinagepore Local Battalion (GOCC of 17 February 1823; GOGG of 14 February 1823). Two companies of the earlier Rungpoor unit (by now renamed Dinagepore) were transferred to the new Rungpoor Local Battalion (ex Cuttack Legion), and in addition the whole of another corps known as the Sylhet Corps was absorbed (see above). There was still no definite record of Gurkhas in any of these units. Bengal Orders of 1823 lay down that "recruiting of Local Corps to be restricted to their home District and its adjacent Zillas". This applied particularly to various Hill Corps. In 1824 the unit moved into Assam and took part in the 1st Burma War, after which it became domiciled in Assam, changing its title to Assam Light Infantry in 1828, at about which time (GOCC No 104 of 16 May 1828) the Commanding Officer was authorised "to recruit Gurkhas under such arrangements as he thought best for the Assam Light Infantry", and "certain men of the Goorkha Tribe" were to be transferred to the Assam Light Infantry from several other units. These Gurkhas were to be formed into two complete companies "which are to be completed with privates by Goorkhas recruited for that purpose". There is a letter written by Lieutenant Colonel S F Hannay in 1857 (Inclosure 596 in No 1 dated 18 June 1857) in which he refers to the service in Burma in 1824–1826. He remarks that "the Gun Detail Ponies, mounted as cavalry, did excellent service against the Burmese, at Rungpore, under Lieutenant Brooke, now Sir James Brooke, Rajah of Sarawak". In November 1828 (GOCC No 234 of 8 November 1828) two complete companies 'intact' were transferred in from the Sylhet Battalion. The latter were intended as reinforcements of trained and well behaved Munipoories to replace men wishing to take their discharge. This was as a result of bad handling by the authorities who arbitrarily removed the inducements for serving in Assam whilst at the same time localising the battalion there - and not giving them the opportunity to return to Rungpore. A caste return of September 1828 gave the majority of the men coming from the provinces of Oude (35), Behar (319), Moorshedabad (178) with only 20 from Napaul and 4 from Bhotaun. (Bengal Military Proceedings No 50 of 13 September 1828).

In 1817 also, the Fatehgarh Levy, which later became 9th Gurkha Rifles, was raised. This became a regiment of the Bengal Line in 1823 enlisting Hindustanis, at that time meaning Brahmins and Rajputs of the Ganges Valley. It did not enlist Gurkhas until much later. The seniority of the 9th Gurkha Rifles over the other Gurkha regiments dates from their becoming a regular regiment in 1823.

As already indicated all the existing Local or Provincial corps were brought into one line of their own in May 1823 (GOCC of 6 May 1823). The first four Gurkha regiments were numbered 6th, 7th, 8th and 9th. This precedence lasted until 1850, new numbers being added up to about 1835 and regiments moving up in number to replace those which were reduced or disbanded. This moving up of numbered units did not seem to continue beyond 1830, after which some numbers remained blank.

In 1823, Garrison Companies were formed in the four senior regiments. (GGO 78 of 1823; GOGG of 31 July 1823; GOCC of 11 August 1823). In February 1824 the Sylhet Local Battalion (later to become 1st Battalion of 8th Gurkha Rifles) was raised as the 16th Local Battalion. The order raising the regiment stated that the men were "to be natives of Sylhet and Cachar frontier including Munulpore and the hill tribes around". Some drafts from existing local corps are mentioned but no Gurkha units are included.

In Bengal General Orders 1824 (p.213) one squadron of Horse each is authorised for the Rungpoor Light Infantry and the Sylhet Local Battalion. Each squadron to consist of 2 troops. This was later cancelled as far as the Rungpoor Light Infantry was concerned (BGO 1824 p.342) and one squadron of Irregular Horse was attached instead.

In 1824, the 6th, 7th and 8th Local Battalions (1st and 2nd Nusseree and Sirmoor Corps) were "augmented to 10 companies of 90 privates each, to be Goorkas". (GGO No 338 of 16 November 1824; GOGG of 11 November 1824; GOCC of 11 November 1824). In 1826 these measures were cancelled and each was to revert to 8 companies of 80 privates per company. (GGO No 113 of 27 May 1826; GOGG of 26 May 1826; GOCC of 27 May 1826). On 22 January 1827 (Bengal General Orders p.18) the artillery details attached to the Gorruckpore and Champarun Local Battalions were transferred to the Sylhet Local Battalion and the guns were handed in at the nearest magazine.

The Champarun Light Infantry took part in the 1st Burma War 1824-1826. Amongst the names on its medal roll are 43 recognisable Gurkha names and 29 others who were Garhwalis. The jats given were:

Thappa (Thapa)	22
Kuttre (Khattri)	7
Rae (Rai)	7
Gurdee (Gharti)	3
Rana	2
Goorung (Gurung)	1
Takoor (Thakur)	1
Routh (Rawat) (Garhwali)	29

The Champarun Light Infantry, formerly the Bettiah Battalion, and the Dinajpore Battalion, formerly the Rungpore Local Battalion, were both disbanded on 1 December 1826. (GGO No 231 dated 29 September 1826).

In 1828 the establishment of the Rungpore Light Infantry was revised and raised to 12 companies of 80 sepoys each, with "10 companies of men of the description of which the corps is now composed and two formed of men of the Goorkha tribe". (GGO No 104 of 7 June 1828). This indicates that no Gurkhas had been enlisted in this corps before this date.

Also in 1828 two companies of the Sylhet Battalion were to be transferred to the Assam Light Infantry - the 9th and 10th Companies to transfer as they stand.

The whole question of class returns generated a lengthy correspondence in the year 1830 when it became apparent that different descriptions were being used in the Nusseree Battalion from that in the Sirmoor Battalion for classifying their soldiers. This correspondence also throws an interesting light on the make-up of these two battalions fifteen years after entering British service. In the Nusseree Battalion there were still 539 men who came across from the 'Goorkah Service' in 1815 out of a total strength of 843; the figures for the Sirmoor Battalion were 346 out of 751. These figures show a remarkably small turn-over with very small recruit intakes in most years.

The major difference between the approach adopted by the two units in classifying their men was that in the Sirmoor Battalion all those who would eat and smoke together covering what would now be called Thakurs/Chhetris, Magars and Gurungs were classed as Rajputs, whereas in the Nusseree Battalion this description is reserved for those 'known to be of unmixed Rajpooth blood'. (Military letter from Bengal No 37 dated 4 September 1830).

The 'Rajpoots' in the Sirmoor Battalion were placed into five different classes listed as:

1st	Sing, Jace, Chund, Mull, Medrasee, Kan, Mean, Mundal, Gosain, Rohilla, Sain.
2nd	Pooar, Chukar, Rawat, Deoba, Bogali, Korial, Bist, Thappa, Burnaut, Khutree, Kunka, Kurkee, Udkaree.
3rd	Rochel, Jur, Suruj, Bunsee, Hummaul.
4th	Rana, Muggur, Newar
5th	Goorun

In both cases the breakdown by place of origin is also given. The totals in 1830 are:

From	Nusseree Battalion	Sirmoor Battalion
Nepal	634	418
Kumaon	8	38
Garhwal	119	272
Sirmoor	28	17
Elsewhere	1	8

The class compositions, placed in general groupings more akin to modern classification, were:

Brahmin	69		65
Rajputs	86	)	
Khas Gurkhas,		)	651
Magar/Gurungs	560	)	
and Garhwalis		)	
Sarkis/Damais etc	54		37

On 1 February 1830 the 2nd Nusseree Battalion was disbanded. All men of less than six years' service were discharged. Men of more than six years' service and who were "residents of the Nypal territory" were to be transferred to the 1st Nusseree and Sirmoor Battalions or to line regiments as they may prefer. The remainder were to go to the Kemaoon Battalion, whose establishment was at the same time reduced to 8 companies (GGO 251 of 1829). In February and March 1830 (Bengal General Orders of 15 February and 12 March 1830) the totals transferred to line regiments were given as:

15th Regiment Native Infantry	-	21
23rd Regiment Native Infantry	-	29
58th Regiment Native Infantry	-	23
60th Regiment Native Infantry	-	22

At the same time (Bengal General Order of 15 February 1830) there is reference to "the officers and men who were received from the Goorkha Army in 1815, are entitled (by the Regulations) when unfit for the active duties of a soldier, to be transferred to the Invalid Establishment, without reference to the time they may have served the British Government".

The 1st Nusseri, Sirmoor and Kemaoon Battalions were at this time numbered as the 4th, 6th and 7th Local Battalions respectively. On the disbandment of the 2nd Nusseri (5th Local) the others did not move up in precedence and the 5th Local number remained unfilled. Although medals for the Sutlej campaign of 1846 show the Sirmoor Battalion as being the 5th, and there are frequent references to this number in other correspondence, the Army Lists retained the number '6th' throughout the period and no authority to change has ever been found.

The Sylhet Light Infantry (later 1st Battalion 8th Gurkha Rifles) had two companies of Gurkhas from 1834.

The Corps of Bengal Pioneers was disbanded in February 1834. It is noted that two of its companies, the 9th, later renumbered 7th, and the 10th, later renumbered 8th, were designated as Hill Companies. They seem to have been composed of Kumaonis and Gurkhas. The 7th was present at Bhurtpore, and the 8th was in the 1st Burma War.

In April 1835, orders were issued for the formation of the Assam Sebundy Corps (later 2nd Battalion, 8th Gurkha Rifles), with 133 volunteers wanted from the Assam Light Infantry, which corps was reduced from 12 companies to 10 companies (GGO of 13 April 1835).

In December 1835 (India Military Consultations Nos 82-83 of 14 December 1835) the Commander-in-Chief requests that "men of the three Goorkha or Hill Corps, who came over to the British Army from that of the Nepaul Government during the campaign of 1815 have now completed twenty years' service, and are consequently entitled to transfer to the Pension Establishment when unfit for Local Service ...". This was agreed under GO No 38 of 8 February 1836.
The Garrison Companies of the Nusseri, Sirmoor and Kemaoon Battalions were renumbered as the 8th Company in early 1836. These Companies were formed in 1823, and indicated a further reduction in strength (GGO No 38 of 1836; GOGG of 8 February 1836).

In February 1836 (GOCC of 13 February 1836) the artillery detachment of the Assam Light Infantry was reorganised. Later, in 1840, (GOCC of 30 November 1840) the gun detachment appears to have been transferred to the Assam Local Artillery Company raised at Dibroo Gurh [Dibrugarh] from 1 October 1840.

There was also a local corps of Sappers and Miners raised in July 1838 "for the settlement of Darjeeling" (GGO No 99 of 1838; GOCC of 2 July 1838; GOCC, of 21 July 1838). This was called the Darjeeling Sebundy Sappers and Miners. Their task was to provide labour for road making in the Darjeeling area. The men were recruited from the border hills unconnected with Nepal. They apparently proved unfit and Captain Napier [later Field Marshal Lord Napier of Magdala] completed the corps with Nepalese. Napier spent four years with this corps. They took part in the campaigns in Sikkim in 1861 and in Bhutan in 1866–66.

In August 1839 a third corps for civil duties in Upper Assam was raised. This was formed from drafts of the Assam Light Infantry (later 6th Gurkha Rifles) and the Assam Sebundy Corps (later 2nd Battalion, 8th Gurkha Rifles). Both regiments contained Gurkhas and this new corps would therefore also have contained a number. The new corps was called The Upper Assam Sebundy Corps, with the original Sebundy Corps being renamed The Lower Assam Sebundy Corps (GOCC No 140 of 1839). The new corps absorbed the Doannea Levy and included "a company of 100 Doanneas and other Border tribes".

Later the same year (GOCC 187 of 23 October 1839) they became the 2nd Assam Sebundy Corps, and, although shown in the Bengal Army Lists between the 8th and 9th Local Battalions, neither the 1st nor the 2nd Assam Sebundy Corps were ever given a local battalion precedence or number. The 2nd Assam Sebundy Corps lasted until August 1844, being disbanded under GOGG No 234 of 9 August 1844, at which time the original Assam Sebundy Corps became light infantry and became the 2nd Assam Light Infantry Battalion, having been between 1839 and 1844 the 1st Assam Sebundy Corps. On disbandment about 100 of the most efficient men were selected to complete the (1st) Assam Light Infantry, and there is evidence that a year later former members of the Assam Light Infantry who had been transferred to the 2nd Assam Sebundy Corps were asking to revert to their original unit.

In 1838 a large contingent of soldiers was raised in India to support the British Claimant for the throne of Afghanistan. Of these, the 4th Regiment (Light Infantry) of Shah Shuja's Contingent (1838-1841) was entirely Gurkha, and Broadfoot's Sappers (1838-1842) had about one third [200 men] Gurkhas. Under GOCC of 28 April 1840, volunteers were called for from the Nusseree and Sirmoor Battalions to serve in this contingent, the men being offered promotion on transfer. From each battalion, 3 Havildars went as Jemadars, 4 Naiks as Havildars and 6 Sepoys as Naiks. The survivors of these units went to the Nusseri, Sirmoor and Kemaoon Battalions after the disasters in Afghanistan. There is also mention of a Corps of Jezailchees, which included a number of Gurkhas, in this campaign.

There is an interesting letter (printed in 1859 papers of the Houses of Parliament relating to the Reorganisation of the Army in India) written by E A Reade of the Bengal Civil Service which refers to recruiting in the period 1840–1843 of men from Gorakhpur for service with Shah Shuja's contingent (both the 4th Regiment and Broadfoot's Sappers) as well as for the Sirmoor Battalion. This letter notes the castes and recruiting districts of the "Nepaul Recruits levied at different times at Gorakpore in 1840, 1841 and 1843".

The tables showing the castes and the districts are:-

Adheekaree	Gayalee	Roon
Allay	Juhusee	Setee
Achayee	Khurka	Sawond
Beend	Khytree	Sahee
Booruh	Khawoss	Sorkee
Bhundaree	Koour	Thapa
Busnaith	Kunaith	Takoor

Beesta	Mull	Tewary
Buhora	Mazee	Misser
Bhatwol	Nurgurkosee	Zysee
Bhutrye	Newar	Kurmee, as carpenter, & c.
Bada	Oochayhee	
Chund	Olee	Kamee, as sohar or souacer
Corkee	Oopudiah	
Cookee	Poon	Bandee, as drummer
Chuttree	Poonar	
Damye	Pookrail	Offree, who digs iron
Doodra	Panda	
Doora	Rana	Augree, who digs copper
Gooroong	Raworth	
Gree	Rajaj	Dhold, as durzee
Ghurtee	Rokaka	
Ghulay		

LIST OF PRINCIPAL RECRUITING DISTRICTS IN NEPAUL

District	Province	District	Province
Toolseepoor* -	Mudhais	Mooseekote -	Rauj in hill
Nyakote - -	Palpah in 2d hill	Phulaban -	Do
Seelguree - -	Dotee hill	Pookreethoke -	Do
Peepulthok -	In upper hill	Goolmee - -	Do
Gurhoon - -	Rauj	Khanchee - -	
Essma - -	Hill do	Dhoorkote - -	Do
Tunhoo - -	Do	Dewgeer - -	
Rohnneekote -	Do	Lumjhommkoto -	Do
Lazurkoto - -	Rauj in hill	Gheering - -	Do
Darmakoto -	In do	Bhirkote - -	Do
Coskee - -	Rauj in hill	Reesing - -	Do
Urgha - -	Do	Srebtar - -	Do
Sylanah - -	Do	Bonkee* - -	Mudhais
Tansein (Toun) -	Do Palpa	Kubeloss - -	In hill
Palpah - -	Do	Mukkwanpoor -	Rauj do
Pewtanah* -	Do	Bootwul* - -	Mudhais
Katmandho -	In Nepaul	Beesing - -	Rauj in hill

The districts marked * are not recommended as recruiting fields. The inhabitants have a good deal of the Tharoo listlessness in them, and few would make good soldiers.

E A READE".

Early in 1842, the establishment of the Nusseree, Sirmoor and Kemaoon Battalions was again raised to 9 companies (GGO No 25 of 1842; GOGG of 21 January 1842; GOCC of 12 February 1842). In May that year Rifle Companies were authorised for the Nusseree and Sirmoor Battalions (GOCC of 25 May 1842). Also in 1844, there is further reference to the Darjeeling Sebundy Sappers and Miners (Bengal General Orders 1840 p.120) which included a number of Gurkha jats. This was the unit previously mentioned which had been raised in 1838.

In 1844 (India Military Proceedings No 44 of 16 August 1844) there are listed 5 Sepoys, formerly of Broadfoot's Sappers transferred 'last year' who were invalided. Again, the same year, (India Military Proceedings No 133 of 18 October 1844) there is noted that medals still required for Afghanistan (implying that some might have already been issued) include 18 Cabool medals for the Sirmoor Battalion and 45 Cabool medals for the Nusseree Battalion. Again, in 1845, (India Military Consultations No 100 of 2 May 1845) the Commanding Officer of the Sirmoor Battalion wrote to exchange 23 Jellalabad medals of men formerly belonging to Broadfoot's Sappers.

The Guides Infantry raised in 1846 always had at least one Gurkha Company, and often two, right up until 1921/1922.

In 1847, the 2nd Infantry of the Frontier Brigade (later the 2nd Sikh Infantry of the Punjab Frontier Force) was raised. They had about 100 Gurkhas. Men from the 10th Supplementary Companies of the Nusseree and Kemaoon Battalions were asked to volunteer (GOCC of 21 May 1847).

THE PERIOD 1850–1864

When the Nusseree Battalion came into the Bengal line in 1850 as the 66th Regiment of Native Infantry, replacing the existing 66th which was mustered out for insubordination, a new Nusseree Battalion was raised, partly from men transferred from the Sirmoor and Kemaoon Battalions. This lasted from 1850 to 1860. The transfers from the Sirmoor and Kemaoon Battalions to the new Nusseree Battalion includes the statement that only Goorkhas be recruited into these three and in the 66th Bengal Native Infantry (GOGG of 15 July 1850).

The order to authorize this transfer stated:-

"The most Noble the Governor General is pleased, in obedience to the wishes of the Honorable the Court of Directors, to resolve, that the Nusseree, Sirmoor and Kemaoon battalions shall hereafter consist of eight companies each, of the following strength:

1 Subadar.
1 Jemadar.
5 Havildars.
5 Naicks.
2 Buglers.
80 Sepoys.

"His Excellency the Commander in Chief is requested, in re-embodying the Nusseree battalion, to transfer to it a proportion of Native commissioned and non-commissioned officers, Buglers and Sepoys, from the Sirmoor and Kemaoon battalions.

"His Lordship directs, according to the orders of the Honorable Court, that the nationality of these corps, and of the 66th or Goorka regiment, shall be kept by the careful exclusion of men as recruits, who are not Goorkas." (GOGG of 15 July 1850; GOCC of 20 July 1850).

The arrangements for making up the "new" Nusseree Battalion which were set out shortly thereafter required transfer from the Sirmoor and Kemaoon Battalions and also from the former Nusseree Battalion, now the 66th or Goorkha Regiment. This meant that the Sirmoor and Kemaoon Battalions transferred out over 225 of their strength during 1850. The instructions issued on 3 August 1850 stated:

"1st . With the sanction of the Most Noble the Governor General of India, and with reference to General Orders by the Governor General, of the 15th ultimo, His Excellency the Commander in Chief is pleased to direct, that transfers to the new Nusseree battalion, directed in General Orders by the Commander in Chief of the 27th February last to be re-embodied, shall take place to the following extent:

	{	2 Subadars.
	{	1 Jemadar.
	{	10 Havildars.
From the Kemaoon battalion,	{	
	{	10 Naicks.
	{	4 Buglers.
	{	200 Sepoys.
	{	1 Subadar.
	{	1 Jemadar.
	{	10 Havildars.
From the Sirmoor battalion,	{	
	{	10 Naiks.
	{	2 Buglers.
	{	200 Sepoys.
	{	2 Jemadars for Subadars.
	{	3 Havildars for Jemadars.
From the 66th or Goorka Regiment,	{	
	{	8 Naicks for Havildars.
	{	8 Sepoys for Naicks.

"2nd. In addition to the above, Major C. O'Brien, commanding the Nusseree battalion, is authorized to select from the 66th or Goorkha regiment, nine men willing to be transferred, eight as Pay Havildars, and one as a recruiting Havildar.

"3rd. To ensure the new regiment obtaining a due proportion of good and experienced Sepoys, the 9th and 10th companies of the Kemaoon and the 9th company of the Sirmoor battalion are to be transferred in their integrity to the Nusseree battalion. The numbers required to complete the transfers, as above directed, are to be made from the supernumeraries which will then remain with the two corps.

"4th. The Band-men of the late Nusseree battalion are to be re-transferred from the 66th or Goorkha regiment to the new corps.

"5th.. The whole of the selected men and transfers are to be struck off the strength of their present corps, from the 1st proximo; they are to be paid up to the above date, and directed to join their new battalion at Juttogh, respectively from Almorah and Deyrah, under command of the senior Native Officers transferred from each corps, at as early a date as possible, provided with certificates of pay, clothing and half mounting; their descriptive rolls in duplicate being furnished, one copy to the Adjutant General of the Army, and the other to the Officer commanding the Nusseree battalion.

"6th. In view to enable Major O'Brien to provide the best description of recruits to complete his regiment to its proper strength, he will, with the sanction of the Most Noble the Governor General, detach a recruiting party, of such strength as he may deem, necessary to Almorah, with as little delay as possible, and General Orders, by the Governor General No.173, dated the 22d March last, are to be fully and carefully explained to the recruits previous to their being enlisted, and again on their being sworn in". (GOCC of 3 August 1850).

Also, in 1850, the new Nusseree Battalion, and the Sirmoor and Kemaoon Battalions received the pay, allowances, pensions and "all other advantages enjoyed by regiments of native infantry of the line". They therefore ceased to be local battalions from this date. This was granted in consideration of their good services and willingness to perform all duties and proceed wherever they may be ordered. Instructions to effect this change had been issued on 6 October 1849, when a letter was issued to "draw out the whole of the men present on parade....explain to them that the (Government) will take the whole of them into the regular service, like the Regular sepoy of the line with the same pay, the same pension, the same allowances in every way". They were required to do the same service and "march wherever they may be ordered like all other regular soldiers", and that "they are to serve wherever they may be ordered....at all times". The actual order was contained in GOGG in Council of 22 March 1850, which stated that "The Sirmoor and Kemaoon Battalions, as well as the New Nusseree Battalion, have been admitted, from 1st March 1850, to the Pay, Batta, Pension and all other advantages enjoyed by regiments of native infantry of the line". Discussion of this idea had begun in 1848 (Indian Military Consultations No 27 of 27 May 1848), with possible reduction in strength to compensate for increased expense. The orders confirming this alteration in conditions of service stated. "The Native officers, non-commissioned officers, and men of the Nusseree, Sirmoor and Kemaoon battalions, which have heretofore been regarded as local infantry, and received the inferior rates of pay and Pensions of corps of that branch of the service, except when employed in the field or with troops of the line, having, as ascertained by his excellency the Commander in Chief, through an officer specially deputed for the purpose, expressed their entire willingness to perform all the duties of a corps of the line, and to proceed where ever they may be ordered, the Most Noble the Governor General of India in Council, in consideration of the good services of those corps; is pleased to resolve that the Sirmoor and Kemaoon battalions, as well as the new Nusseree battalion, directed to be raised by General Order by His Excellency the Commander in Chief of the 27th ultimo, shall, on these conditions, be admitted from the 1st instant to the pay, batta, pension, and all other privileges enjoyed by regiments of native infantry of the line". (GGO No 173 of 1850; GOGG of 22 March 1850; GOCC of 28 March 1850) It is noteworthy that this order refers to the increases as "privileges". In earlier correspondence they are referred to as "advantages".

In the period 1850-1851 there was further correspondence about the class composition of the four Gurkha regiments which were then serving - the 66th BNI (formerly the Nusseree Battalion), the Sirmoor Battalion, the Kemaoon Battalion, and the new Nusseree Battalion.

For the Sirmoor Battalion, the remarks column against the breakdown by strengths states "Goorkhas (or the inhabitants of Nepal proper), Doteeallies and Ghurwallies are chiefly recruited for service in the Sirmoor Battalion and are all classed under the head of Rajpoots". Much the same comment is given for the Kemaoon Battalion, adding only 'Kumaonees'.

The actual class composition in May 1851 is given as:

	Sirmoor Battalion	Kemaoon Battalion
Brahmin	63	71
Rajput	595	720
Inferior Caste	77	15
Others	-	3

For the new Nusseree Battalion a rather different classification is used, based on four classes which were really categories of soldiers. The description of these 'classes' and the totals given for May 1851 is: Class 1 was pure Rajputs and Magar/Gurungs (described as Nepaulese). Class 2 was the children of the old Nusseree Battalion, 'commonly called Goorkahs', who came into British Service in 1815 (75). Class 3 were hillmen (152) and Class 4 plainsmen (13). Of those in Class 1 and 2 the totals for Brahmins are 10, Rajputs 31, Khas/Magar/Gurung or their descendants 382, and Damais 48.

The return for the 66th Bengal Native Infantry is much more detailed and contains a breakdown by jats and thars, some of which might nowadays be classified differently.

The geographical breakdown, presumably by place of origin, was given as:

Gurkhas (?Nepal)	412
Dotias (?W Nepal)	45
Kumaon	19
Garhwal	128
Sirmoor	115
Born in Regiment	181

Of these totals, the breakdown by major groupings includes Brahmins 90, Rajputs 134, Khas/Magar/Gurungs 677 and a fair number of others.

This series of correspondence also contained comment on the desirability of enlisting men other than from Nepal proper. It was noted that "real Goorkhas can not be got in any numbers. There are ... very few of them and what there are the Court of Katmandoo will not let go if it can help it". (Minute by Governor General Lord Dalhousie of 5 May 1852). It goes on to say that there is anyway a strong case for taking a proportion of our own hill subjects who are as good soldiers because it was not expedient to have these corps "all foreigners". The guidelines given by the Governor-General-in-Council were that a "judicious division of classes would be effected for laying down that, as nearly as may be possible, one third of each of the four Gurkha regiments shall be real Goorkhas, and the remaining two thirds shall be made up of the descendants of Goorkhas bred among ourselves and Paharees from the hills now belonging to the British Government lying between the Indus and Nepal".

There is a GOCC dated 2 March 1858 which states that the increase in strength ordered by the GOC Upper Provinces on 10 September 1857 for the Sirmoor, Kemaoon and "new Goorka battalion" to 1000 Sepoys each, was stated, "with a full proportion of Native officers and non-commissioned officers allowed for corps of the line". Also during 1858 the Extra Goorkha Regiment (later 4th Gurkha Rifles) was allowed an establishment of 10 companies. Under GOCC dated 15 March 1858, officers were appointed to the "1st extra Goorkha regiment of officers from 66th or Goorkha regiment, and from 29th and 68th Native Infantry".

Both the 4th and 5th Gurkha Rifles stem from regiments raised during the Mutiny in 1857. They enlisted Gurkhas exclusively from their inception. There was incidentally a good deal of objection from the existing regiments about this, since it was felt that they would encroach upon the existing recruiting areas and dilute the quality of recruits available.

In the period of the 1850s there was considerable concern expressed about raising new Gurkha Regiments. This concern was on the difficulty of obtaining "real Goorkahs". The authorities in Nepal were reluctant to allow Gurkhas to leave the traditional recruiting areas. It was thought that the Government "could never keep up more than 4 Regiments of real Goorkas, each a thousand strong". (Letter from C Reid dated 5 August 1857 at that time in Hindu Rao's House during the Mutiny). This letter also states that "I would never myself enlist any but real Goorkas and none but fighting castes. Sarkees and Damais I do not take". Opinion was also expressed that Hill men from "Gurhwal and Kumaon" were not held in high esteem. A further letter from the same officer made a comment about those who had applied to enlist. "the greater portion (although they hold themselves out to be Goorkahs) are Gurhwall and Kumaon men, others again are Dhoteeals – none of whom I ever enlist". (Letter from Major C Reid, dated 13 August 1857).

The same officer records that in 1851/52 he was recruiting at the outpost of Petora Gurh and was asked to enlist men for the 66th Goorkahs and Corps of Guides. He states that he was recruiting for nearly ten months and "only procured 155 men – all were genuine Goorkahs". (Letter dated 25 January 1858).

The Nepal Authorities had long been against allowing recruiting in the Hill areas of Nepal where the majority of Gurungs and Magars lived.

There is a letter written in 1858 which states that "about four years ago when Jung Bahadur was on a visit to Almorah he asked to be allowed to inspect the Sirmoor Battalion ...... The late Lt Colonel Evans, then commanding ..... consented. After passing down the ranks and looking minutely into every man's face, he turned round to Lieut Colonel Evans and said "I see you have got all the best Gurkhas in my Country – I must put a stop to this. I look on these men as Deserters". (Letter of Major C Reid dated 25 January 1853).

There was at this time always a difficulty for potential recruits to leave the hill areas. It was recorded that "There are always difficulties thrown in the way of their crossing the upper ghats, and the lower at this season of the year (August) they never attempt it". (Letter from Major C Reid from Hindoo Rao's House dated 5 August 1857). There were stated to be "but three small Goorkah Districts " and once it was known by the authorities in Nepal that more regiments were to be raised with a new recruiting depot at Petrogarh then "the Guards of the different Ghauts will be strengthened, and the authorities will be even more vigilant than before in preventing the real Goorkah from leaving the country........ "(Letter from Lt Col C Reid, Commanding Sirmoor Bn from the Palace Delhi dated 11 June 1858). This was reinforced by the experience of the previous recruiting season when it was recorded that "the Nepaul Government now appear more determined than ever that we shall not have men out of the Country. Difficulties were always thrown in the way of their crossing the frontier, but now the Guards at the Ghats are more viligant than ever and up to the present time I have only succeeded in procuring 11 Goorkas from Nepaul .... " (Letter from Maj C Reid Commanding Sirmoor Bn dated 25 January 1858).

At the time of the Mutiny The Guides Infantry is noted as having one company (E Company) of Gurkhas (Magar/Gurung) as one of their eight companies. The other companies were A Dogras from Kangra and Jammu; B Yusufzais and Riverine Akora Khattaks; C Punjabi Musalmans and Cis–Sutlej Khattaks; D Afridis; F Jat Sikhs; G mixed classes and H Jat Sikhs.

A contemporary account, published in 1858, alludes to the difficulty of recruiting Gurkhas from Nepal.

"The jealousy of enlistment for our army shown by the Nepaulese Government, who are naturally desirous of keeping as many as possible of the real Ghoorkalee for their regiment, renders recruiting from that class difficult, and Hill Rajpoots or Coolies are often taken into our Hill Corps. The Ghoorkhas of the Sirmoor Battalion, however, appear to be a corps of picked men even amongst their own countrymen". However, this same publication later makes a distinction between what would now be referred to as Thakur/Chhetri and Magar/Gurung. The author notes that

"By 'Ghoorkas' I mean the class usually called so by Anglo-Indians. They are not the real Ghoorka, however, but much superior to them in strength, activity and courage: they are very short, Tartar-featured, of great muscular development, and come chiefly from the district of Nuggur in Nepaul. The real Ghoorkhas, ... have regular and handsome features ....".

There is a letter dated 18 June 1857 from the Commanding Officer of 1st Assam Light Infantry (later 6th Gurkha Rifles) who were stationed in North East Assam at Debrooghur [Dibrugarh]. He quotes the early history of the regiment stating that its original composition as the Cuttack Legion in 1817 was "principally of Hindoostanies", but at the time of writing in 1857 the regiment was composed as follows:-

Hindoostanees, including Sylhet men, about	600
Nepalese	250
Manipoories and Jarooahs, or Natives of Gowalparah District	260

Jarooahs are Assamese. They appear variously as Jurwahs, Jharwahs, Jaruas, Jarwahs and Jherowahs.

In the papers printed in 1859 covering the report to the Houses of Parliament on the Re-Organisation of the Army in India, there is a table showing the Races and Castes of which the Native Army was composed on 1 April 1858. This table probably covers only the Bengal Army. It has three Columns which have a relevance to Gurkha units, although there may be others which could apply. The infantry are listed as Regular and Irregular; and the relevant columns are headed Hill States of Nepal, Goorkhas, and Hillmen. The Regular Infantry at this date could only refer to the 66th Bengal Native Infantry (later 1st Gurkha Rifles). The Hill States of Nepal possibly refer to those areas formerly subject to Nepal; and the title Hillmen could embrace a number of different people including Garhwalis and Kumaonis who are not otherwise identified.

The relevant extracts are:

	Hill States of Nepal	Goorkhas	Hillmen
Infantry (Regular)		590	
Infantry (Irregular)	358	271	3677

In November 1858 there were proclamations made throughout India to mark the end of the Mutiny. Under GGO No 1490 of 1858 dated 1 November 1858, the troops drawn up in Fort William, Calcutta, include "Detachment 73rd Native Infantry (Goorkhas)." There is no other record of Gurkhas being in this regiment. Two Companies had mutinied in November 1857 at Dacca, but the regiment survived the Mutiny (and served on until 3 May 1861). It had been stationed at Jalpagiri with a wing at Darjeeling, so it is possible that they recruited some Gurkhas. They were known to have supplied men for the Sebundy Sappers and Miners at Darjeeling, and these were known to have enlisted Gurkhas since 1838.

There are also references in the records to a unit entitled the Landour Rangers (or Landour Levy) during 1858 and 1859. The first mention appears in Government letter No. 735 of 19 October 1857 and their raising is dated 8 June 1858. (Punjaub Gazette No. 6 of 26 September 1858, Punjaub GO No 185 of 24 September 1858), where orders are issued to raise a Levy of recruits of 'Goorkas, Sirmoores, and other hillmen' at Landour. They were referred to as L' Estrange's Goorkha Levy, named after their Commanding Officer. The next reference to this unit is in GGO No 286 dated 4 March 1859 when it is referred to as The Corps of Landour Rangers. Then in June 1859 an instruction was issued to break up this unit (GOCC dated 3 June 1859) with the men being permitted to volunteer for any corps including police. The effective date of disbandment was 30 June 1859.

There is also reference to another regiment which enlisted Gurkhas. This was referred to as the Mussoorie Hill Regiment. It appears in 1858 and it may be the same as the Landour Rangers since it was raised by Lieutenant Colonel L'Estrange. This was apparently not without objection from the existing Gurkha Regiments. There is a letter to the Commander-in-Chief dated 11 June 1858 from Lieutenant Colonel Charles Reid stating that boys "belonging to the Regiment" have been enticed to enlist in the Mussoorie Hill Regiment, commanded by Lieutenant Colonel L'Estrange, "as also in the Meerut Police Corps which now has a recruiting party at Deyrah [Dehra Dun] ". These boys were apparently all considered to "belong to the Regiment..... many of these were waiting my inspection".

There is a further letter dated 20 July 1858 from the same Commanding Officer which comments about the "injurious practice which at present exists in the newly raised Mussoorie Regiment, and other Police Corps, of enlisting men who have been dismissed by sentence of court martial from the four old Goorkah Corps". (letter from Lt Col C Reid Commanding Sirmoor Battalion to Commander-in-Chief dated 20 July 1858). This letter goes on to name six men formerly belonging to the Sirmoor Battalion, all of bad character who are held in the Mussoorie Regiment, some of whom have been promoted. All were dismissed within "the last ten and fifteen years" and were presumably still living in Dehra Dun.

It is not known whether the Mussoorie Hill Regiment, or Mussoorie Regiment, are the same as the Landour Hill Rangers.

Nor is it known whether the Meerut Police Corps were entitled to enlist Gurkhas. The "other Police Corps" are not identified.

In the period immediately after the Mutiny there was a considerable reorganisation and a new Bengal line was constituted. The Sirmoor Battalion became officially a rifle regiment, although some Gurkha battalions had been clothed and equipped as riflemen for some time. This started a movement which eventually spread to all other Gurkha regiments.

Partly because it remained difficult to recruit from the Hill areas of Nepal, there was encouragement to encourage settlement at the regimental depots to provide suitable line boys for enlistment.

This practice was already well established as it was recorded in the Sirmoor Battalion that "out of seven men who obtained the Order of Merit during the Sutlej Campaign four of them were Line boys and in the late operations before Delhi they have proved themselves equally good. " (Letter from Major C Reid dated 25 January 1858).

Under GOCC dated 5 November 1858 the 66th or Goorkha Regiment (later 1st Gurkha Rifles) was constituted as Light Infantry Corps, "as an acknowledgement of its good Services" and was thereafter to be titled 66th or Goorka Light Infantry Regiment.

In the 2nd Goorkha letter book there is a letter from Lt Col Reid, Commandant Sirmoor Battalion, dated 1 June 1858 which asks the Adjutant General at Army Headquarters to "solicit His Excellency the Cin C to authorize me to abolish the grade termed "Sepoy" and to substitute 'Goorka' for the same. The Native Officers and men of the Battalion I have the honour to Command are desirous of this change which may I trust be sanctioned".

On the back of this letter is a note stating "The Commander in Chief desires that the men of this Regt may either be designated 'Riflemen' or Privates". This note is undated.

The new Nusseree Battalion was broken up in 1860. It had behaved badly and, being in an isolated hill station, had given the inhabitants there a great fright, so much so that the good name won by Gurkhas earlier, in the Punjab campaign of 1846 and elsewhere during the Mutiny, was in danger of being lost. It was noted in 1858 that "the Nusseeree Battalion does not possess so many of those brave little fellows, the Ghoorkas, as the Sirmoor and other Hill corps; had there been none but Ghoorkas in the regiment, it is possible no cause for anxiety would have arisen."

The Commander-in-Chief, writing on 5 October 1861 (Proceedings of the Government of India Military Department for November 1862 No 721), had advised that in future all personnel of all native corps (cavalry and infantry) should be of mixed composition "to the greatest extent possible". He set out his views in some detail and adds,

"With respect to the Goorkha regiments, in which nationality has been preserved very closely, it is believed the Government is averse to any change; but his Excellency cannot agree to a principle so full of risk, and he ventures to be of a different opinion, and to instance in support of his views the conduct of the Nusseeree Battalion during the mutiny. As these corps are generally stationed in the hills at isolated cantonments, any disaffection on their part would be doubly dangerous to the peace of the country. The Assam and Sylhet Corps are similarly isolated; but the Commander-in-Chief would advise Government that they should not be allowed to remain local longer than the difficulty of effecting their relief may render necessary."

However, he quickly modified this view in respect of the Sirmoor Battalion, because in a letter dated 19 October 1861 an amendment was issued which stated:

"The Commander-in-Chief wishes to modify his opinion as conveyed in my letter of the 12 October that a mixed composition should be introduced into the Goorkha regiments; he would except the 17th regiment (Sirmoor), because he considers the Government, chiefly on account of their excellent conduct before Delhi, held out hopes to them through their commanding officer that they were to retain their nationality and form a Goorkha colony."

It was in fact decided that the five remaining Gurkha regiments should be brought into the line. This happened in May 1861 but lasted only until October of the same year. Then they were set apart as a separate Gurkha line and given the numbers which they have retained. At the same time (under GGO 990 of 1861), the precedence of these five regiments was laid down. The 1st Gurkha Rifles ranking after the 10th Regiment Bengal Native Infantry; the 2nd, 3rd, 4th Gurkha Rifles ranking after the 15th Regiment Bengal Native Infantry; and the 5th Gurkha Rifles ranking after the 32nd (Punjab) Regiment Native Infantry.

In 1864, there was an important move to lay down the class composition of regiments more clearly. Under AG Circular No 117 dated 9 September 1864, the first five regiments were to enlist just 'Gurkhas'; the 42nd, 43rd, and 44th Regiments (later to become 6th Gurkha Rifles and 2nd and 1st Battalions of 8th Gurkha Rifles) were to have "chiefly Gurkhas and Hillmen (Assamese), with a proportion not exceeding one-fourth of strength of Hindustanis", the 9th Regiment (later to become 9th Gurkha Rifles) had two companies of Hindustani Brahmins and Rajputs, one company Hindustani-Mussulmans, two companies Bundelahs, one company Jats, one company Gurkhas and Hillmen, and one company Dogras and Hillmen. Under the same AG's Circular there were a number of other regiments which had Gurkhas. The Guides Infantry in the Punjab Frontier Force of course continued to keep their Gurkhas. They had one company (E Company) made up of Magars and Gurungs. They also had another Company (G Company) of mixed classes. [Their other class companies were A Dogras, B Yusufzais and Khattaks, C Punjabi Musulmans and Cis Indus Khattaks, D Afridis, F & H Jat Sikhs]. In the Bengal line the 18th Regiment had two Gurkha companies, and the 5th, 13th, 39th and 41st Regiments had one company each.

THE PERIOD 1864-1890

During this period, there occurred the gradual exclusion of Gurkhas from all but the Gurkha line and the Assam Regiments.

The Darjeeling Sibundy Sappers and Miners, after service in Sikkim in 1861 and in Bhutan in 1864–1866 were ordered to be reduced on 21 March 1867. It was hoped that the men would transfer to the 42nd and 43rd Assam Light Infantry. Most however opted to join the police or go on pension. Item No. 178 of the Proceedings of the 17 January 1867 contains a lot of information on their worth including a remark by the Brigadier commanding on the Eastern Frontier who thought the Gurkhas acted as a check on the Sikhs of whom he thought there were too many in the Assam Regiment. Paragraph 3 of a letter dated 21 May 1866 from Brigadier C Reid, CB, commanding the 2nd Frontier Brigade reads "The corps is composed chiefly of hill-men, Nepaulese and Goorkhas, and many of the latter are of the fighting class. They have had great experience in hill road-making, and the officers who have served with them, speak most highly of the men; indeed, they consider the Goorkha Sapper equal to two Roorkee sappers, and when properly drilled and organized they will be a valuable body of men, and I would beg to suggest that the corps should be augmented to 200 privates, the present strength being 180". Paragraph 6 of the same letter is as follows "So long as the hill-men, Goorkhas in particular, know that their wives and children (to whom they are devotedly attached) are well cared for, they will serve anywhere and at any distance from their hills, but as soon as the service and the excitement of war is over, they should be permitted to return to their "Bhustee" ".

The Digest of Services for the 2nd Goorkhas gives an indication of how many Line Boys, ie those born in the Regimental Lines, were included in the enlistments. It states that "From 1861 to 1 January 1870 the number of Recruits enlisted was 341, of these, fifty were line boys and the remainder natives of Nepaul".

In class returns of 1873, 1874 and 1875 of the Bengal Army, the 1st, 2nd, 3rd and 4th Goorkhas are all simply given as Goorkhas. The 42nd Native Infantry (Assam) is given as two companies each of Punjabees and Hindustanees, one company of Jharwahs and three companies of Goorkhas, The 43rd Native Infantry (Assam) is listed as General Mixture with Goorkhas, Jharwahs, Hindustanee Muslims and Hindus; and the 44th Native Infantry (Assam) is also listed as General Mixture with Goorkhas, Jharwahs and Hindustanees. The 5th Native Infantry had one company of Goorkhas and Hillmen; the 9th Native Infantry one company of Goorkhas, the 18th Native Infantry had two companies of Goorkhas and Hillmen; the 39th Native Infantry had one company of Goorkhas and so did the 41st Native Infantry. In 1877 there is a return (Organisation of the Native Army 1877), which shows the average number of recruits present on the 1st of each month during the past five years.

This gives:

42nd Native Infantry	89
43rd " "	64
44th " "	67
1st Goorkhas	73
2nd "	50
3rd "	28
4th "	28

In the same publication and for the same year (Organisation of the Native Army 1877) there is an interesting abstract of replies from officers commanding regiments as to the difficulty or otherwise of obtaining good recruits. These returns throw some light on the varied quality and difficulty of recruiting Gurkhas. These extracts include:

9th Native Infantry	No difficulty to speak of; though Goorkhas from Nepal and Dograhs of good stamina are not easy to get.
42nd " "	It has been found very difficult to obtain "Goorkhas" of good physique. Also the "Jurwahs" who present themselves for enlistment are not such good men as of former years.
43rd " "	No difficulty has been experienced in securing recruits of good physique; the physique of the regiment generally has materially improved within the last few years.
44th " "	No difficulty has been experienced by the recruiting parties sent out annually of late years to obtain recruits; but few recruits of the Goorkha caste, of which the regiment is mainly composed, have presented themselves for enlistment at headquarters since the regiment left Shillong and descended to the plains.
1st Goorkhas	During the six years and nine months I have commanded the regiment I have never experienced any difficulty in procuring Goorkha recruits of good physique and proper caste. On this date there is not a single vacancy in any grade in the regiment.
2nd "	This regiment is recruited principally from Nepaul; men who go on furlough bring back their relatives, and recruiting parties are sent down to attend the fairs held along the British and Nepaul borders. I cannot state positively that we have had great difficulty in securing recruits of good physique of late years. This regiment has not required any great number in any one year. I may mention that it has just taken us nearly four months to obtain 20 young Goorkhas.
3rd "	No difficulty in procuring the number required. Physique of recruits last joined excellent, regiment up to established strength, and 10 good lads waiting for vacancies.
4th "	No difficulty has been experienced of late years in securing recruits of good physique.

A summary of the total numbers serving in 1875 shows that in the Bengal Army and Frontier Corps there were, 9,166 Goorkhas and Hillmen. This was further broken down as 5,188 Goorkhas, 3,126 Dogras and 852 Hillmen of other classes. In the Bombay Army at the same date it was noted that "of Hillmen there are 3 Goorkhas and 44 Dograhs".

In 1880 the establishment of Privates (Riflemen) in Gurkha Regiments was stated to be 800. (2nd Gurkha Rifles letter book entry dated 2 January 1880). There were in addition a further 25 Supernumerary Recruits "which have been allowed by Government for Goorkha Regts for a long time".

By 1883, Gurkhas were excluded from the 5th, 39th and 41st Regiments. They were also wasting out of the 18th which was allowed two companies of Hillmen and the 13th which kept one such company. The 18th still had Gurkhas in 1885 since there is a record of an IOM award to a Gurkha in the regiment in that year. At the same time (GO of 29 January 1883) the three Assam Regiments (42nd, 43rd and 44th) were each given seven companies of Gurkhas and one company of Jarwahs of Assam. On 2 January 1889 this last Company became Gurkha. The Jarwahs were distributed throughout the regiments and gradually wasted out.

The 9th Regiment meanwhile had ceased to enlist Gurkhas between 1881 and 1893. Their composition was given as one company Hindustani Brahmins, one company Mussulmans, two companies Jats and Ahirs, two companies Hindustani Rajputs and two companies Nepalese Newars. Under GO of 29 January 1883, two companies are shown as Hillmen, presumably the two Newar companies. There is no other record of enlistment of Newars as a policy. In the early 1890s, the Government of India suggested that the 9th became a class Newar regiment, but the recruiting officer stated that in his opinion Khas Gurkhas, at that time no longer enlisted, had a better claim. In June 1892 (effective early 1893) they became a class regiment of Khas Gurkhas, two thirds Khas (Chhetri) and one third Thakur.

In 1886 the decision was taken to raise 2nd Battalions of the first five Gurkha Regiments. In 1887, the remaining Garhwalis (whose enlistment had ceased in 1883) in the first three regiments were all transferred to the new 2nd Battalion of the 3rd Gurkha Rifles. This new battalion was brought into the line to take the place of the 39th Bengal Infantry in 1890, and later became the 39th (later 18th) Royal Garhwal Rifles. A new 2nd Battalion of the 3rd Gurkha Rifles, this time exclusively Gurkha, was raised in 1891.

Also in 1886, a central recruiting depot was established at Gorakhpur and this remained the main recruiting centre until 1949. In about 1890 a small office was opened in Darjeeling, and shortly thereafter the Recruiting Officer became responsible for recruiting for Burma and Assam units.

In the India Office Library Collections in the British Library there are Annual Class Composition Returns for all the regiments in the Bengal, Madras and Bombay Armies, as well as the Punjab Frontier Force. Some other local units were also included in the early returns.

The annual returns start in 1875 and continue in one form or another until 1942.

These returns are listed in the catalogues as Annual Caste Returns although their printed title is Annual Class Return. They are all dated "as at 1 January".

The documents are either printed (L/MIL/7/17081-17085 Collection 415) which covers 1889 to 1908 and 1933 to 1942; or on micro film (L/MIL/7/206 – 236) which covers 1875 to 1942.

Each year's return, by separate Armies up to 1903, contains much detailed information printed in columns for each unit showing breakdown by ranks for each class. The columns and lines are quite close together and it could be that there are some unintentional misprints. For instance in 1876 the 1st, 2nd, 3rd and 4th Hyderabad Infantry show a large number of Gurkhas and Hillmen (some 966 in all). However, in the years before there are none shown. A few appear in 1877 and again in 1883, but not in between.

Similarly, the 1877 entry shows 128 men from Nepal in the Central India Horse; and the 1878 entry show 86 men from Nepal in the 2nd Bombay Light Cavalry. None of these entries appear again. These entries are likely to be misprints.

The returns and abstracts for the years from 1875 to 1903 have separate entries for "Goorkhas and Nepalese" (variously spelt) and "Hillmen in British Territory". The latter can be taken to be Kumaonis and Garhwalis, but also include Jarwahs from Assam. These also appear with different spellings as already noted.

Each class return up to 1903 also contains a table which gives the place from which the classes are recruited or where they are domiciled. There is a separate entry on each page entitled "From Nepal". There is a close relationship between this entry and the entry under Gurkhas and Nepalese, but there are some interesting anomalies. Some units show all their men as coming from Nepal. Others clearly list line-boys and Indian domiciled Gurkhas differently.

At the end of each year's returns there is an Abstract showing the total "Native officers" and other ranks. Again it is difficult to reconcile exactly all these figures with the vast number of individual entries which precede the Abstract, but they can be taken to be an accurate return.

It must have taken some while to complete these annual returns. There are letters on record complaining how late these were printed. In some years they did not reach the India Office in London for eighteen months.

Also of interest are the number of non-Gurkhas shown in various Gurkha Regiments. Complete extracts of these have not been collected, but some examples from the earlier years of the 6th, 8th, and 9th Gurkha Rifles are included in the Tables which follow.

The annual Abstracts for total numbers for the period 1875 to 1890 are shown in the next table; and the breakdown by units which were either already identified as Gurkha units or who later became Gurkha units is shown in the table which follows. These cover only the Gurkhas and Hillmen entries. The many other units which had Gurkhas recorded amongst their totals are separately listed; as are the non-Gurkhas in Gurkha units.

TOTAL GURKHA STRENGTHS AS AT 1 JANUARY 1875-1890

	Native Officers			Native Non-Commissioned Offices, Rank and File, Drummers & Buglers		
	Gurkhas & Nepalese	Hillmen in British Territory	From Nepal	Gurkhas & Nepalese	Hillmen in British Territory	From Nepal
1875	85	25	-	5035	609	4972
1876	86	31	80	5485	663	4919
1877	81	20	80	5173	501	5141
1878	82	25	84	5292	485	5515
1879	86	21	85	5212	464	5242
1880	96	22	94	5455	575	5511
1881	100	22	85	5846	519	5691
1882	104	21	90	6186	509	6005
1883	106	19	90	6378	569	6215
1884	108	15	93	6456	587	6313
1885	125	12	98	6559	584	6430
1886	119	27	105	7326	780	6813
1887	157	19	135	9844	785	9141
1888	139	4	168	8228	1282	9814
1889	169	10	172	10228	1667	10288
1890	199	18	178	10600	1435	10455

STRENGTHS IN GURKHA UNITS AS AT 1 JANUARY 1875-1890

	1875			1876			1877			1878		
	GURKHAS & NEPALESE	HILLMEN IN BRITISH TERRITORY	FROM NEPAL	GURKHAS & NEPALESE	HILLMEN IN BRITISH TERRITORY	FROM NEPAL	GURKHAS & NEPALESE	HILLMEN IN BRITISH TERRITORY	FROM NEPAL	GURKHAS & NEPALESE	HILLMEN IN BRITISH TERRITORY	FROM NEPAL
1 GR	691	36	691	657	35	657	679	-	679	706	-	706
2 GR	713	-	469	683	9	683	699	5	483	704	3	707
3 GR	558	151	558	560	139	560	575	131	575	574	116	574
4 GR	647	58	647	654	43	654	674	37	674	695	33	695
5 GR	635	-	635	606	80	(?)	682	68	682	693	62	693
42 BNI (6 GR)	293	-	293	257	-	257	310	-	310	306	8	306
43 BNI (2/8 GR)	368	-	368	381	-	381	358	-	358	395	-	395
44 BNI (1/8 GR)	598	9	598	596	7	596	618	9	618	653	11	653
9 BNI (9 GR)	43	-	43	41	35	41	41	43	41	42	45	87
Guides Inf	98	-	98	93	8	-	94	8	94	97	8	97

	1879			1880			1881			1882		
	GURKHAS & NEPALESE	HILLMEN IN BRITISH TERRITORY	FROM NEPAL	GURKHAS & NEPALESE	HILLMEN IN BRITISH TERRITORY	FROM NEPAL	GURKHAS & NEPALESE	HILLMEN IN BRITISH TERRITORY	FROM NEPAL	GURKHAS & NEPALESE	HILLMEN IN BRITISH TERRITORY	FROM NEPAL
1 GR	708	-	708	644	4	644	748	-	748	816	-	817
2 GR	689	3	689	732	4	732	744	6	589	805	4	615
3 GR	595	112	595	661	150	661	661	112	666	727	104	738
4 GR	711	33	711	737	32	737	792	29	792	850	64	850
5 GR	660	48	660	702	40	702	778	30	778	813	31	813
42 BNI (6 GR)	288	-	288	318	12	330	373	5	378	430	5	435
43 BNI (2/8 GR)	401	-	401	434	-	434	504	-	504	515	-	515
44 BNI (1/8 GR)	645	9	645	603	13	603	617	15	617	656	12	656
9 BNI (9 GR)	37	54	37	61	59	61	50	54	50	45	50	45
Guides Inf	99	-	91	77	7	77	80	23	80	119	23	119

STRENGTHS IN GURKHA UNITS AS AT 1 JANUARY 1875-1890

	1883			1884			1885			1886		
	GURKHAS & NEPALESE	HILLMEN IN BRITISH TERRITORY	FROM NEPAL	GURKHAS & NEPALESE	HILLMEN IN BRITISH TERRITORY	FROM NEPAL	GURKHAS & NEPALESE	HILLMEN IN BRITISH TERRITORY	FROM NEPAL	GURKHAS & NEPALESE	HILLMEN IN BRITISH TERRITORY	FROM NEPAL
1 GR	841	4	842	827	4	828	834	4	835	924	4	924
2 GR	833	3	673	869	2	674	856	2	664	719	194	720
3 GR	729	94	740	780	92	790	788	84	796	764	72	772
4 GR	800	60	800	818	57	723	812	33	812	880	29	880
5 GR	819	26	819	837	24	840	847	23	849	865	20	865
42 GLI (6 GR)	498	-	498	546	4	550	621	3	624	691	4	695
43 GR (2/8 GR)	571	-	571	565	-	565	589	-	589	656	-	656
44 GR (1/8 GR	680	11	680	719	10	719	685	6	757	795	12	795
9 BNI (9 GR)	42	50	42	88	39	88	123	39	123	118	29	126
39 BNI (39 Garhwal R)	-	-	-	1	114	5	-	117	4	-	133	3
Guides Infantry	116	19	111	106	16	101	97	19	94	115	18	112

STRENGTHS IN GURKHA UNITS AS AT 1 JANUARY 1875-1890

	1887			1888			1889			1890		
	GURKHAS & NEPALESE	HILLMEN IN BRITISH TERRITORY	FROM NEPAL	GURKHAS & NEPALESE	HILLMEN IN BRITISH TERRITORY	FROM NEPAL	GURKHAS & NEPALESE	HILLMEN IN BRITISH TERRITORY	FROM NEPAL	GURKHAS & NEPALESE	HILLMEN IN BRITISH TERRITORY	FROM NEPAL
1 GR & 1/1 GR	826	2	826	865	1	865	871	1	873	811	1	871
2/1 GR	926	-	926	871	-	871	900	-	900	853	-	853
2 GR & 1/2 GR	866	18	715	743	132	741	773	141	774	889	6	762
2/2 GR	896	8	814	786	115	736	790	138	790	884	15	774
3 GR & 1/3 GR	803	68	803	831	32	831	836	27	836	908	13	908
2/3 GR				63	360	56	40	718	40	100	712	68
4 GR & 1/4 GR	863	26	863	861	-	861	875	-	875	867	1	876
2/4 GR	791	90	723	833	4	833	866	4	866	898	4	898
5 GR & 1/5 GR	754	14	754	867	12	867	877	11	877	870	10	870
2/5 GR	170	2	170	604	5	558	845	7	845	905	10	905
42 GLI (6 GR)	710	4	714	741	24	744	799	3	802	821	3	824
43 GR (2/8 GR)	656	-	656	752	-	752	761	-	761	827	-	827
44 GR (1/8 GR)	742	12	742	738	11	738	800	10	800	822	8	822
9 BNI (9 GR)	-	211	130	-	211	94	-	216	90	-	233	95
39 BNI (39 Garhwal R)	-	144	3	-	223	2	-	203	2	-	198	-
Guides Infantry	111	17	108	98	18	95	115	17	112	109	17	106

Although there were some non-Gurkhas in all the Gurkha Regiments, the most significant numbers occur in the three Assam based regiments, 42nd, 43rd, 44th Bengal Infantry (later 6th Gurkha Rifles, 2/8th and 1/8th Gurkha Rifles). The totals recorded in the Class Returns from 1875 to 1890 are:

NON GURKHAS IN GURKHA UNITS AS AT 1 JANUARY 1875-1890

		1875	1876	1877	1878	1879	1880	1881	1882
42 BNI	Assamese & Jarwahs	105	104	98	102	90	83	67	64
	Muslims	130	120	122	120	105	105	72	63
	Sikhs	196	181	162	213	205	205	190	183
	Other Hindus	151	141	161	133	149	118	58	61
43 BNI	Assamese & Jarwahs	287	318	311	287	263	251	213	176
	Muslims	39	34	32	39	45	47	47	42
	Other Hindus	174	167	152	150	140	124	104	92
44 BNI	Assamese & Jarwahs	9	91	92	91	91	13	82	65
	Muslims	20	20	21	22	20	19	17	16
	Other Hindus	146	116	116	102	76	62	52	42

		1883	1884	1885	1886	1887	1888	1889	1890
42 GLI	Assamese & Jarwahs	59	57	52	43	33	1	17	16
	Muslims	42	50	45	41	33	22	19	18
	Sikhs	127	105	98	9	4	2	2	1
	Other Hindus	58	41	37	36	20	9	11	9
43 GR	Assamese & Jarwahs	165	145	131	111	111	80	48	31
	Muslims	28	24	23	20	20	24	23	19
	Other Hindus	64	49	39	11	11	10	9	6
44 GR	Assamese & Jarwahs	48	40	37	70	70	54	44	43
	Muslims	12	12	8	7	8	6	6	6
	Other Hindus	35	30	23	21	13	5	4	4

The Regiments which show Gurkhas or "Hillmen in British Territory" in the Class Returns between 1875 and 1890 are shown below. Almost all the Gurkhas were also shown as being "From Nepal". This list is probably not absolutely complete, and some Regiments, already referred to in previous paragraphs as being probable misprints, have been omitted.

NUMBER OF GURKHAS SHOWN IN NON-GURKHA UNITS 1875-1890

	1875	1876	1877	1878	1879	1880	1881	1882	1883	1884	1885	1886	1887	1888	1889	1890
10 Ben Cav	2	2	2	2	2	1	-	1	-	-	-	-	-	-	-	-
17 Ben Cav	1	1	-	-	-	-	-	-	-	-	-	-	-	-	-	-
2 Bo Cav	1	1	1	1	1	-	-	-	-	-	-	-	-	-	-	-
3 Bo Cav	1	-	-	-	-	-	-	-	-	-	-	-	-	-	-	-
Guides Cav	-	-	-	-	2	1	2	1	1	-	-	-	-	-	-	-
Bo Arty	2	2	-	-	-	-	-	-	-	-	-	-	-	-	64	-
Ben S & M	16	-	16	20	20	22	-	15	23	24	14	10	10	8	6	6
2 BNI	2	2	2	2	2	2	-	-	-	1	1	1	1	-	-	-
4 BNI	12	-	12	-	-	-	-	-	-	-	-	-	-	-	-	-
5 BNI	22	18	17	14	12	12	12	11	-	-	-	-	-	-	17	14
8 BNI	59	60	58	57	49	47	46	42	44	40	37	40	18	14	12	9
9 BNI	43	41	41	42	37	61	50	45	42	88	123	118	-	-	-	-
10 BNI	2	1	2	1	1	1	-	-	-	-	-	-	-	-	-	-
13 BNI	80	75	72	87	87	126	142	114	102	97	90	87	89	86	85	84
15 BNI	3	2	2	2	2	2	-	-	-	1	1	2	2	2	2	2
16 BNI	1	1	-	-	-	-	-	-	-	-	-	-	-	-	-	-
17 BNI	-	-	-	-	-	-	-	-	-	1	-	-	-	-	-	-
18 BNI	167	155	175	169	165	221	220	172	150	139	107	99	84	75	56	52
19 BNI	1	1	1	1	1	-	1	-	-	-	-	-	-	-	-	-
20 BNI	1	-	-	-	-	-	-	-	-	-	-	-	-	-	-	-
21 BNI	-	-	-	-	-	-	-	-	1	1	-	-	-	-	-	-
33 BNI	-	-	-	1	1	1	1	1	1	1	1	1	-	-	-	-
37 BNI	1	-	-	-	-	-	-	-	-	-	-	-	-	-	-	-
38 BNI	94	89	147	137	109	145	141	124	110	97	90	87	-	-	-	-
39 BNI	6	5	5	5	5	5	5	5	5	1	-	-	-	-	-	-
41 BNI	5	5	7	6	5	2	-	-	-	-	-	-	-	-	-	-
45 BNI	1	-	-	-	-	-	-	1	1	1	1	1	1	1	1	-
6 Pun Inf	1	1	1	1	1	1	1	1	1	1	-	-	-	-	-	-
3 Bo NI	-	-	-	1	-	1	1	-	1	-	-	-	-	-	-	-
24 Bo NI	-	-	-	-	-	-	-	-	-	1	1	1	1	1	1	1
27 Bo NI	3	-	2	2	2	1	1	1	1	1	1	1	1	2	1	4
28 Bo NI	-	-	-	-	-	-	-	-	2	-	3	2	2	2	2	2

ASSAM MILITARY POLICE AND ASSAM RIFLES

In 1835 the earliest of the many constituent units which later became The Assam Rifles was raised. They had a particularly complicated lineage which is given in the Lineage Lists, with many amalgamations, dispersals and change of title. They were by no means all Gurkha and the forerunner units such as the Cachar Levy (1835), the Jorhat Militia (1838) and the Kuki Levy (1850) had few if any Gurkhas in them. Gurkhas begin to figure in the class composition about 1852 in the Nowgong Frontier Police, later the Naga Hills Frontier Police which became the 3rd Battalion Assam Rifles. This was intended to 'protect' the regular Gurkha battalions. The enlistment of Kiranti (Limbus and Rais) was increased and more Cacharis, Jarwahs (Jaruas) and other locals were taken in. Nevertheless Magar and Gurung names continued to occur on unit rolls in large numbers. In 1864 the Lakhimpur Armed Police had some Gurkhas from its inception. This later became the 2nd Battalion Assam Rifles. In 1866 the Frontier Police of Bengal started to enlist Nepalese, and after many changes of title, through Chittagong Hill Tracts Frontier Police and South Lushai Hills Military Police together with the Surma Valley Frontier Police became eventually the 1st Battalion Assam Rifles. In 1879 the forerunner of the Garo Hills Military Police was raised, also including Nepalese in its ranks, and this eventually descended via the Darrang Military Police to become the 4th Battalion Assam Rifles. At one stage enlistment of Magars and Gurungs was prohibited by order of the Government of India (1887).

The North Cachar Hills Frontier Police (1852) descended from the Cachar Levy and later became the Surma Valley Frontier Police (1873) who became Military Police in 1883. They had a strength of 797 in 1889. The Bengal Armed Police (1860) became the Chittagong Hill Tracts Frontier Police in 1866 with a strength of 550. The Lakhimpur Armed Police (1864) became Frontier Police in 1873 and Military Police in 1883 rising to a strength of 818 in 1889. The Nowgong Frontier Police (1852) also descended from the old Cachar Levy and later became the Naga Hills Frontier Police in 1868. They received a draft from the Garo Hills Military Police in the later 1870s and changed their name to Military Police in 1883. Their strength in 1889 was 671.

The Garo Hills Military Police was raised from Armed Civil Police in the 1870s. Their title dates from 1883. Originally composed chiefly of Nepalese and Cacharis they later enlisted Sikhs, Punjabis, Dogras and some Muslims. Their strength was given as 300 in 1879 and 243 in 1889.

The History of Upper Assam, Upper Burmah and North Eastern India by L W Shakespear (1914) notes that in 1810–1881 the "Regulars" were reduced to be in the 42nd, 43rd and 44th Assam Light Infantry. It also states that the old Frontier Force was divided into three Military Police Battalions which were:

Lakhimpur MP Battalion at Dibrughar
Naga Hills MP Battalion at Kohima
Lushai MP Battalion at Aijal

In addition there were two battalions "at lesser strength" which were

Garo Hills MP Battalion at Tura
Cachar MP Battalion at Silchar

The composition of these units is given as "at first mixed enlistments, then Gurkhas and Jarwas (the fighting clans of Assam)".

The Chittagong Hill Tracts Frontier Police became the South Lushai Hills Military Police in 1891 in which year their strength was given as 540. Their composition changed from Nepalese, Jarwahs (Jaruas), Chakmas and Muslims to Gurkhas and Jarwahs only. The major portion of the Surma Valley Military Police became the North Lushai Hills Military Police in 1891. Their composition is given as Gurkhas and Jarwahs. The remnant of the Surma Valley Military Police was reduced to 350. The North and South Lushai Hills Military Police were amalgamated in 1898 and became the Lushai Hills Military Police. The Naga Hills Military Police in 1892 was composed of three companies of Gurkhas, two companies of Jarwahs, and one company of Dogras and Garhwalis.

The units along the Assam and Bengal border continued to evolve. The state of Manipur is noted around 1905 as having a State Military Police at a strength of 377 but it is not known if they enlisted Gurkhas. There was also a Military Police Battalion, or perhaps a Civil Armed Police force at Ranchi which had a number of Gurkhas serving in it. The forerunners of the Assam Rifles progressed towards their final form. The Lushai Hills Military Police was reduced in strength in 1901 to 850. In 1905 its composition is given as mostly Gurkhas with Garos, Rabhas, Meches and Cacharis. The old Surma Valley Military Police was incorporated (less a small detachment) in 1903 into the Dacca Military Police when East Bengal was transferred to Assam. The last detachment of 4 and 73 was finally incorporated in the Darrang Military Police in 1913. The Lakhimpur Military Police was composed in 1905 of 78% Gurkha, the remainder being Garos, Rabhas, Meches and Cacharis with a strength of 847. This was reduced in 1910 to 673 but raised again in 1911 to 850 by which time the composition is given as four companies of Gurkhas and three companies of Jarwahs. The Naga Hills Military Police strength in 1905 is given as 671. The following year the composition is four companies of Gurkhas and three companies of Jarwahs. The strength in 1910 is given as 704. The last Dogras were enlisted in 1912. The Garo Hills Military Police sent a draft to the Dacca Military Police in 1908. Its composition in 1912 is given as ¾ Gurkha and ¼ Jarwahs. The strength is given in 1901 as 203 going down to 102 by 1911 by which time it is noted as a detachment from the Dacca Military Police. This remaining detachment of 4 and 130 were transferred in 1913 to the newly formed Darrang Military Police.

The strength of the Assam Military Police battalions in 1906 is given in the Handbook on Gurkhas (Vansittart) as:

ASSAM MILITARY POLICE BATTALIONS IN 1906

Name of Battalion	Location	Establishment	
		Companies	Total
Garo Hills Battalion	Tura	2	202
Lakhimpur Battalion	Dibrugarh	8	880
Lushai Hills Battalion	Aijal	8	840
Naga Hills Battalion	Kohima	7	670
Silchar Battalion	Silchar	4	389
Establishment of Gurkhas at 80%	Total	29	2,981
			2,385

BURMA MILITARY POLICE AND BURMA FRONTIER FORCE

From 1886 a number of units were raised specifically for service in the newly annexed provinces of Burma. Under GOCC of 15 March 1886, two levies of military police each with a strength of 561 were raised in Upper Burma. These first two levies were composed of Punjabis and Hindustanis respectively and were open to all classes except Gurkhas. At the same time military district police were raised in both Upper and Lower Burma. In August 1886 (under GOCC of 19 August 1886), two additional battalions were raised for service in Burma, one of which was initially called the Punjab Battalion and enlisted Punjabis. The other was called the Assam Battalion and was raised from the 42nd and 44th Regiments (Gurkhas), also from the Assam Police Battalions and from "newly enlisted men who may be either

Nepalese or natives of Assam, or Manipuris, or tribesmen of the Assam frontier".

In the History of Upper Assam, Upper Burmah and North Eastern Frontier by L W Shakespear (1914) the Military Police in Upper Burma in 1886 were listed as:

> Chindwyn MP Battalion at Monywa
> Myitkyina MP Battalion at Myitkyina
> Bhamo MP Battalion at Lashio
> Southern Shan States MP Battalion

This history also states that the Upper and Lower Chindwyn MP Battalions had been amalgamated in 1886, and the Mogaung Levy had been absorbed into the Myitkyina MP Battalion in the same year (1886).

It was also noted that these units mostly enlisted men from Northern India with two companies of Gurkhas from Eastern Nepal. The Myitkyina MP Battalion was composed entirely of Eastern Gurkhas and the Bhamo MP Battalion had two companies of Kachins.

Back in March 1886 the Mogaung Levy about 500 strong was raised and this too is given as a Gurkha unit. It may be that this is the same unit as the Assam Battalion already mentioned. These then were the first Gurkhas in the Burma units. The year 1886 was evidently a busy one because in addition to the five 2nd Battalions of the regular Gurkha regiments, the first one (or two) Gurkha Burma Police units were raised.

In the early part of 1887 there was a further considerable expansion in the Burma Military Police. Under GOCC of 8 January 1887, 3,000 more were authorised to be raised, 1,000 each from the Punjab, North West Provinces and Oudh, and again under GOCC of 27 May 1887 a further 3,000 were authorised; this time 2,000 from North West Provinces and 1,000 from Oudh. None of these would have had any Gurkhas. However under GOCC of 7 March 1887, a further 2,000 of all classes were authorised to be raised and there were probably some Gurkhas amongst these. Under GOCC of 9 April 1887 the Kubo Valley Military Police Battalion was formed for service in the Kubo (nowadays Kabaw) Valley and Upper Chindwin. It may be that the 500 or so men in this battalion were drawn from those authorised in the previous month. The battalion was raised from volunteers from the 42nd and 44th Regiments (Gurkhas), not more than 75 from each and from the Frontier Police, and by newly enlisted men, who, it is noted, "will be composed of Assam Jhurwahs, Cacharis, Kookis and other tribes". This sounds remarkably like the composition of the previous Assam Battalions. It is believed that the Gurkha elements were mostly Kiranti from Eastern Nepal.

In March 1890 it was announced that a number of regular Madras Regiments were to be "localised" in Burma. This was achieved initially by transferring the newly raised Burma Military Police battalions onto the Madras establishment and mustering out the soldiers of the Madras Regiments who were to be replaced. Amongst the first of such transfers was the move of the Kubo Valley Military Police Battalion to take the place of the 10th Madras Regiment of Infantry. This was authorised under Madras GO No 231 of 14 March 1890. The composition of the new regiment was given as three companies Gurkhas and five companies of Assamese hillmen. The future enlistment of Karens, Shans and Kachins for the new regiment was also sanctioned. The regiment kept the number of the old Madras Regiment and also inherited its colours, funds, mess and band property. They could perhaps have kept their precedence and honours. Had they been allowed to do so, or had they chosen to do so, the 10th Gurkha Rifles would have become the senior Gurkha regiment in British Service, because precedence was set by the date of raising as a regular regiment.

The 10th Gurkha Rifles were permitted to assume the honours of the 10th Madras Regiment in 1988. However they were specifically not granted the precedence of the old regiment.

The new 10th Regiment sent out its first recruiting parties in 1891 seeking Gurkhas from Eastern Nepal and Jharwahs (Jherowahs) from Assam. The latter being difficult to obtain, authority was given to raise a company of Khas Gurkhas. Later the same year the composition was altered to allow half the battalion to be Gurkhas of any class. By early 1895, the composition of this unit was given as four companies of Gurkhas and four companies of Assamese.

The Army List of April 1895 shows that the native officers were mainly Western Gurkhas (9 Magars and 3 Gurungs) with only 2 Khas Gurkhas and 2 unidentified names (possibly Assamese).

The Mogaung Levy appears to have amalgamated with the Bhamo Battalion of the Military Police and this remained in existence up to 1942. There were Gurkhas in this unit from 1918 to 1942.

Another unit which appeared in 1887 was the Ruby Mines Battalion. This originally enlisted Sikhs, Punjabi and Hindustani Muslims, but in 1888 it is noted that 85 Gurkhas were added. By 1893 the composition had changed and the strength was given as 160 Sikhs, 295 Gurkhas and 304 Karens. In 1899 the Karens were transferred to the Karen Battalion, leaving a unit largely of Gurkhas and Garhwalis with one and a half companies of Sikhs and Rajputs. The Gurkha content is down to two companies by 1909, and in the next year one company was transferred to the newly raised Northern Shan States Battalion. Shortly thereafter, in 1914, the Ruby Mines Battalion was absorbed by the Mandalay Battalion which was directly descended from the very first Burma Police Levies and which in turn survived until 1942. This Battalion did not enlist Gurkhas between 1915 and 1932 after which it recruited Gurkhas up to 1942. Another unit raised in 1887 at Yamethin became the Upper Burma Reserve Battalion and later the Reserve Battalion. This too survived until 1942, and there were certainly Gurkhas in this Battalion from 1916 to 1942.

To complete the picture, the Toungoo-Karen Battalions raised in 1893 certainly had some Gurkhas serving in 1914, when 138 are noted, after which this battalion disappears perhaps absorbed into the Putao Battalion. The Myitkyina Battalion (1893-1926) also had Gurkhas, and no less than 1,500 are shown in the class return for 1919. This battalion split into two (Eastern and Western) in 1926 and came together again in 1938. It continued up to 1942.

Other Burma Military Police and Burma Force units which had Gurkha connections, some of whose badges included the crossed kukri motif, included:

Putao Military Police	1915-1925
Chin Hills Military Police	1895-1942
Chindwin Military Police	1916-1922
Northern Shan States Military Police	1904-1939
Southern Shan States Military Police	1906-1942
Rangoon Military Police (from 1932 1st & 2nd)	1918-1942
Arakan Hill Tracts Military Police	1904-1928
North West Border Military Police	1922 1925

The units of the Burma Frontier Force enlisting Gurkhas in 1939 were the Bhamo, Chin Hills, Myitkyina, Northern Shan States, Southern Shan States, 1st and 2nd Rangoon and Reserve Battalions. Two more units appear in the last Class Returns, Lashio Battalion from 1940 and Kokine Battalion from 1941. Both had Gurkhas enlisted.

The 1906 strength of the Burma Military Police given in the Handbook on Gurkhas (Vansittart) was:

BURMA MILITARY POLICE BATTALIONS IN 1906

Name of Battalion	Location	Establishment	
		Companies	Total
Arakan Hill Tracts Battalion	Palewa	2	200
Chin Hills Battalion	Falam	3	339
Mandalay Battalion	Mandalay	3	339
Myitkyina Battalion	Myitkyina	13	1,469
Northern Shan States Battalion	Lashio	2	226
Ruby Mines Battalion	Mogok	3	339
Toungoo Battalion	Toungoo	2	220
Establishment of Gurkhas	Total	28	3,132
at 80%			2,506

THE PERIOD 1891-1914

The situation during the last decade of the 19th Century was that there were in the Bengal Army the 9th, 42nd, 43rd and 44th Regiments, all Gurkha and of one battalion each, as well as the 1st, 2nd, 3rd, 4th and 5th Gurkha Rifles, with two battalions each. The official spellings had changed to 'Gurkha' and they were all now Rifle Regiments.

In 1900 a double company system was introduced in most Indian Army regiments and in the Guides Infantry the two companies A and E had Dogras and Gurkhas.

On 15 May 1902 the 8th Madras Infantry was mustered out and a day later a new regiment called 8th Gurkha Rifles was formed, taking some 200 men in from 10th Gurkha Rifles. These two regiments were linked and were to have identical organisations and conditions of service. A year later in July 1903 this 8th Gurkha Rifles became the 2nd Battalion 10th Gurkha Rifles. A few months later in October 1903 the great reorganisation of the Indian Army took place and this brought the whole of the Bengal, Madras and Bombay Regiments, as well as the Punjab Frontier Force, into one consecutively numbered line. The Gurkha Regiments were however reorganised into their own line and numbered separately. The first five regiments remained unchanged as Western Gurkha regiments, each of two battalions. The 42nd, 43rd and 44th Gurkha Rifles came into this new line as the 6th, 7th and 8th Gurkha Rifles at one battalion each. In the case of the new 8th Gurkha Rifles this was a completely different regiment from the one raised in 1902 which had been absorbed by the 10th Gurkha Rifles only three months previously. The 9th came in from the Bengal Line keeping its previous number. It remained a Khas Gurkha Regiment and in due course raised a 2nd Battalion.

The 10th came across from the Madras Army with the two battalions already mentioned. It was largely an Eastern Gurkha regiment. Four years later in 1907 a further set of complicated changes took place. The 2nd Battalion 10th Gurkha Rifles, raised only in 1902 as 8th Gurkha Rifles, split into two wings, each becoming a battalion of a new regiment called the 7th Gurkha Rifles, this time also composed of Eastern Gurkhas. Meanwhile the existing 7th Gurkha Rifles (formerly the 43rd) became the 2nd Battalion of the 8th Gurkha Rifles (formerly the 44th). The 10th Gurkha Rifles then raised another 2nd Battalion of its own in 1908, during which year the regiment was delocalised from being a unit serving exclusively in Burma. By the end of the period all the regiments had two regular battalions and this remained the basis until 1947/1948.

Sunwars were first enlisted in Gurkha regiments in 1909.

In 1911 the double company system in the Guides was re-arranged and C and E companies were linked recruiting Punjabi Musulmen and Gurkhas. In 1914 two extra platoons of B Company of the Guides became Gurkhas.

The annual Abstracts for total numbers (as at 1 January each year) for the period 1891 to 1910 are given in the next table. In 1896 and 1897 the numbers for Hillmen in British Territory include Kumaonis and Garhwalis. In other years these are shown separately. From about 1900 onwards the Abstracts begin to include Gurkhas enlisted in the Indian States Forces (Imperial Service Troops) (IST). From about 1904 the Abstracts also show Gurkhas serving in the Military Police units in Assam and Burma (MP). From the same year these Abstracts omit the separate classification of Native officers. From about 1905 the Hillmen in British Territory category reverted to including Kumaonis and Garhwalis.

These tables taken from the Annual Class Returns have to be compared with the annual enlistment numbers which are recorded in the Handbook on Gurkhas (1935 edition. Morris). This book gives a list of all classes enlisted to cover the years from 1886–1887 and up to 1934–35. The first extract takes the numbers up to 1910. Thakurs, Chhetris and Sunwars first appear in 1904–05 as separate entries.

The Annual Class Returns from 1911 onwards classify all the tribes or jats in separate columns and this system was used for all units of the Indian Army, as well as for the State Forces and Military Police Units. Initially, from 1911 to 1912, the different classes were listed as Magar, Gurung, Khas Thakur, Limbu, Rai, Sunwar and Other Gurkhas. In 1912 two more classes were shown separately and these were Newar and Lama. These nine separate categories continued until 1930. when the Khas Thakur class was split into Thakur and Chhetri.

ANNUAL RECRUITING NUMBERS

Recruiting Season	NUMBER AND CLASS OF RECRUITS					TOTALS
	MAGARS	GURUNGS	LIMBUS	RAIS	OTHERS	
1886 – 87	No Records					1,082
1887 – 88						1,025
1888 – 89	622	226			24	872
1889 – 90	725	264			18	1,007
1890 – 91 1891 – 92 1892 – 93 1893 – 94	Records Incomplete					1,889 1,786 1,732 1,731
1894 – 95	592	338	230	225	498	1,883
1895 – 96	503	293	263	213	391	1,663
1896 – 97	516	333	197	150	368	1,564
1897 – 98	550	322	229	184	152	1,437
1898 – 99	688	417	147	110	200	1,562
1899 – 1900	696	375	240	236	312	1,859
1900 – 01	734	417	199	205	264	1,819
1901 – 02	420	246	117	132	187	1,102
1902 – 03	632	385	357	259	157	1,790
1903 – 04	584	398	238	262	143	1,625
Total 1888–94	Records Incomplete					11,124
Total 1894–95 to 1903–04	5,915	3,524	2,217	1,976	2,672	16,304
TOTAL						27,428

Recruiting Season	NUMBER AND CLASS OF RECRUITS								TOTAL
	THAKURS	CHHETRIS	MAGARS	GURUNGS	LIMBUS	RAIS	SUNWARS	OTHERS	
1904-05	-	-	1,111	656	133	127	-	894	2,921
1905-06	-	-	666	463	342	222	-	143	1,836
1906-07	50	54	753	385	199	171	-	61	1,673
1907-08	68	138	1,016	638	544	607	54	77	3,142
1908-09	62	143	893	707	486	550	49	90	2,980
1909-10	57	81	649	550	243	441	58	80	2,159
1910-11	44	74	625	458	110	193	30	16	1,550

ABSTRACT OF TOTAL GURKHAS 1891–1910 AS AT 1 JANUARY

	Native Officers			Native Non Commissioned Officers, Rank & File, Drummers & Buglers		
	GURKHAS & NEPALESE	HILLMEN IN BRITISH TERRITORY	FROM NEPAL	GURKHAS & NEPALESE	HILLMEN IN BRITISH TERRITORY	FROM NEPAL
1891	208	16	189	11211	1462	11296
1892	219	16	201	11720	419	11972
1893	232	10	220	12334	355	12233
1894	232	6	218	12632	141	12327
1895	240	5	221	12624	125	12314
1896	224	6	226	12823	938	12553
1897	224	17	223	12686	747	12559
1898	228	4	209	13045	121	12707
1899	130 (?)	4	212	12887	129	12534
1900	234	2	216	13019	94	12693
1901	230	1	216	13021	86	12581
1902	235	2	219	13356	89	13047
1903	239	-	222	13325	74	13001

	INDIAN ARMY	IMPERIAL SERVICE TROOPS	MILITARY POLICE	TOTAL	HILLMEN IN BRITISH TERRITORY	FROM NEPAL
1904	14224	883	4854	19961	1901	19572
1905	16190	898	4816	21904	5540	19888
1906	15617	896	4812	21325	2696	20925
1907	16145	898	4887	21930	3357	21385
1908	16470	962	4685	22117	2837	22022
1909	17418	1013	4556	22987	2748	20239
1910	17821	1025	5276	24122	2831	21291

STRENGTHS IN GURKHA UNITS 1891–1910 AS AT 1 JANUARY

1891-1894	1891			1892			1893			1894		
	GURKHAS & NEPALESE	HILLMEN IN BRITISH TERRITORY	FROM NEPAL	GURKHAS & NEPALESE	HILLMEN IN BRITISH TERRITORY	FROM NEPAL	GURKHAS & NEPALESE	HILLMEN IN BRITISH TERRITORY	FROM NEPAL	GURKHAS & NEPALESE	HILLMEN IN BRITISH TERRITORY	FROM NEPAL
1/1 GR	860	1	860	903	1	903	906	1	906	902	1	902
2/1 GR	904	-	904	921	-	921	923	-	923	897	-	897
1/2 GR	921	5	800	856	4	735	919	4	802	898	4	778
2/2 GR	908	15	778	916	15	784	910	16	782	887	15	763
1/3 GR	901	13	901	866	7	866	904	7	904	887	6	887
2/3 GR	287	707	257	873	1	873	866	1	866	923	1	923
1/4 GR	895	1	895	895	1	895	888	-	888	887	1	887
2/4 GR	880	4	880	896	4	896	897	3	897	919	3	919
1/5 GR	901	10	901	891	4	891	879	4	879	903	4	903
2/5 GR	894	16	894	888	16	888	865	17	865	892	19	892
42 GLI (6 GR)	906	2	908	830	2	832	864	2	866	881	2	883
43 GR (2/8 GR)	855	-	855	806	-	806	856	-	856	875	-	875
44 GR (1/8 GR)	853	8	853	854	8	854	878	9	878	862	7	862
9 Bengal Inf (9 GR)	-	225	81	-	212	77	114	157	114	388	105	317
39 Bengal Inf (39 Garhwal R)	-	194	-	16	834	16	28	864	28	7	747	7
Guides Inf	123	17	121	122	7	120	102	18	101	115	18	115
10 Madras Inf (10 GR)	172	392	355	227	515	560	622	143	625	661	157	661

STRENGTHS IN GURKHA UNITS 1891–1910 AS AT 1 JANUARY cont../

1895-1898	1895 GURKHAS & NEPALESE	1895 HILLMEN IN BRITISH TERRITORY	1895 FROM NEPAL	1896 GURKHAS & NEPALESE	1896 HILLMEN IN BRITISH TERRITORY	1896 FROM NEPAL	1897 GURKHAS & NEPALESE	1897 HILLMEN IN BRITISH TERRITORY	1897 FROM NEPAL E	1897 FROM NEPAL W	1898 GURKHAS & NEPALESE	1898 HILLMEN IN BRITISH TERRITORY	1898 FROM NEPAL E	1898 FROM NEPAL W
1/1 GR	888	-	888	882	1	882	897	1	21	876	888	1	19	869
2/1 GR	924	-	925	889	-	890	888	-	680	209	911	-	106	805
1/2 GR	907	4	786	912	4	787	776	4	36	740	895	5	37	731
2/2 GR	901	14	775	887	15	755	762	14	-	707	897	13	56	714
1/3 GR	886	4	886	895	4	895	902	3	-	902	874	3	-	874
2/3 GR	896	1	896	885	1	885	913	1	2	868	896	1	2	842
1/4 GR	900	1	900	888	-	888	905	2	405	500	894	1	131	763
2/4 GR	878	3	878	884	-	884	882	11	79	772	888	10	85	772
1/5 GR	914	4	914	912	5	912	905	3	348	557	921	1	7	914
2/5 GR	889	14	889	883	13	883	892	13	9	883	890	13	9	881
42 GR (6 GR)	893	2	893	922	1	922	905	3	12	893	891	2	11	882
43 GR (2/8 GR)	848	-	848	869	-	869	869	-	69	800	890	-	70	820
44 GR (1/8 GR)	891	8	891	861	8	861	862	8	-	862	865	17	34	831
9 GR	378	79	308	563	119	563	658	56	36	622	776	57	24	743
39 Garhwal R	8	881	8	6	882	6	7	865	7	-	8	903	8	-
Guides Inf	93	15	93	109	15	109	99	16	82	17	94	12	821	14
10 Madras Inf (10 GR)	714	90	690	752	81	729	688	-	688		734	-	734	

STRENGTHS IN GURKHA UNITS 1891–1910 AS AT 1 JANUARY cont../

1899-1902	1899				1900				1901				1902			
	GURKHAS & NEPALESE	HILLMAN IN BRITISH TERRITORY	FROM NEPAL		GURKHAS & NEPALESE	HILLMAN IN BRITISH TERRITORY	FROM NEPAL		GURKHAS & NEPALESE	HILLMAN IN BRITISH TERRITORY	FROM NEPAL		GURKHAS & NEPALESE	HILLMAN IN BRITISH TERRITORY	FROM NEPAL	
			E	W			E	W			E	W			E	W
1/1 GR	882	1	19	863	897	1	19	878	889	1	18	871	901	-	16	885
2/1 GR	883	2	101	783	903	3	100	894	895	3	105	791	905	3	67	839
1/2 GR	880	4	29	722	889	3	28	726	868	3	27	611	880	-	22	745
2/2 GR	888	13	53	701	875	13	44	690	868	11	44	705	908	12	57	704
1/3 GR	877	6	-	877	876	5	-	876	870	5	-	870	891	5	-	891
2/3 GR	884	2	2	824	904	2	1	843	906	2	1	837	896	2	1	833
1/4 GR	901	2	3	898	879	4	2	877	903	4	10	893	952	4	-	952
2/4 GR	873	10	85	758	877	7	71	806	898	6	7	827	1056	3	58	998
1/5 GR	883	-	7	876	920	-	7	913	895	-	6	889	893	2	3	890
2/5 GR	888	13	13	879	913	-	9	904	886	-	9	877	900	-	9	891
42 GR (6 GR)	868	2	16	852	839	2	14	825	881	2	13	868	899	2	16	884
43 GR (2/8 GR)	886	-	59	827	846	-	48	797	888	1	45	843	885	-	32	853
44 GR (1/8 GR)	841	6	46	795	893	15	43	850	872	15	43	829	887	5	40	843
9 GR	796	54	23	765	823	39	23	793	781	36	22	755	807	33	19	788
39 Garhwal R	6	901	6	-	6	894	6	-	4	899	4	-	8	866	7	1
Guides Inf	94	13	-	94	92	10	-	92	101	7	-	101	105	5	-	105
10 Burma Inf (10 GR)	728	-	728		771	-	771		765	-	765		774	36	743	31

STRENGTHS IN GURKHA UNITS 1891–1910 AS AT 1 JANUARY cont../

1903-1906	1903				1904			1905			1906		
	GURKHAS & NEPALESE	HILLMAN IN BRITISH TERRITORY	FROM NEPAL E	FROM NEPAL W	GURKHAS & NEPALESE	HILLMAN IN BRITISH TERRITORY	FROM NEPAL	GURKHAS & NEPALESE	HILLMAN IN BRITISH TERRITORY	FROM NEPAL	GURKHAS & NEPALESE	HILLMAN IN BRITISH TERRITORY	FROM NEPAL
1/1 GR	892	-	11	881	901	-	901	910	-	910	899	1	899
2/1 GR	889	2	62	828	892	2	893	887	-	888	912	2	913
1/2 GR	875	-	17	745	913	-	816	917	-	822	914	2	825
2/2 GR	892	4	66	676	877	3	880	905	3	762	906	2	779
1/3 GR	880	4	-	880	881	3	881	900	3	900	881	-	881
2/3 GR	900	2	1	837	905	2	836	913	1	833	900	3	834
1/4 GR	849	4	3	846	896	4	896	903	2	903	901	2	901
2/4 GR	1041	2	51	990	947	4	947	892	-	892	886	1	886
1/5 GR	867	2	2	865	874	4	864	855	-	855	860	-	860
2/5 GR	873	-	4	869	900	-	900	908	-	908	910	-	910
1/6 GR	876	-	7	869	886	2	886	500	-	502	840	-	840
2/6 GR	-	-	-	-	-	-	-	483	-	483	857	-	857
43 GR/7 GR	850	-	21	879	879	2	879	896	2	896	703	2	703
44 GR/8 GR	871	5	40	831	920	-	923	850	-	854	829	6	829
1/9 GR	808	34	12	759	817	44	775	517	2	512	901	1	871
2/9 GR	-	-	-	-	-	-	-	504	4	497	820	51	820
1/10 GR	587	33	33	555	761	31	761	755	32	755	698	5	699
2/10 GR	433	-	92	341	798	-	798	840	1	840	847	-	847
Guides Inf	113	3	113	-	104	1	104	105	1	105	101	2	101

STRENGTHS IN GURKHA UNITS 1891–1910 AS AT 1 JANUARY cont../

1907-1910	1907			1908			1909			1910		
	GURKHAS & NEPALESE	HILLMEN IN BRITISH TERRITORY	FROM NEPAL	GURKHAS & NEPALESE	HILLMEN IN BRITISH TERRITORY	FROM NEPAL	GURKHAS & NEPALESE	HILLMEN IN BRITISH TERRITORY	FROM NEPAL	GURKHAS & NEPALESE	HILLMEN IN BRITISH TERRITORY	FROM NEPAL
1/1 GR	915	3	914	893	4	892	903	4	902	894	6	894
2/1 GR	916	2	917	895	-	896	888	-	889	896	-	897
1/2 GR	922	2	834	922	-	833	892	-	823	900	2	830
2/2 GR	892	7	776	902	5	795	911	1	822	896	1	792
1/3 GR	904	-	904	880	-	880	906	-	906	891	-	891
2/3 GR	910	2	910	906	3	846	911	3	840	904	3	837
1/4 GR	901	2	901	882	-	882	914	1	914	903	1	903
2/4 GR	893	-	893	857	-	856	901	-	901	876	-	876
1/5 GR	900	-	900	862	-	862	918	-	918	927	-	927
2/5 GR	867	-	867	898	-	898	883	-	883	896	-	896
1/6 GR	900	-	900	856	-	856	877	-	877	895	-	895
2/6 GR	920	-	920	838	-	838	875	-	875	919	-	919
1/7 GR	852	2	852	657	4	657	865	4	865	833	4	833
2/7 GR	-	-	-	687	2	687	906	2	906	849	4	849
1/8 GR	875	-	873	894	-	894	884	-	884	888	-	888
2/8 GR	-	-	-	921	-	921	926	-	926	914	-	914
1/9 GR	875	2	876	885	-	845	906	1	909	902	2	877
2/9 GR	890	27	890	893	26	893	897	21	897	860	34	860
1/10 GR	725	4	723	769	5	773	557	-	557	755	10	755
2/10 GR	894	-	894	-	-	-	519	14	519	833	9	796
Guides Inf	112	2	112	91	1	91	115	2	115	102	2	102

The above extracts from the annual returns cover those regiments which formed the numbered Gurkha Regiments who retained these numbers for the next century. They also include the Garhwal Rifles up to 1902.

Between 1897 and 1904 the entry "From Nepal" was divided into East and West Nepal. This shows that the great majority of Gurkhas in regular Indian Army regiments were domiciled in or recruited from West Nepal. There are some anomalies between the entry for "Gurkhas and Nepalese" and those listed as "From Nepal". In some regiments the numerical entry is identical or nearly so, indicating that all the soldiers were domiciled in or recruited from Nepal. In some years the "From Nepal" totals do include Line Boys. The entry for 1st and 2nd Battalions, 1st Gurkha Rifles for 1899, 1905 and 1906 have a foot note which shows that the "From Nepal" totals do include Line Boys. Other regiments, most notably 2nd Gurkha Rifles, appear to leave out Indian-domiciled recruits and Line Boys. Their totals "From Nepal" are consistently lower than the "Gurkhas and Nepalese" totals.

The presence of non-Gurkhas in small numbers continues to be shown in the returns of many of the Regiments shown in the above table. There are still some Muslims and "Other Hindus" shown in the Assam based regiments (later 6th, 2/8th and 1/8th Gurkha Rifles) but these numbers decline very shortly after 1890, as do the numbers of Assam Jharuas who had previously featured in these regiments.

The 9th Gurkha Rifles had also been largely composed of "Hindus" up to about 1893, with a few Muslims and Christians. In the years 1888 to 1893 they included their Gurkha element in the Total "Hindus", as shown below.

9GR	1888	1889	1890	1891	1892	1893
Total Hindus	750	758	773	757	750	745
Including Gurkhas	211	216	233	225	212	114 (+ 157 Hillmen)

The Imperial Service Troops of the Indian States were included in the annual returns with effect from 1900 (Gazette of India No 101 dated 10 July 1900). These returns all included "as at 1st January" but for some reasons from 1902 they are actually dated "as at 1st April". The Ulwar (Alwar) Imperial Service Lancers showed 12 Gurkhas in 1900, 7 in 1901, and 75 in 1902 after which they no longer appear. The Sirmur Imperial Service Sappers and Miners show:

	1900	1901	1902	1903	1904	1905	1906	1907	1908	1909	1910
Gurkha/ Nepalese	138(?)	12	12	12	20	20	20	30	38	35	51
Kumaonis/ Garhwalis	-	1	1	2	6	-	2	-	7	6	6

The Kashmir Imperial Service Troops shows the number of Gurkhas listed below as well as a few other "Hillmen".

	1900	1901	1902	1903	1904	1905	1906	1907	1908	1909	1910
1st Kashmir Inf	2	2	2	2	2	2	2	2	3	2	1
2nd Kashmir Rifles	326	327	303	316	291	328	338	325	431	423	451
4th Kashmir Rifles	314	314	321	320	315	333	325	327	-	-	-
5th Kashmir LI	200	200	203	205	210	212	211	214	-	-	-
3rd Kashmir Rifles									428	430	432
Kashmir Inf Depot									62	118	85
Kashmir Totals	842	843	829	843	818	875	876	868	924	973	969
Total Indian State Forces		847	897	855	883	898	896	898	962	1013	1025

The compositions of the Burma, Assam and Bengal Military Police Battalions were included in the Annual Class composition returns from 1904 onwards. These were originally dated "as at 1st April" but later changed to conform to the 1 January date used by all other units. The tables which follow show the Gurkha and Garhwali entries for these units.

In the Bengal Military Police there are very few Gurkhas shown – in 1904 and 1905 only 1, and in 1906 19. In the New Dacca Military Police there are no Gurkhas shown.

There is one entry for the Peshawar Border Military Police in 1908 showing 2 Gurkhas.

For the Assam Military Police the returns show the totals below. The Naga Hills MP Battalion appears to have switched from Gurkhas to Garhwalis in 1908.

	1904		1905		1906		1907		1908		1909		1910	
Assam M P Battalion	GURKHAS	GARHWALIS	GURKHAS	GARHWALIS	GURKHAS	GARHWALIS	GURKHAS	GARHWALIS	GURKHAS	GARHWALIS	GURKHAS	GARHWALIS	GURKHAS	GARHWALIS
Silchar	322	-	194	-	113	-	107	-	119	-	125	-	118	-
Lushai Hills	684	32	686	40	672	39	673	41	687	44	596	16	647	42
Lakimpur	684	-	681	-	687	-	710	-	690	-	730	-	713	-
Naga Hills	269	89	294	79	309	83	319	69	52	353	395	60	364	65
Garo Hills	92	-	104	-	97	1	97	3	123	4	154	7	138	7
Salween	-	-	-	-	-	-	-	-	-	-	65	1	62	1
Bengal	-	-	-	-	-	-	-	-	-	-	100	-	-	-

The Burma Military Police Battalions are listed below. There were no Gurkhas or Garhwalis shown in the MP Battalions of Bhamo, Chindwin, Magwe, Rangoon, nor in the Reserve Battalion. The Shwebo Battalion had 4 Gurkhas in 1904 and 1905, 2 in 1906, 3 in 1907 and 1908. In these extracts almost all the Gurkhas are listed as coming "From Nepal".

	1904		1905		1906		1907		1908		1909		1910	
Burma MP Battalion	GURKHAS	GARHWALIS	GURKHAS	GARHWALIS	GURKHAS	GARHWALIS	GURKHAS	GARHWALIS	GURKHAS	GARHWALIS	GURKHAS	GARHWALIS	GURKHAS	GARHWALIS
Myitkyina	1288	26	1285	11	1306	16	1328	11	1344	9	1351	14	1357	10
Ruby Mines	309	352	309	347	328	335	320	224	329	222	335	223	222	217
Chin Hills	309	218	318	189	328	234	337	198	318	195	265	162	317	200
North Shan States	213	155	201	115	215	115	214	115	214	144	204	112	203	115
South Shan States	-	-	-	-	494	5	500	6	501	5	426	9	710	9
Mandalay	315	-	337	324	-	-	-	-	-	-	-	-	-	-
Toungoo	161	3	206	19	60	15	95	14	112	12	141	-	92	2
Arakan Hill Tracts	192	-	196	-	186	-	184	-	193	-	192	-	193	-
Shwebo	4	-	4	-	2	-	3	-	3	-	3	-	3	-

As in the previous Class Returns before 1890 there are Gurkhas shown in a number of other units. Most of these are also noted to be "From Nepal". There continue to be some anomalies in these returns and almost certainly some misprints. There were some Gurkhas in the various Mule Corps (6 in 1907, 8 in 1908, 5 in 1909 and 14 in 1910).

NUMBER OF GURKHAS SHOWN 1891-1910

	1891	1892	1893	1894	1895	1896	1897	1898	1899	1900
5 Ben Cav	-	-	-	-	-	-	-	11	-	-
19 Ben Cav	-	-	-	-	-	-	1	1	1	1
Ben S & M	4	4	3	3	4	5	10	10	10	10
4 Ben Inf	-	-	-	-	-	-	-	-	-	-
5 Ben Inf	14	4	1	1	1	1	-	-	1	1
8 Ben Inf	9	6	5	4	1	1	1	-	-	-
13 Ben Inf	82	-	72	69	35	32	29	26	24	-
15 Sikhs	2	2	2	1	-	-	22	4	4	5
18 Ben Inf	40	36	34	10	5	4	2	1	1	1
22 Ben Inf	-	2	1	1	1	1	1	-	-	-
30 Ben Inf	-	-	1	2	-	3	3	3	3	3
31 Ben Inf	-	1	-	-	-	-	-	-	-	-
8 Madras Inf	-	-	-	-	-	-	1	-	-	-
12 Madras Inf	-	-	-	4	-	1	-	-	-	-
29 Madras Inf	-	-	-	-	-	1	1	1	1	1
31 Madras Inf	-	-	4	3	3	1	1	3	3	3
6 Madras Inf	-	-	-	-	-	-	-	-	-	-
33 Madras Inf	-	-	-	-	-	-	-	-	1	1
20 Punjabis	-	-	-	-	-	-	-	-	-	-
1 Punjab Inf	-	-	-	-	-	-	-	-	-	-
4 Punjab Inf	-	-	-	-	-	-	1	-	-	-
Bo Arty	-	40	-	-	-	-	-	-	-	-
107 Pioneers	-	-	-	-	-	-	-	-	-	-
113 Inf	-	-	-	-	-	-	-	-	-	-
17 Bo Inf	-	1	-	1	1	1	-	-	-	-
24 Bo Inf	1	6	10	-	8	7	-	-	-	-
27 Bo Inf	2	2	1	-	-	-	-	-	-	-
28 Bo Inf	2	2	2	2	2	2	-	-	-	-

	1901	1902	1903	1904	1905	1906	1907	1908	1909	1910
5 Ben Cav	-	-	-	-	-	-	-	-	-	-
19 Ben Cav	1	1	1	-	-	-	-	-	-	-
Ben S & M	9	8	8	10	8	6	6	7	6	6
4 Ben Inf	1	1	-	-	-	-	2	3	7	4
5 Ben Inf	2	-	-	-	-	-	-	-	-	-
8 Ben Inf	-	-	-	-	-	-	-	-	-	-
13 Ben Inf	24	21	-	24	23	23	17	22	17	1
15 Sikhs	-	-	5	-	5	4	4	4	3	3
18 Ben Inf	1	1	1	1	-	-	-	-	-	-
22 Ben Inf	-	-	-	-	-	-	-	-	-	-
30 Ben Inf	2	2	1	1	1	-	-	-	-	-
31 Ben Inf	-	-	-	-	-	-	-	-	-	-
8 Madras Inf	-	-	-	-	-	-	-	-	-	-
12 Madras Inf	-	-	-	-	-	-	-	-	-	-
29 Madras Inf	1	1	1	1	2	1	1	1	-	-
31 Madras Inf	2	-	-	-	4	8	8	6	7	5
6 Madras Inf	-	-	1	1	1	1	1	-	-	-
33 Madras Inf	1	-	1	-	-	-	-	-	-	-
20 Punjabis	-	-	-	10	-	-	-	-	-	-
1 Punjab Inf	-	1	1	-	-	-	-	-	-	-
4 Punjab Inf	-	-	-	-	-	-	-	-	-	-
Bo Arty	-	-	-	-	-	-	-	-	-	-
107 Pioneers	-	-	-	-	-	-	4	-	-	-
113 Inf	-	-	-	-	-	1	-	-	-	-
17 Bo Inf	-	-	-	-	-	-	-	-	-	-
24 Bo Inf	-	-	-	-	-	-	-	-	-	-
27 Bo Inf	-	-	-	-	-	-	-	-	-	-
28 Bo Inf	-	-	-	-	-	-	-	-	-	-

The establishment for the Infantry Battalions in the newly reorganized Indian Army was published in 1905. In this there were 20 Gurkha Battalions authorized, each of which were permitted "20 supernumaries except where the line boy system operated" when the number allowed was 14. Three infantry regiments, of which the 2nd Gurkha Rifles was the only Gurkha unit, were permitted one extra Jemadar to carry the "Hon Colour".

The establishment included.

Commandant	1	Followers	
Double Company Commander	4	English Master	1
Double Company Wing Officer	5	Vernacular Master	1
Adjutant	1	Pundit	1
Quartermaster	1		
Medical Officer	1		
	—		
Total	13		
Hospital Bhisti	2	Cook	2
Subedar Major	1	Sweeper	2
Subedar	7		
Jemadar	8	Tindal	1
	—		
Total	16	Lascar	4
Rank and File		Bhisti	8
Havildar	40	Sweeper	8
Naik	40	Chowdries	1
Bugler/Drummer	16	Mutsuddies	1
Sepoys	800		
Hospital Assistant	1		
Total	897	Total	30 .

FIRST WORLD WAR

All the ten regular regiments were authorised to raise a third Battalion during the war. All except the 4th Gurkha Rifles and the 10th Gurkha Rifles did so. By some extraordinary error, the 3rd/4th was gazetted as the 4th/3rd and this error was never corrected. After the war and the Third Afghan War, these war-raised battalions were all disbanded.

2nd Battalion 7th Gurkha Rifles was re-raised after the original battalion was captured at Kut in Mesopotamia.

There was also the 11th Gurkha Rifles, raised in the Middle East and Mesopotamia from 1918 onwards. There were four battalions all raised from existing battalions of other regiments. These were disbanded between 1919 and 1922.

In 1917 owing to the shortage of Sikhs, extra Gurkhas were enlisted in the Guides, with two more platoons in D Company. Many of these men came from Burma Military Police and Assam Military Police Units.

The Regimental History of the 10th Gurkha Rifles contains some interesting comments on recruiting during the First World War.

Their depot sent out 2149 of all ranks, 56 percent went to their own regiment and 43 percent to other units. About the recruits available the history states:

"At first, the quality was excellent, but, as recruiting became more and more intensive, orders were received that all classes were to be recruited and that men of below standard physique, who might be expected to improve with training, were to be accepted. In the event this was justified, for not more than 50 men from first to last were found unfit to take the field. In pursuance of this policy, a recruiting party was sent round the Gurkha bastis of the Shan States and the Namtu mines and brought in some good recruits"

The tables which follow give the composition by clan/jat of each of the regular Gurkha battalions, plus the Guides Infantry, for the period from 1911 to 1920, covering the First World War. In some years the Residents Escort, Nepal is included - even though this unit never had more than two Gurkhas on its strength. In 1917 there are two new entries for 1st Reserve and 2nd Reserve Battalions. The 1st Reserve Battalion became 4th Battalion 3rd Gurkha Rifles and 2nd Reserve Battalion became 3rd Battalion 5th Gurkha Rifles.

In the two annual returns for 1918 and 1919 there are misprints or mistakes in that the order of columns for Sunwars and Newars are reversed in the printed document. It is not known if the class returns have been changed or not. In these tables the original order has been used.

In the London Gazette of 30 July 1920 there is a long list of those mentioned in despatches which lists recipients by regiment. After the 3rd Battalion 11th Gurkha Rifles there is an entry for "Corps of Gurkha Scouts". Three Officers names appear each with the name of a parent regiment. This unit of Gurkha Scouts does not appear in any of the Annual Class Returns and no other record has been found.

At the end of these tables an example of the number of non-Gurkhas enlisted in the Regular Gurkha Regiments is given. This is an extract from the 1 January 1919 Class Returns. Similar tables could be extracted from the other annual returns between 1911 and 1920.

The first table is taken from the Handbook on Gurkhas (1935 edition Morris) which lists all classes enlisted (up to 1934–35). In 1915–16 Newars and Tamangs are separately recorded. The recruiting for 1919–1920 is included later. It is assumed that these figures refer only to the Gurkhas recruited through the regular recruiting organizations.

The Indian Army strengths during the First World War are recorded on a board in the Imperial War Museum. This shows the strengths as at:

	August 1914	November 1918
Combatants	193,901	877,068
Non-Combatants	45,460	563,369
Totals	239,561	1,440,437

Taking the Combatant totals, and comparing them against recorded Gurkha strengths at roughly the same dates (1914 – 24,305; 1918/1919 – 68,903) it can be calculated that at the beginning of the First World War, Gurkhas provided 12.5% of the combatant strength of the Indian Army and 7.8% at the end of the war.

TOTAL GURKHAS RECRUITED 1911–1919

Recruiting Season	NUMBER AND CLASS OF RECRUITS										
	THAKUR	CHHETRI	MAGAR	GURUNG	LIMBU	RAI	SUNWAR	NEWAR	TAMANG	OTHER	TOTAL
1911 – 12	66	60	464	400	256	421	29	X	X	61	1,757
1912 – 13	38	93	702	521	236	289	16	X	X	39	1,934
1913 – 14	70	129	591	434	243	418	23	X	X	45	1,953
1914 – 15	299	1,421	3,972	1,565	828	1,346	148	X	X	392	9,971
1915 – 16	909	4,324	6,546	2,506	748	1,280	229	427	492	835	18,296
1916 – 17	469	2,273	4,704	2,081	665	1,398	149	115	752	1,060	13,666
1917 – 18	422	2,420	4,080	2,016	704	1,431	195	300	684	2,142	14,394
1918 – 19	102	753	968	599	401	574	74	76	637	311	4,495

This table shows that 60,822 Gurkhas were recruited by the Gurkha Recruiting Staff between 1914 and 1919.

The next tables show the Gurkha strengths in Gurkha Regiments each year from 1911 to 1920, including also the Resident's Escort in Nepal and the Guides Infantry.

GURKHA STRENGTHS IN GURKHA REGIMENTS 1911–1920 (AS AT 1 JANUARY)

1911	MAGAR	GURUNG	KHAS THAKUR	LIMBU	RAI	SUNWAR	OTHER GURKHAS	TOTAL
Resident's Escort	2	-	-	-	-	-	-	2
1/1 GR	525	314	27	9	-	-	32	907
2/1 GR	548	273	39	18	12	1	27	918
1/2 GR	488	376	51	-	-	-	-	915
2/2 GR	372	464	33	-	-	-	35	904
1/3 GR	513	347	23	-	-	-	16	899
2/3 GR	536	352	30	-	-	-	8	926
1/4 GR	453	397	21	-	-	-	29	900
2/4 GR	483	276	44	-	3	-	38	844
1/5 GR	555	347	21	-	-	-	-	923
2/5 GR	562	293	42	1	1	-	22	921
1/6 GR	593	279	-	-	2	-	13	887
2/6 GR	564	318	1	-	2	1	6	892
1/7 GR	41	30	13	320	377	73	26	880
2/7 GR	35	34	21	329	368	57	22	866
1/8 GR	520	339	33	3	1	-	24	920
2/8 GR	557	304	38	1	-	-	19	919
1/9 GR	11	4	867	-	-	-	6	888
2/9 GR	5	-	868	-	-	-	12	885
1/10 GR	30	30	12	376	297	10	58	813
2/10 GR	72	26	29	370	319	23	38	877
Guides Inf	69	28	5	-	-	-	2	104

1912	MAGAR	GURUNG	KHAS THAKUR	LIMBU	RAI	SUNWAR	NEWAR	LAMA	OTHER GURKHAS	TOTAL
Resident's Escort	2	-	-	-	-	-	-	-	-	2
1/1 GR	531	308	21	9	1	-	9	-	19	898
2/1 GR	551	276	33	15	9	-	10	-	13	907
1/2 GR	488	376	29	1	-	-	1	1	25	921
2/2 GR	383	474	34	-	-	-	7	-	26	924
1/3 GR	504	367	25	-	-	-	-	-	15	911
2/3 GR	519	362	30	-	-	-	6	-	7	924
1/4 GR	441	391	18	-	-	-	8	-	27	885
2/4 GR	509	328	44	-	2	-	18	-	12	913
1/5 GR	532	340	25	-	-	-	-	-	29	926
2/5 GR	573	286	33	1	-	-	8	1	20	922
1/6 GR	598	285	-	-	2	-	-	-	10	895
2/6 GR	561	314	-	-	2	-	-	-	5	882
1/7 GR	36	26	-	326	370	70	-	9	21	858
2/7 GR	28	28	25	324	401	59	-	10	14	889
1/8 GR	536	355	33	9	5	-	3	1	10	952
2/8 GR	557	309	34	1	-	-	1	3	14	919
1/9 GR	10	4	836	-	-	-	5	-	4	859
2/9 GR	1	3	903	-	-	-	1	-	10	918
1/10 GR	30	24	14	364	310	9	1	23	21	796
2/10 GR	80	27	30	359	313	20	-	18	6	853
Guides Inf	69	33	4	-	-	-	-	-	1	107

1913	MAGAR	GURUNG	KHAS THAKUR	LIMBU	RAI	SUNWAR	NEWAR	LAMA	OTHER GURKHAS	TOTAL
Resident's Escort	2	-	-	-	-	-	-	-	-	2
1/1 GR	521	326	23	6	1	-	-	1	26	904
2/1 GR	551	285	34	15	8	-	11	-	12	916
1/2 GR	472	398	27	1	-	-	1	-	26	925
2/2 GR	394	463	83	-	-	-	7	-	25	972
1/3 GR	506	354	18	-	-	-	-	-	16	894
2/3 GR	520	342	30	-	-	-	4	-	8	904
1/4 GR	441	442	16	-	-	-	7	-	25	931
2/4 GR	521	309	37	-	2	-	1	-	12	882
1/5 GR	522	351	20	-	-	-	-	-	27	920
2/5 GR	569	299	32	1	-	-	7	1	19	928
1/6 GR	571	298	-	-	-	-	-	-	10	879
2/6 GR	541	315	-	-	2	-	-	-	5	863
1/7 GR	40	24	13	339	374	67	1	8	7	873
2/7 GR	27	24	19	350	395	61	-	7	11	894
1/8 GR	512	340	35	4	-	-	-	-	26	917
2/8 GR	540	314	40	1	-	-	-	3	13	911
1/9 GR	10	4	873	-	-	-	5	-	4	896
2/9 GR	2	3	892	-	-	-	-	-	14	911
1/10 GR	29	25	15	360	342	7	1	27	22	828
2/10 GR	74	31	21	346	344	20	-	25	22	883
Guides Inf	63	35	5	-	-	-	-	-	2	105

1914	MAGAR	GURUNG	KHAS THAKUR	LIMBU	RAI	SUNWAR	NEWAR	LAMA	OTHER GURKHAS	TOTAL
Resident's Escort	2	-	-	-	-	-	-	-	-	2
1/1 GR	519	320	23	6	-	-	8	1	18	895
2/1 GR	543	283	36	11	8	-	11	-	13	905
1/2 GR	474	372	27	1	-	-	2	-	31	907
2/2 GR	383	461	32	-	-	-	6	-	23	905
1/3 GR	516	363	13	-	-	-	1	-	13	906
2/3 GR	513	366	33	-	1	-	2	-	8	923
1/4 GR	446	417	9	-	-	-	7	-	29	908
2/4 GR	514	319	34	-	1	-	-	-	12	880
1/5 GR	487	392	20	-	-	-	-	-	24	923
2/5 GR	543	322	22	1	-	-	11	1	16	916
1/6 GR	576	322	-	-	2	-	-	-	9	909
2/6 GR	537	291	-	-	2	-	-	-	8	838
1/7 GR	38	19	12	373	367	66	2	8	7	892
2/7 GR	19	17	13	369	408	59	-	7	8	900
1/8 GR	518	336	33	-	-	-	-	-	33	920
2/8 GR	523	326	42	1	-	-	-	3	13	908
1/9 GR	8	10	867	-	-	-	4	-	5	894
2/9 GR	-	4	896	-	-	-	-	-	18	918
1/10 GR	31	31	16	328	353	7	-	26	19	811
2/10 GR	85	49	19	317	365	22	-	20	9	886
Guides Inf	63	37	3	-	-	-	-	-	3	106

1915	MAGAR	GURUNG	KHAS THAKUR	LIMBU	RAI	SUNWAR	NEWAR	LAMA	OTHER GURKHAS	TOTAL
Resident's Escort	2	-	-	-	-	-	-	-	-	2
1/1 GR	678	414	44	6	-	-	7	-	18	1167
2/1 GR	536	284	27	11	9	-	11	-	13	891
1/2 GR	528	352	33	1	-	-	2	-	31	947
2/2 GR	521	567	67	-	3	-	6	-	27	1191
1/3 GR	322	210	18	-	-	-	1	-	14	565
2/3 GR	686	446	63	-	1	-	2	-	8	1206
1/4 GR	686	479	11	-	-	-	5	-	19	1200
2/4 GR	476	248	34	1	2	-	3	1	14	779
1/5 GR	545	413	18	-	-	-	-	-	20	996
2/5 GR	592	328	37	1	-	-	8	1	17	984
1/6 GR	615	345	2	-	2	9	-	-	17	990
2/6 GR	604	349	-	-	2	-	-	-	9	964
1/7 GR	31	21	17	367	413	61	-	10	85	1005
2/7 GR	34	19	25	397	489	66	-	8	11	1049
1/8 GR	509	333	56	3	4	-	4	9	19	937
2/8 GR	570	324	56	-	-	2	1	3	14	970
1/9 GR	8	5	1203	-	-	-	4	-	5	1225
2/9 GR	-	4	827	-	-	-	4	-	6	841
1/10 GR	43	34	26	381	470	13	2	33	20	1022
2/10 GR	85	54	36	414	462	29	2	45	15	1142
Guides Inf	61	43	2	-	-	-	1	-	4	111

1916	MAGAR	GURUNG	KHAS THAKUR	LIMBU	RAI	SUNWAR	NEWAR	LAMA	OTHER GURKHAS	TOTAL
Resident's Escort	2	-	-	-	-	-	-	-	-	2
1/1 GR	816	417	183	22	9	9	20	9	23	1508
2/1 GR	947	446	111	24	26	-	37	-	23	1614
1/2 GR	991	622	122	14	22	1	19	2	53	1846
2/2 GR	659	554	148	19	29	1	22	7	47	1486
1/3 GR	1030	572	111	10	7	2	15	1	14	1762
2/3 GR	858	507	152	21	21	2	35	12	15	1623
1/4 GR	877	570	105	18	13	2	22	20	50	1677
2/4 GR	1209	594	147	25	3	1	9	3	21	2012
1/5 GR	771	511	91	-	62	8	5	6	28	1482
2/5 GR	686	375	142	3	66	1	27	18	17	1335
1/6 GR	341	209	8	3	15	9	7	5	70	667
2/6 GR	782	330	24	2	50	-	3	5	64	1260
1/7 GR	49	26	9	628	755	106	-	14	67	1654
2/7 GR	22	20	44	618	626	51	-	57	15	1453
1/8 GR	993	525	213	30	14	4	16	6	25	1826
2/8 GR	715	348	201	-	31	4	9	1	28	1337
1/9 GR	7	4	1465	-	-	-	2	-	5	1483
2/9 GR	-	5	1689	-	-	-	5	-	6	1705
1/10 GR	49	37	28	528	696	19	5	29	21	1412
2/10 GR	63	44	20	216	318	27	3	178	11	880
Guides Inf	116	44	2	-	-	-	1	-	2	165

1917	MAGAR	GURUNG	KHAS THAKUR	LIMBU	RAI	SUNWAR	NEWAR	LAMA	OTHER GURKHAS	TOTAL
1/1 GR	1579	737	252	87	122	10	53	12	35	2887
2/1 GR	844	365	100	14	20	-	32	-	27	1402
1/2 GR	1416	663	249	44	63	8	34	-	69	2546
2/2 GR	811	639	184	13	37	4	25	17	32	1762
1/3 GR	956	359	154	11	6	2	23	2	18	1531
2/3 GR	1107	557	255	17	16	4	53	19	40	2068
1/4 GR	926	598	110	17	15	6	17	5	62	1756
2/4 GR	1465	664	190	23	3	-	31	3	14	2393
1/5 GR	910	477	104	-	35	3	24	7	36	1596
2/5 GR	1107	546	224	8	64	6	47	34	22	2058
1/6 GR	1103	555	80	8	38	15	25	4	31	1859
2/6 GR	1412	569	40	3	45	-	24	4	127	2224
1/7 GR	40	30	11	481	602	-	69	60	7	1300
2/7 GR	68	63	19	402	610	65	10	410	-	1647
1/8 GR	1169	670	276	44	55	-	41	15	21	2291
2/8 GR	838	397	163	2	30	2	40	-	23	1495
1/9 GR	4	2	1702	-	-	-	3	-	7	1718
2/9 GR	-	8	2687	-	-	-	4	-	8	2707
1/10 GR	94	60	79	719	710	42	71	11	-	1786
2/10 GR	81	66	-	320	503	67	3	472	15	1527
1 Reserve	562	249	22	11	43	4	14	14	77	996
2 Reserve	319	131	302	39	97	18	15	119	10	1050
Guides Inf	90	82	-	-	-	2	-	-	-	174
Resident's Escort	2	-	-	-	-	-	-	-	-	2

1918	MAGAR	GURUNG	KHAS THAKUR	LIMBU	RAI	SUNWAR	NEWAR	LAMA	OTHER GUR-KHAS	TOTAL
1/1 GR	1468	675	258	57	82	50	5	12	32	2639
2/1 GR	937	397	108	13	17	42	-	-	24	1538
3/1 GR	483	250	85	2	4	20	4	1	8	857
1/2 GR	1255	620	259	8	11	37	2	-	72	2264
2/2 GR	743	525	149	6	14	25	-	12	37	1511
3/2 GR	393	219	108	2	4	11	-	-	17	754
1/3 GR	1146	619	146	1	5	19	1	-	12	1949
2/3 GR	881	463	205	10	16	44	2	16	48	1685
3/3 GR	388	167	67	9	5	22	2	3	14	677
4/3 GR	643	289	30	10	45	19	3	50	124	1213
1/4 GR	955	527	78	12	13	14	3	18	34	1654
2/4 GR	1587	666	272	53	39	48	3	16	19	2703
1/5 GR	1042	567	160	17	55	33	8	30	32	1944
2/5 GR	1245	632	258	22	82	59	7	50	42	2397
3/5 GR	387	189	347	49	91	22	17	119	15	1236
1/6 GR	503	222	12	3	4	16	10	1	86	857
2/6 GR	1187	498	39	5	40	14	-	9	144	1936
3/6 GR	349	150	255	38	83	17	11	75	8	986
1/7 GR	78	58	48	540	703	16	69	193	18	1723
2/7 GR	96	114	25	776	1108	2	190	286	104	2701
3/7 GR	46	44	77	188	364	17	50	330	39	1155
1/8 GR	1075	517	177	14	11	30	5	13	32	1874
2/8 GR	682	303	117	1	23	28	1	-	14	1169
3/8 GR	410	183	26	1	2	8	-	-	66	696
1/9 GR	12	4	1467	-	1	3	-	-	6	1493
2/9 GR	5	2	2331	-	-	4	-	-	-	2342
3/9 GR	-	-	913	-	-	-	-	-	3	916
1/10 GR	149	116	141	759	1033	16	71	266	54	2605
2/10 GR	86	89	43	276	656	15	75	613	9	1862
1/Guides Inf	215	216	14	17	23	19	4	29	90	627
2/Guides Inf	181	124	10	-	2	21	-	-	10	348
Guides Inf Depot	46	17	1	-	1	7	3	44	23	142
Resident's Escort	1	1	-	-	-	-	-	-	-	2

1919	MAGAR	GURUNG	KHAS THAKUR	LIMBU	RAI	SUNWAR	NEWAR	LAMA	OTHER GURKHAS	TOTAL
1/1 GR	1073	465	171	22	23	2	50	2	28	1836
2/1 GR	837	863	111	15	16	-	44	-	34	1920
3/1 GR	791	334	143	2	9	8	33	16	40	1376
1/2 GR	1018	532	217	4	7	3	32	9	64	1886
2/2 GR	729	514	140	4	10	-	28	13	38	1476
3/2 GR	560	395	199	2	24	-	28	22	25	1255
1/3 GR	1130	673	199	20	10	3	69	20	14	2138
2/3 GR	1108	496	236	9	16	1	59	74	69	2068
3/3 GR	437	217	157	20	34	6	32	2	16	921
4/3 GR	653	294	48	12	66	12	37	170	148	1440
1/4 GR	930	453	122	9	13	3	30	50	50	1660
2/4 GR	1280	577	222	23	27	4	38	17	22	2210
1/5 GR	1020	555	194	56	93	24	52	71	37	2102
2/5 GR	1099	546	237	12	63	6	55	52	44	2114
3/5 GR	485	219	360	65	108	27	29	144	24	1461
1/6 GR	1059	505	90	6	31	18	39	12	133	1893
2/6 GR	1099	486	48	1	24	-	49	37	199	1943
3/6 GR	467	258	316	92	191	12	29	107	44	1516
1/7 GR	93	67	68	545	672	65	16	203	22	1751
2/7 GR	143	118	71	700	957	101	8	392	80	2570
3/7 GR	66	70	133	295	588	69	32	488	43	1784
1/8 GR	991	474	240	13	27	10	34	23	42	1854
2/8 GR	995	408	185	3	21	5	42	17	28	1704
3/8 GR	571	237	27	27	71	15	39	182	106	1275
1/9 GR	9	4	1181	-	-	-	2	-	13	1209
2/9 GR	5	2	2244	-	-	-	4	-	-	2255
3/9 GR	-	-	1240	-	-	-	-	-	9	1249
1/10 GR	107	97	97	563	880	64	30	209	87	2134
2/10 GR	98	68	56	209	464	53	19	367	8	1342
1/11 GR	574	262	57	6	21	3	19	11	53	1006
2/11 GR	469	186	90	100	114	16	14	19	14	1022
3/11 GR	61	85	368	206	283	26	5	120	13	1167
4/11 GR	489	258	190	191	313	28	47	197	127	1840
1 Guides Inf	192	154	12	3	12	3	33	33	74	516
2 Guides Inf	214	192	8	-	3	-	15	19	12	463
3 Guides Inf	70	51	50	26	48	6	20	85	5	361
4 Guides Inf	15	3	-	-	-	-	-	-	1	19
Resident's Escort	1	1	-	-	-	-	-	-	-	2

1920	MAGAR	GURUNG	KHAS THAKUR	LIMBU	RAI	SUNWAR	NEWAR	LAMA	OTHER GURKHAS	TOTAL
1/1 GR	1158	548	151	20	19	4	41	11	31	1983
2/1 GR	573	266	77	8	14	6	25	3	25	997
3/1 GR	437	205	79	3	11	8	16	8	30	797
1/2 GR	883	645	251	8	9	10	36	6	72	1920
2/2 GR	492	373	82	4	4	3	18	4	19	999
3/2 GR	445	252	99	2	17	-	15	13	13	856
1/3 GR	1046	506	100	3	4	-	16	-	19	1694
2/3 GR	969	476	174	6	11	1	59	59	40	1795
3/3 GR	377	180	114	15	24	3	16	12	20	761
4/3 GR	468	244	64	17	49	9	15	66	33	965
1/4 GR	675	389	86	7	8	-	20	4	39	1228
2/4 GR	972	443	132	18	22	2	15	7	22	1633
1/5 GR	718	377	88	10	24	3	15	8	27	1270
2/5 GR	789	417	159	2	17	2	38	13	28	1465
3/5 GR	458	212	226	45	101	25	17	70	30	1184
1/6 GR	889	446	20	2	23	14	30	11	101	1536
2/6 GR	955	464	149	12	13	4	22	16	24	1659
3/6 GR	431	209	169	63	140	11	20	69	29	1141
1/7 GR	79	59	37	574	683	68	15	181	17	1713
2/7 GR	81	51	42	384	551	62	4	219	17	1411
3/7 GR	20	39	20	181	325	34	3	175	17	814
1/8 GR	837	412	189	9	18	5	25	19	31	1545
2/8 GR	591	250	140	3	18	1	27	7	27	1064
3/8 GR	380	186	39	24	46	4	9	72	46	806
1/9 GR	12	3	935	-	-	-	1	-	6	957
2/9 GR	-	2	1700	-	-	-	5	-	4	1711
3/9 GR	-	-	924	-	-	-	-	-	9	933
1/10 GR	80	85	66	482	757	46	7	180	33	1736
2/10 GR	77	50	38	214	426	46	12	346	17	1226
1/11 GR	490	231	56	6	18	3	12	6	19	841
2/11 GR	340	160	58	98	92	14	2	24	32	820
3/11 GR	34	36	312	156	208	15	6	64	12	843
4/11 GR	264	128	43	109	116	19	14	37	12	742
1 Guides Inf	163	166	12	22	-	8	13	36	-	420
2 Guides Inf	203	175	10	-	5	-	10	19	7	429
3 Guides Inf	79	58	37	23	29	4	13	25	-	268
Resident's Escort	-	-	-	-	-	-	-	2	-	2

The Burma Military Police units are also shown in these Annual Class Returns with the Gurkha clans/jats shown in the same columns as for the regular units. These separate columns are not shown in the table which follows which shows only the total number of Gurkhas in each unit. None of these units were 100% Gurkha but the other classes enlisted are not shown. The table which follows lists the total Gurkhas shown in Burma Military Police units in the period 1911 to 1920. All classes/jats are represented but the largest numbers are Limbus and Rais. The units which do not appear in the annual returns are marked "X". Those which have no Gurkhas are marked "-"

GURKHAS IN BURMA MILITARY POLICE AS AT 1 JANUARY

Burma Military Police Battalion	1911	1912	1913	1914	1915	1916	1917	1918	1919	1920
Myitkyina	1343	1369	1357	1420	1120	1538	1395	1382	1514	1527
Bhamo	1	1	-	1	1	1	1	231	263	244
Ruby Mines	110	105	112	111	X	X	X	X	X	X
Chindwin	-	X	X	X	X	X	X	301	366	382
Shwebo	1	1	-	-	-	-	-	-	-	-
North Shan States	300	313	332	318	346	315	317	384	371	366
South Shan States	694	693	697	710	666	833	759	708	848	866
Toungoo	110	107	140	138	-	-	-	-	-	-
Arakan Hill Tracts	188	194	160	158	159	154	148	153	159	162
Chin Hills	249	264	270	259	290	336	307	283	277	8
Salween	18	65	61	90	99	69	75	116	-	-
Putao	X	X	X	X	664	821	704	684	707	685
Mandalay	-	-	-	-	-	1	1	-	-	-
Reserve Bn	-	-	-	-	-	434	380	480	511	481
Recruit Bn	X	X	X	X	X	X	207	X	X	X
Rangoon	-	-	-	-	-	-	-	524	524	485

The Assam Rifles (Assam Military Police) units also show a high proportion of Gurkhas, again with other non-Gurkhas in each unit. The largest number of Limbus and Rais are found in the 1st and 2nd Battalions (Lushai Hills and Lakhimpur). This table also lists Gurkhas in the Bengal Military Police Units (Dacca) and the Ranchi Military Police. It is recorded in the history of the Assam Rifles that they sent 3197 officers and men as reinforcements to the regular Gurkha Regiments during the First World War. Again those units which do not appear in the annual returns are marked "X". Those which have no Gurkhas are marked "-".

GURKHAS IN ASSAM RIFLES ETC. AS AT 1 JANUARY

Assam Rifles Battalion	1911	1912	1913	1914	1915	1916	1917	1918	1919	1920
Lushai Hills (1st Bn)	622	614	649	659	623	1095	887	1015	1092	1081
Lakhimpur (2nd Bn)	696	750	730	786	742	730	942	865	905	947
Naga Hills (3rd Bn)	319	308	331	395	383	631	725	676	745	649
Darrang (4th Bn)	X	X	-	-	370	580	778	724	872	765
Silchar	X	X	111	132	X	X	X	X	X	X
Garo Hills	X	X	82	X	X	X	X	X	X	X
Dibrugarh	X	X	X	121	X	X	X	X	X	X
Bengal MP	110	100	-	-	-	-	-	-	-	-
Dacca MP	284	301	105	133	188	160	160	161	168	194
Ranchi MP	X	X	-	109	106	105	105	111	378	211

As in the previous Annual Class Returns, there are Gurkhas shown on the strength of many units of the Indian Army. The table below shows units which had Gurkhas recorded in the years between 1911 and 1920. The detailed annual returns show all these listed under separate classes/jats. This summary gives total numbers. The Bengal Sappers and Miners always had a few Gurkhas and their total rose to 120 in 1919. The Signals Units first appear in 1916 and by 1920 they show 233 Gurkhas in different Signals Units. In the Infantry the 4th Rajputs, 10th Jats, 13th Rajputs and 91st Punjabis had a few Gurkhas throughout. Other units which had a large number were the 85th Burman Rifles (447 in 1918; 569 in 1919), the 51st FF Sikhs and 53rd FF Sikhs in 1917, 1918 and the war-raised 151st Punjabi Rifles and 152nd Punjabis. Again in the annual returns all these totals are listed by separate class/jat. In this table only the total numbers are shown.

NUMBER OF GURKHAS IN NON GURKHA REGULAR UNITS 1911-1920
AS AT 1 JANUARY

	1911	1912	1913	1914	1915	1916	1917	1918	1919	1920
19 Lancers	-	1	1	1	1	1	1	2	4	4
43 Cav	-	-	-	-	-	-	-	-	1	-
Ben S & M	2	8	15	6	24	4	106	112	120	100
Arty Units	-	-	-	-	-	-	-	85	17	7
Signal Units	-	-	-	-	-	10	134	195	185	233
4 Rajputs	3	3	5	5	3	3	10	6	4	2
8 Rajputs	-	-	-	-	-	-	1	-	1	1
10 Jats	3	2	3	4	4	4	3	3	3	3
13 Rajputs	22	22	23	23	25	22	13	-	19	16
15 Sikhs	2	1	-	-	-	1	1	-	1	1
16 Rajputs	-	-	-	-	-	3	2	2	4	2
22 Punjabis	-	-	-	-	-	-	-	-	-	1
26 Punjabis	1	1	1	1	1	-	-	-	1	-
39 Garhwal Rifles	-	-	17	18	-	5	7	5	9	-
41 Dogras	-	-	-	-	-	-	-	-	-	1
42 Deoli	-	-	-	-	-	-	-	1	-	-
43 Erinpura	-	-	-	-	-	-	-	-	-	1
50 Kumaon Rifles	-	-	-	-	-	-	-	-	1	50
51 FF Sikhs	-	-	-	-	-	-	-	185	-	2
53 FF Sikhs	-	-	-	-	-	-	100	137	-	-
69 Punjabis	-	-	-	-	-	-	-	-	1	1
70 Burma Rifles	-	-	-	-	-	-	-	-	8	1
85 Burman Rifles	-	-	-	-	-	-	-	447	569	-
89 Punjabis	-	-	-	-	-	-	5	-	-	-
91 Punjabis	2	3	3	2	1	1	-	2	-	-
97 Deccan Inf	-	-	-	-	-	-	-	-	-	1
105 Mahratta LI	-	-	-	-	-	-	-	-	-	2
107 Pioneers	-	-	-	-	-	-	-	1	-	-
131 UP Regt	-	-	-	-	-	-	-	-	69	-
151 Punjabi Rifles	-	-	-	-	-	-	-	-	207	90
152 Punjabis	-	-	-	-	-	-	-	-	123	-

The same period included a number classed as Gurkhas enlisted in the various transport and works units. Again these are shown by separate classes/jats with the majority being classed as "other Gurkhas". There are however a respectable number of Khas/Thakur in these units. A number of units had a high percentage of Gurkhas although none were exclusively so. The 2nd Mule Depot had 69 Gurkhas in 1917 and 64 in 1918; the 3rd Mule Depot had 298 in 1918 and 372 in 1920; 27th Mule Company had 63 in 1917 and 74 in 1919; 43rd Mule Company had 69 in 1917 and 64 in 1918; 61st Mule Company had 74 in 1918; 63rd Pony Company had 74 in 1919; 84th United Provinces Works Battalion had

84 in 1920; 12th Draught Bullock Corps had 72 in 1920.

The following table lists the total number of Gurkhas in transport and works units between 1911 and 1920:

NUMBER OF GURKHAS IN TRANSPORT AND WORKS UNITS 1911-1920 AS AT 1 JANUARY

	1911	1912	1913	1914	1915	1916	1917	1918	1919	1920
Mule Depots	-	-	-	-	-	-	-	366	139	399
Mule Corps	-	9	15	27	9	33	219	231	413	255
Pony Corps	-	-	-	-	-	-	-	80	165	108
Camel Corps	-	-	-	-	-	-	-	5	-	-
Draught Bullock Corps	-	-	-	-	-	-	-	2	15	138
Remount Depot	-	-	-	-	-	-	-	-	13	-
Works Bn	-	-	-	-	-	-	-	-	-	97
MT School	-	-	-	-	-	-	-	10	10	47
MT Companies	-	-	-	-	-	-	-	1	-	20

The States Forces also had a number of Gurkhas in the ranks in the period 1911 to 1920. At this time those State Force units which had offered units to the Government, and who had attained/maintained a suitable standard of proficiency, were classed as Imperial Service Troops (IST). These are the only units recorded in the Annual Class Returns. As in all other returns the Gurkhas are shown by their separate class/jats. In the table which follows only the total numbers classed as Gurkhas are shown. The total number in 1911 was 1008 and in 1920 it was 843.

GURKHAS IN INDIAN STATES' FORCES 1911–1920 AS AT 1 JANUARY

	1911	1912	1913	1914	1915	1916	1917	1918	1919	1920
Bikaner Camel Corps	-	-	-	-	-	1	1	1	1	-
Sirmoor S & M	55	56	56	57	164	75	116	107	120	82
Tehri Garhwal S & M	4	4	4	4	2	2	-	4	-	-
1st Kashmir IS Inf	1	-	-	-	-	-	-	203	111	226
2nd Kashmir Rifles	438	433	440	449	437	449	415	520	137	317
3rd Kashmir Rifles	425	449	448	447	447	441	446	441	533	207
Kashmir Inf Depot	83	73	79	55	145	188	70	-	-	-
Nabha IS Inf	1	-	-	-	-	-	-	-	-	-
Jaipur IS Inf	1	1	1	1	3	2	2	-	-	-
Jaipur IS Tpt Corps	-	-	-	-	-	-	-	-	8	11

There were a number of non-Gurkhas enlisted in regular Gurkha units and an example is given in the next table to show these non-Gurkhas in the January 1919 class return.

OTHER CLASSES ON STRENGTH OF GURKHA REGIMENTS IN WORLD WAR 1
AS AT 1 JANUARY 1919

BATTALION	DOGRAS	GARHWALIS	KUMAONIS	BRAHMINS	RAJPUTS	SIKHS	JATS	AHIRS	MAHRATTAS	TAMILS	OTHER HINDUS	PUNJABI MUSLIMS	HINDUSTANI MUSLIMS	OTHER MUSLIMS	OTHERS
1/1	15	1													
2/1	7														
3/1	7														
1/2				4											
2/2				287											
3/2	1														
1/3															
2/3															
3/3															
4/3	2			14		1						13			
1/4	2					4									
2/4	8			34		1	1					1		1	
1/5	7			14								9			
2/5	9			4		1					1	4			
3/5	4			2	4							2		2	
1/6				1	8							12	1	4	
2/6				2		2		1			5	10	1		
3/6						1									
1/7	1	3		1		4					5	3			
2/7											25				
3/7			2	1		3	1				17	4	1		
1/8			2								9			1	203
2/8		16	8		7		1								
3/8	1	3	5		3							1		1	432
1/9			29		36										
2/9		4	7		2										
3/9		7	3		1										
1/10	1													2	
2/10		1		3		1					2	2	1		
1/11					9	1						1			
2/11											2	1			1
3/11									1	2	1				1
4/11															
Total	65	35	56	367	70	19	3	1	1	2	67	63	4	11	637

The totals shown in the various abstracts, including Gurkhas in Indian States' Forces, in the period 1911 to 1920 are given in the next table.

ABSTRACT OF TOTAL GURKHAS AS AT 1 JANUARY

JANUARY	INDIAN ARMY	IMPERIAL SERVICE TROOPS	MILITARY POLICE	TOTAL
1911	18043	1008	5037	24088
1912	18111	1017	5191	24319
1913	18142	1028	5135	24305
1914	18156	1013	5540	24709
1915	20263	1098	5752	27113
1916	30280	1156	7864	39300
1917	41230	1080	7861	50171
1918	50285	1275	8801	60361
1919	58299	910	9694	68903
1920	43768	943	9324	54035

These totals show that the number of Gurkhas serving more than doubled between 1915 and 1918, and reached its highest number in 1919.

To try to reconcile all these figures is difficult. The figures for the number of Gurkhas recruited between 1914 and 1919 contained in the Handbook (1935 edition, Morris) is 60122. The number of Gurkhas in named Gurkha units of the Indian Army on 1 January 1919 is 56326. The total number of Gurkhas, at the same date, serving in Indian Army Regular Units is 58299; and in Military Police units is 9694; and in Imperial Service Troops is 910; making a grand total of 68903.

When the war memorial at Kunraghat was unveiled in 1928, the official figure for enlistments in the named Gurkha infantry regiments between August 1914 and November 1918 was given as 55,589. This figure is taken from the official publication of 1923 entitled India's Contribution to the Great War. It appears in the table showing recruitment of fighting men by classes up to November 1918. Elsewhere in the same publication there is an entry which reads "a total of 58,904 recruits have been obtained from Nepal".

This illustrates the complexities of assessing Gurkha enlistment figures. Not all Gurkhas were domiciled in Nepal; not all joined named Gurkha units; not all recruits from Nepal were necessarily classed as Gurkhas. In addition it is not known how many recruits came through the official recruiting system. A number were probably locally enlisted. This almost certainly applies to those serving in the Imperial Service Troops and probably to a number of those enlisted in the Assam Rifles and Burma Military Police. Even within the thirty three battalions of the Gurkha Brigade at the end of the First World War (where there were 57398 classed as Gurkhas on their books), there are differences which will have depended on how soldiers were shown in the battalion long roll in the orderly room. This will particularly apply to those classed as "Other Gurkhas".

Then there were transfers made between units. For example there were 3197 officers and men sent as reinforcements to Gurkha Regiments from the Assam Rifles during the war. It is not certain whether these were shown on their parent unit strengths or were permanently transferred. The figures in reinforcements sent from the Burma Military Police battalions do not seem to be recorded, but it is known that there was a substantial number.

In addition during the First World War a large number of Dotiyals was recruited in the Far West of Nepal to serve in medical and labour units. These do not appear in the recruiting totals presumably because they were classed as non-military.

Another aspect of these complicated figures is that some Gurkha depots took in other classes for training. The 10th Gurkhas' Depot maintained a tradition of fathering other units. In 1917, at Mandalay, a company of Burmese was attached to it for training, equipment and discipline. This company formed the nucleus of what was known as the Burma Pioneers, and later the 1st Battalion of the 70th Burma Rifles. In June 1919 a company of Chins arrived from the 3/70th Burma Rifles. These, too, were trained at the Depot and became, in 1921, the 4/70th Chin Rifles. Similarly, in September 1919, a company of Kachins came from the 85th Burman Rifles, and they were afterwards raised to the strength of a battalion and became the 3/70th Kachin Rifles.

These anomalies also probably explain why there were 287 Brahmins listed in 2nd Battalion 2nd Gurkhas in the strength return table for 1 January 1919 (see page 77). There is an entry in the battalion's Digest of Services for September 1918 which states that "A special company of Mahratta Brahmins was attached to the battalion for training and discipline from this month". The battalion at that date was stationed at Tank in North West Frontier Province.

It is not possible to reconcile all these figures but there were probably around 60,000 Gurkha enlistments during the First World War. To this can be added the pre-war total strengths of regular units enlisting Gurkhas (Gurkha Brigade, Guides Infantry) of about 18,000, plus just over 5000 in the Assam Rifles and Burma Military Police; and another 1000 in the Imperial Service Troops; and another 100 in non-Gurkha regular units of the Indian Army, giving a total of about 84,100.

THE INTER WAR YEARS 1919-1939

The Guides Infantry lost its Gurkha companies in 1921/1922.

Between 1921 and 1928 there were two Gurkha companies in G Divisional Signals of the Indian Signal Corps, for which British Officers were seconded from Gurkha Regiments.

Gurkhas continued to be enlisted in Bengal, Assam and Burma units. A 5th Battalion Assam Rifles was raised in June 1920 for duty on the Darrang and Kamrup borders from drafts of the 3rd and 4th Battalions with the remainder directly recruited to make up a strength of 510. All Assam Rifles battalions were organised in 1920 as 8 companies (of 16 platoons); each was to have 4 companies Gurkhas, 3 companies Jharuas, 1 company Cacharis plus a few locals. The Eastern Frontier Rifles (Bengal Battalion) was formed in 1920. It enlisted Gurkhas (Gurungs, Magars, Limbus and Rais), as well as Jharuas of various clans including Meches (Kacharis), Rabhas, Koches (Rajbansis), Jaldas and Garos.

In the class composition of the Burma Frontier Force for 31 December 1939 the following Gurkhas were shown:

Bhamo Battalion	151
Chin Hills Battalion	163
Myitkyina Battalion	620
Northern Shan States Battalion	432
Southern Shan States Battalion	489
Reserve Battalion	472
Headquarters	1
Total	2,328

There were in addition some 438 Garhwalis and 450 Kumaonis in the Burma Frontier Force.

Up to the beginning of the Second World War there was a Gurkha Reserve consisting of 100 men per battalion who were registered at the recruiting depots and who were called up for training every other year. This reserve was not re-raised after the Second World War.

In the Handbook on Gurkhas 1935 (Morris) a list of all classes enlisted is given to cover the years from 1886–87 up to 1934–35.

The table which follows shows the number by class/jat enlisted from 1919–20 to 1934–35. The separate entries used up to 1918–19 for Newars and Tamangs are no longer shown. The first year 1919–20 shows the last of the war time enhanced recruiting.

TOTAL GURKHAS RECRUITED 1919-1935

Recruiting Season	NUMBER AND CLASS								
	THAKURS	CHHETRIS	MAGARS	GURUNGS	LIMBUS	RAIS	SUNWARS	OTHERS	TOTAL
1919–20	203	622	2,513	1,735	497	714	61	376	6,721
1920–21	15	97	484	295	336	349	3	374	1,953
1921–22	45	87	723	432	167	246	39	60	1,799
1922–23	67	114	865	589	188	278	2	185	2,288
1923–24	41	108	636	473	150	238	-	66	1,712
1924–25	48	145	621	517	174	361	11	74	1,951
1925–26	59	149	603	507	142	405	78	84	2,027
1926–27	51	110	542	606	177	240	34	349	2,109
1927–28	49	107	505	538	190	260	39	10	1,698
1928–29	62	114	521	441	194	184	26	22	1,564
1929–30	42	96	520	447	123	165	38	10	1,441
1930–31	69	164	852	588	138	250	25	5	2.091
1931–32	43	108	711	522	146	173	6	12	1,721
1932–33	38	104	566	446	211	179	59	21	1,624
1933–34	65	123	490	390	82	76	5	11	1,242
1934–35	62	97	549	441	177	244	25	10	1,605

The Annual Class Returns continue throughout this period. They start with the same separate categories as in the First World War, but in 1930 the entries for Khas Thakur are separated out into two separate columns of Thakur and Chhetri. From the same year the categories of Newar and Lama are omitted and two new categories are added, which were Dura and Ranabhatt. It is unclear who these last two categories were supposed to include, and clearly this posed a problem to the regular Gurkha Units since there is hardly an entry under the new categories in the next ten years' annual returns. The total entries between 1930 and 1939 for these categories are:

Dura   1 in 2/2 GR in 1930; 36 in 1/10 GR in 1935;
            8 in 2/10 GR in 1938; 2 in 1/8 GR in 1939

Ranabhatt   14 in 2/4 GR in 1930; 6 in 1/9 GR in 1932

The class of Lama, but not Newar, was reintroduced in 1938, having been omitted since 1930.

The next set of tables shows the strengths of regular Gurkha Regiments, plus Guides Infantry and Nepal Escort, in the years 1921 to 1939:

GURKHAS IN GURKHA UNITS 1921–1939
AS AT 1 JANUARY

1921	MAGAR	GURUNG	KHAS THAKUR	LIMBU	RAI	SUNWAR	NEWAR	LAMA	OTHER GURKHAS	TOTAL
1/1 GR	501	255	61	5	9	1	19	3	20	874
2/1 GR	518	253	68	10	9	-	24	2	20	904
3/1 GR	545	246	39	19	22	5	12	4	20	912
1/2 GR	714	351	151	7	11	4	15	8	40	1301
2/2 GR	416	330	68	3	5	1	22	7	28	880
1/3 GR	701	402	50	-	1	-	12	-	17	1183
2/3 GR	450	307	84	2	10	1	15	9	19	897
4/3 GR	542	245	52	31	61	13	10	30	20	1004
1/4 GR	613	367	63	8	12	-	9	3	39	1114
2/4 GR	565	297	74	3	1	-	8	2	12	962
1/5 GR	483	339	38	7	17	1	5	4	25	919
2/5 GR	447	250	69	1	6	-	22	3	23	821
3/5 GR	398	197	189	53	103	26	12	66	19	1063
1/6 GR	501	263	21	5	14	2	10	10	23	849
2/6 GR	505	296	61	6	8	1	12	1	16	906
1/7 GR	53	54	31	385	436	43	10	82	11	1105
2/7 GR	73	38	20	269	423	20	4	62	12	921
1/8 GR	607	314	63	4	3	-	7	9	20	1027
2/8 GR	533	250	94	1	12	2	17	6	17	932
3/8 GR	427	190	58	36	60	6	7	53	25	862
1/9 GR	8	3	898	-	-	-	1	-	7	917
2/9 GR	1	3	889	-	-	-	4	-	5	902
1/10 GR	56	64	20	383	476	42	7	125	21	1194
2/10 GR	66	51	35	209	313	21	8	122	17	842
1/11 GR	562	292	58	11	20	2	12	13	14	984
2/11 GR	432	199	138	115	169	14	4	-	4	1075
3/11 GR	44	39	160	148	171	13	11	57	4	647
1 Guides Inf	158	143	8	-	-	2	9	3	20	343
2 Guides Inf	186	150	8	-	5	-	11	16	12	388
3 Guides Inf	83	83	21	26	44	3	8	26	1	295
Resident's Escort	1	1	-	-	-	-	-	-	-	2

1922	MAGAR	GURUNG	KHAS THAKUR	LIMBU	RAI	SUNWAR	NEWAR	LAMA	OTHER GURKHAS	TOTAL
1/1 GR	531	263	60	5	9	2	18	-	15	903
2/1 GR	561	257	61	7	7	1	18	2	22	936
1/2 GR	473	303	145	4	1	2	11	3	33	975
2/2 GR	417	329	58	3	5	1	7	7	29	856
1/3 GR	488	226	23	1	-	-	7	-	17	762
2/3 GR	471	310	72	1	8	2	11	7	19	901
4/3 GR	470	280	40	30	56	13	7	41	35	972
1/4 GR	576	278	38	7	9	3	10	2	23	946
2/4 GR	579	339	57	2	4	2	4	2	9	998
1/5 GR	506	328	38	6	23	2	4	6	21	934
2/5 GR	554	255	64	-	8	-	22	4	20	927
1/6 GR	507	263	27	5	14	2	13	11	10	852
2/6 GR	459	336	65	3	8	-	8	5	18	902
1/7 GR	55	48	25	314	380	32	7	43	10	914
2/7 GR	73	40	24	267	433	20	4	49	16	926
1/8 GR	536	272	47	5	3	-	5	10	19	897
2/8 GR	586	268	80	-	10	1	11	2	13	971
1/9 GR	5	3	910	-	-	-	1	-	8	927
2/9 GR	1	3	869	-	-	-	3	-	6	882
1/10 GR	47	43	11	263	414	31	6	73	27	915
2/10 GR	65	43	37	206	313	19	7	119	17	826
1/11 GR	57	46	139	128	170	12	6	50	6	614
1 Guides Inf	-	-	-	-	-	-	-	-	-	-
2 Guides Inf	-	-	-	-	-	-	-	-	-	-
British Envoy at Court of Nepal	2	-	-	-	-	-	-	-	-	2

1923	MAGAR	GURUNG	KHAS THAKUR	LIMBU	RAI	SUNWAR	NEWAR	LAMA	OTHER GURKHAS	TOTAL
1/1 GR	443	266	29	5	3	1	6	1	138	892
2/1 GR	561	264	54	4	6	-	18	-	22	929
1/2 GR	496	287	77	4	10	2	9	2	29	916
2/2 GR	459	342	49	2	4	2	6	5	31	900
1/3 GR	561	331	22	-	-	-	3	-	19	936
2/3 GR	494	335	57	1	8	2	12	6	17	932
1/4 GR	663	348	45	2	2	2	9	2	21	1094
2/4 GR	526	317	45	4	2	1	4	2	11	912
1/5 RGR	521	351	34	5	20	1	3	3	17	955
2/5 RGR	565	245	63	-	7	-	19	5	23	927
1/6 GR	491	279	41	4	14	2	10	10	13	864
2/6 GR	485	315	66	-	8	-	8	5	28	915
1/7 GR	42	40	13	346	428	26	2	18	11	926
2/7 GR	39	28	32	285	430	48	3	56	8	929
1/8 GR	557	300	36	5	3	2	2	9	16	930
2/8 GR	555	271	68	-	2	1	8	-	15	920
1/9 GR	1	2	914	-	-	-	1	-	10	928
2/9 GR	2	2	882	-	-	-	2	-	4	892
1/10 GR	39	38	13	310	433	31	7	50	10	931
2/10 GR	51	47	27	267	385	33	8	86	17	921
*BEE, N	1	1	-	-	-	-	-	-	-	2

1924	MAGAR	GURUNG	KHAS THAKUR	LIMBU	RAI	SUNWAR	NEWAR	LAMA	OTHER GURKHAS	TOTAL
1/1 GR	431	308	26	5	7	1	5	2	133	918
2/1 GR	558	266	51	3	5	-	13	1	17	914
1/2 GR	479	342	48	4	7	1	9	-	27	917
2/2 GR	466	356	48	2	2	2	6	6	32	920
1/3 GR	564	270	29	-	-	-	3	3	18	887
2/3 GR	461	346	43	1	7	1	13	5	11	888
1/4 GR	520	323	32	1	4	-	7	2	25	914
2/4 GR	500	326	46	2	1	1	3	1	25	905
1/5 RGR	506	339	32	3	23	1	3	4	22	933
2/5 RGR	553	244	62	1	8	-	19	5	23	915
1/6 GR	535	279	23	4	14	2	5	11	18	891
2/6 GR	538	326	17	-	7	2	4	-	17	911
1/7 GR	44	32	10	343	436	26	2	16	11	920
2/7 GR	49	28	19	287	433	18	1	58	7	900
1/8 GR	553	301	27	5	3	-	4	8	13	914
2/8 GR	530	286	67	-	2	1	8	-	11	905
1/9 GR	14	2	885	-	-	-	2	-	12	915
2/9 GR	2	3	886	-	-	-	3	-	6	900
1/10 GR	27	37	13	295	432	25	6	39	12	886
2/10 GR	46	37	29	263	382	23	7	74	12	873
*BEE, N	3	-	-	-	-	-	-	-	-	3

*British Envoy's Escort Nepal

1925	MAGAR	GURUNG	KHAS THAKUR	LIMBU	RAI	SUNWAR	NEWAR	LAMA	OTHER GURKHAS	TOTAL
1/1 GR	463	364	53	6	8	-	11	-	12	917
2/1 GR	562	294	44	3	5	-	11	2	15	936
1/2 GR	436	372	53	4	8	1	10	-	30	914
2/2 GR	474	361	46	2	2	2	5	6	33	931
1/3 GR	533	325	35	-	-	-	3	2	16	914
2/3 GR	486	386	46	1	5	1	10	4	7	946
1/4 GR	530	314	36	1	3	-	4	1	20	909
2/4 GR	533	311	28	3	1	1	2	1	35	915
1/5 RGR	490	352	32	4	18	2	3	3	25	929
2/5 RGR	574	239	53	1	10	-	17	2	16	912
1/6 GR	559	293	14	4	13	2	3	10	18	916
2/6 GR	523	319	19	-	4	2	6	-	29	902
1/7 GR	37	30	11	324	421	24	1	11	11	870
2/7 GR	32	24	19	290	456	15	1	42	11	890
1/8 GR	535	304	26	4	2	-	4	8	14	897
2/8 GR	529	270	59	-	2	1	9	-	11	881
1/9 GR	2	1	889	-	-	1	1	-	11	905
2/9 GR	4	2	917	-	-	-	3	-	8	934
1/10 GR	25	33	15	316	441	21	5	35	11	902
2/10 GR	37	31	25	275	427	23	7	61	7	893
*BEE, N	3	-	-	-	-	-	-	-	-	3

1926	MAGAR	GURUNG	KHAS THAKUR	LIMBU	RAI	SUNWAR	NEWAR	LAMA	OTHER GURKHAS	TOTAL
1/1 GR	472	359	44	5	10	-	11	-	22	923
2/1 GR	526	313	44	3	4	-	9	1	21	921
1/2 GR	447	378	48	2	6	-	10	-	29	920
2/2 GR	463	370	42	2	2	1	4	6	34	924
1/3 GR	498	376	34	-	-	-	3	-	14	925
2/3 GR	471	394	35	1	5	1	12	2	10	931
1/4 GR	512	347	33	1	2	-	7	-	32	934
2/4 GR	441	334	25	6	-	-	1	2	94	903
1/5 RGR	480	349	32	2	16	-	5	4	18	906
2/5 RGR	535	281	52	1	9	-	14	2	19	913
1/6 GR	563	281	11	2	10	2	3	9	19	900
2/6 GR	500	312	32	-	6	1	3	1	22	877
1/7 GR	39	29	10	334	444	27	1	10	10	904
2/7 GR	37	19	16	256	440	17	1	36	8	830
1/8 GR	547	313	30	4	2	-	3	8	15	922
2/8 GR	555	286	56	1	4	1	6	1	10	920
1/9 GR	3	2	890	-	-	-	1	-	11	907
2/9 GR	-	2	912	-	-	-	2	-	10	926
1/10 GR	29	30	16	334	419	19	3	26	6	882
2/10 GR	30	38	24	260	414	30	7	55	11	869
*BEE, N	1	1	-	-	-	-	-	-	-	2

*British Envoy's Escort Nepal

1927	MAGAR	GURUNG	KHAS THAKUR	LIMBU	RAI	SUNWAR	NEWAR	LAMA	OTHER GURKHAS	TOTAL
1/1 GR	456	371	48	6	7	-	11	4	26	929
2/1 GR	532	310	44	4	4	-	9	1	18	922
1/2 GR	441	381	51	2	5	-	9	-	28	917
2/2 GR	454	323	33	2	1	1	3	6	30	853
1/3 GR	459	397	32	-	-	-	3	1	18	910
2/3 GR	452	398	32	1	4	1	10	1	12	911
1/4 GR	490	359	42	-	2	-	5	1	20	919
2/4 GR	515	317	29	3	2	1	1	-	29	897
1/5 RGR	445	394	27	2	13	-	4	4	22	911
2/5 RGR	521	287	45	-	8	-	13	2	19	895
1/6 GR	553	307	10	2	10	2	3	6	24	917
2/6 GR	498	359	22	-	2	-	2	1	25	909
1/7 GR	38	29	10	331	409	31	1	11	11	871
2/7 GR	33	18	17	256	470	26	1	31	6	858
1/8 GR	546	308	30	3	3	-	2	9	12	913
2/8 GR	550	294	50	1	4	1	7	2	12	921
1/9 GR	15	2	894	-	-	1	2	-	12	926
2/9 GR	3	3	894	-	-	-	2	-	10	912
1/10 GR	33	35	21	308	442	18	4	31	8	900
2/10 GR	32	38	21	222	442	34	10	54	8	861
*BEE, N	1	1	-	-	-	-	-	-	-	2

1928	MAGAR	GURUNG	KHAS THAKUR	LIMBU	RAI	SUNWAR	NEWAR	LAMA	OTHER GURKHAS	TOTAL
1/1 GR	462	356	44	6	6	5	6	1	25	911
2/1 GR	540	313	45	4	4	-	10	2	21	939
1/2 GR	449	413	50	2	-	-	8	-	28	950
2/2 GR	441	366	36	2	1	1	3	-	30	880
1/3 GR	456	441	25	-	-	-	2	-	18	942
2/3 GR	386	422	30	1	5	1	11	2	10	868
1/4 GR	473	393	36	-	2	-	5	1	25	935
2/4 GR	514	352	30	2	3	3	1	-	19	924
1/5 RGR	466	397	29	-	11	-	3	4	23	933
2/5 RGR	537	308	44	-	7	-	13	4	18	931
1/6 GR	548	331	10	2	9	2	3	3	22	930
2/6 GR	525	371	20	-	2	-	-	-	21	939
1/7 GR	36	26	9	340	453	36	1	9	10	920
2/7 GR	36	16	7	280	502	33	1	31	5	911
1/8 GR	553	311	28	2	3	-	1	9	11	918
2/8 GR	547	307	51	1	5	-	7	5	11	934
1/9 GR	16	2	913	-	-	1	1	-	11	944
2/9 GR	4	3	921	-	-	-	4	-	10	942
1/10 GR	34	34	25	354	451	17	4	26	9	954
2/10 GR	38	47	21	212	436	59	6	55	7	881
*BEE, N	-	-	-	-	-	-	-	-	2	2

*British Envoy's Escort Nepal

1929	MAGAR	GURUNG	KHAS THAKUR	LIMBU	RAI	SUNWAR	NEWAR	LAMA	OTHER GURKHAS	TOTAL
1/1 GR	469	374	42	6	5	-	8	4	24	932
2/1 GR	529	323	49	4	3	-	8	1	21	938
1/2 GR	444	407	50	2	-	-	8	-	26	937
2/2 GR	480	402	33	1	1	1	3	-	29	950
1/3 GR	435	467	18	-	-	-	1	-	17	938
2/3 GR	429	428	33	1	5	1	12	1	11	921
1/4 GR	477	406	33	-	1	-	4	1	22	944
2/4 GR	485	375	33	4	1	-	1	-	17	916
1/5 RGR	447	435	17	2	11	-	2	6	24	944
2/5 RGR	521	332	42	-	7	-	12	4	20	938
1/6 GR	587	328	9	2	8	1	3	3	20	961
2/6 GR	486	385	24	-	2	-	-	-	20	917
1/7 GR	22	35	8	346	435	46	1	10	10	913
2/7 GR	31	16	12	297	497	36	1	28	8	926
1/8 GR	580	299	27	2	2	-	-	8	14	932
2/8 GR	522	301	50	1	5	-	8	4	11	902
1/9 GR	18	5	898	-	-	-	3	-	12	936
2/9 GR	4	4	920	-	-	-	3	-	10	941
1/10 GR	36	32	25	333	432	18	6	36	8	926
2/10 GR	36	51	25	252	438	60	6	69	7	944
*BEE, N	2	-	-	-	-	-	-	-	-	2

1930	MAGAR	GURUNG	THAKUR	LIMBU	RAI	SUNWAR	CHHETRI	DURA	RANABHAT	OTHER GURKHA	TOTAL
1/1 GR	473	367	4	5	5	-	35	-	-	32	921
2/1 GR	546	317	18	3	2	-	30	-	-	32	948
1/2 GR	431	416	47	2	-	-	-	-	-	33	929
2/2 GR	467	397	14	1	-	-	21	1	-	26	927
1/3 GR	458	440	16	-	-	-	3	-	-	18	935
2/3 GR	443	444	24	1	5	1	4	-	-	23	945
1/4 GR	460	389	13	-	1	1	20	-	-	26	910
2/4 GR	488	368	27	3	1	1	3	-	14	23	928
1/5 RGR	436	409	16	1	10	-	11	-	-	35	918
2/5 RGR	514	336	40	4	10	-	-	-	-	31	935
1/6 GR	549	342	1	1	8	2	9	-	-	24	936
2/6 GR	463	399	25	-	1	-	2	-	-	16	906
1/7 GR	21	38	7	356	435	53	-	-	-	21	931
2/7 GR	37	12	-	275	499	48	12	-	-	36	919
1/8 GR	575	319	16	2	2	-	10	-	-	21	945
2/8 GR	526	311	46	2	5	-	-	-	-	25	915
1/9 GR	16	2	287	-	-	-	636	-	-	15	956
2/9 GR	4	3	284	-	-	-	628	-	-	13	932
1/10 GR	37	31	8	324	453	17	23	-	-	51	944
2/10 GR	32	52	5	276	438	62	27	-	-	78	970
*BEE, N	-	-	-	-	-	-	-	-	-	2	2

*British Envoy's Escort Nepal

1931	MAGAR	GURUNG	THAKUR	LIMBU	RAI	SUNWAR	CHHETRI	DURA	RANABHAT	OTHER GURKHA	TOTAL
1/1 GR	472	386	8	2	5	-	31	-	-	31	935
2/1 GR	538	312	20	3	2	-	21	-	-	28	924
1/2 GR	448	421	52	2	-	-	-	-	-	29	952
2/2 GR	499	374	19	-	-	-	16	-	-	28	936
1/3 GR	469	426	19	-	-	-	1	-	-	19	934
2/3 GR	450	431	24	1	4	1	5	-	-	22	938
1/4 GR	461	402	26	-	1	1	9	-	-	28	928
2/4 GR	512	390	28	2	-	1	-	-	-	15	948
1/5 RGR	441	424	20	-	9	-	9	-	-	34	937
2/5 RGR	489	357	21	-	7	-	12	-	-	30	916
1/6 GR	583	354	1	-	7	2	7	-	-	23	977
2/6 GR	525	376	24	-	1	-	1	-	-	17	944
1/7 GR	26	27	1	374	436	62	6	-	-	19	951
2/7 GR	31	12	1	305	502	36	14	-	-	33	934
1/8 GR	558	325	16	1	2	-	5	-	-	23	930
2/8 GR	556	297	21	1	4	-	17	-	-	26	922
1/9 GR	14	2	274	-	-	-	634	-	-	12	936
2/9 GR	3	3	291	-	-	-	654	-	-	12	963
1/10 GR	48	27	4	316	433	18	31	-	-	51	928
2/10 GR	42	41	4	257	418	56	18	-	-	72	908
*BEE, N	3	-	-	-	-	-	-	-	-	-	3

1932	MAGAR	GURUNG	THAKUR	LIMBU	RAI	SUNWAR	CHHETRI	DURA	RANABHAT	OTHER GURKHA	TOTAL
1/1 GR	457	371	6	3	3	-	27	-	-	25	892
2/1 GR	535	317	36	3	1	-	8	-	-	34	934
1/2 GR	437	400	23	2	-	-	-	-	-	29	891
2/2 GR	494	486	12	-	-	-	19	-	-	29	1040
1/3 GR	437	436	12	-	-	-	11	-	-	19	915
2/3 GR	450	435	24	1	2	-	6	-	-	22	940
1/4 GR	478	406	10	-	1	1	13	-	-	26	935
2/4 GR	491	409	21	2	-	2	-	-	-	13	938
1/5 RGR	430	433	22	-	9	-	4	-	-	27	925
2/5 RGR	485	368	23	-	7	1	8	-	-	32	924
1/6 GR	518	316	2	-	7	2	9	-	-	20	874
2/6 GR	503	362	21	-	1	-	-	-	-	13	900
1/7 GR	26	25	-	339	456	60	5	-	-	18	929
2/7 GR	31	17	1	308	475	33	11	-	-	30	906
1/8 GR	540	340	11	8	2	-	6	-	-	12	919
2/8 GR	566	302	20	1	4	-	15	-	-	20	928
1/9 GR	9	1	269	-	-	-	629	-	6	14	928
2/9 GR	3	2	230	-	-	-	617	-	-	13	865
1/10 GR	50	28	10	311	430	17	26	-	-	52	924
2/10 GR	38	44	1	286	432	57	24	-	-	76	958
*BEE, N	-	-	-	-	-	-	-	-	-	2	2

*British Envoys' Escort Nepal

1933	MAGAR	GURUNG	THAKUR	LIMBU	RAI	SUNWAR	CHHETRI	DURA	RANABHAT	OTHER GURKHA	TOTAL
1/1 GR	480	361	5	5	3	-	18	-	-	24	896
2/1 GR	529	325	13	4	1	-	28	-	-	28	928
1/2 GR	441	407	26	2	-	-	-	-	-	27	903
2/2 GR	474	388	9	-	-	-	21	-	-	26	918
1/3 GR	458	440	16	-	-	-	2	-	-	18	934
2/3 GR	446	407	14	2	3	-	8	-	-	24	904
1/4 GR	468	399	7	-	1	1	10	-	-	24	910
2/4 GR	503	382	19	2	-	2	-	-	-	18	926
1/5 RGR	416	447	19	-	9	-	5	-	-	30	926
2/5 RGR	478	363	21	-	6	1	6	-	-	31	906
1/6 GR	548	332	1	3	7	1	10	-	-	21	923
2/6 GR	480	398	20	-	1	-	-	-	-	10	909
1/7 GR	28	27	-	378	443	79	6	-	-	15	976
2/7 GR	21	17	-	315	534	26	10	-	-	28	951
1/8 GR	518	357	15	9	2	-	7	-	-	10	918
2/8 GR	570	326	13	1	4	-	13	-	-	23	950
1/9 GR	6	1	268	-	-	-	634	-	-	12	921
2/9 GR	-	2	305	-	-	-	613	-	-	14	934
1/10 GR	45	29	9	324	433	31	35	-	-	51	957
2/10 GR	32	43	1	300	392	65	22	-	-	74	929
*BEE, N	-	-	-	-	-	-	-	-	-	2	2

1934	MAGAR	GURUNG	THAKUR	LIMBU	RAI	SUNWAR	CHHETRI	DURA	RANABHAT	OTHER GURKHA	TOTAL
1/1 GR	496	376	5	2	5	-	21	-	-	20	925
2/1 GR	544	312	13	4	1	-	24	-	-	27	925
1/2 GR	459	437	22	2	-	-	-	-	-	25	945
2/2 GR	488	373	10	-	-	-	17	-	-	33	921
1/3 GR	445	450	12	1	-	-	5	-	-	16	929
2/3 GR	464	413	15	2	3	-	13	-	-	22	932
1/4 GR	489	415	9	-	-	1	9	-	-	21	944
2/4 GR	485	403	10	1	-	4	1	-	-	19	923
1/5 RGR	386	475	21	-	7	-	8	-	-	33	930
2/5 RGR	497	373	20	-	4	1	7	-	-	31	933
1/6 GR	543	339	-	2	6	2	8	-	-	20	920
2/6 GR	488	390	17	-	1	-	-	-	-	10	906
1/7 GR	18	26	-	340	415	79	8	-	-	13	899
2/7 GR	22	20	-	331	477	24	9	-	-	20	903
1/8 GR	526	335	14	-	2	-	5	-	-	19	901
2/8 GR	575	310	12	1	3	-	9	-	-	21	931
1/9 GR	7	1	292	-	-	-	623	-	-	12	935
2/9 GR	-	1	280	-	-	-	638	-	-	12	931
1/10 GR	46	29	15	319	395	28	28	-	-	52	912
2/10 GR	38	47	5	296	380	64	30	-	-	74	934
*BEE, N	2	-	-	-	-	-	-	-	-	-	2

*British Envoy's Escort Nepal

1935	MAGAR	GURUNG	THAKUR	LIMBU	RAI	SUNWAR	CHHETRI	DURA	RANABHAT	OTHER GURKHA	TOTAL
1/1 GR	517	372	5	2	4	-	23	-	-	18	941
2/1 GR	558	329	13	3	1	-	16	-	-	24	944
1/2 GR	426	417	22	2	-	-	-	-	-	15	882
2/2 GR	501	372	11	-	-	-	15	-	-	28	927
1/3 GR	455	443	11	1	-	-	2	-	-	16	928
2/3 GR	467	408	17	2	2	-	16	-	-	19	931
1/4 GR	493	413	9	-	-	1	7	-	-	19	942
2/4 GR	478	404	12	1	-	1	1	-	-	24	921
1/5 RGR	389	493	18	-	5	-	7	-	-	30	942
2/5 RGR	487	357	16	-	4	1	6	-	-	30	901
1/6 GR	562	338	-	2	5	2	7	-	-	17	933
2/6 GR	482	390	22	-	1	-	2	-	-	8	905
1/7 GR	19	23	-	342	414	82	7	-	-	14	901
2/7 GR	24	21	-	317	495	27	12	-	-	16	912
1/8 GR	557	326	13	-	3	-	4	-	-	14	917
2/8 GR	554	335	11	1	3	-	10	-	-	20	934
1/9 GR	8	1	292	-	-	-	596	-	-	11	908
2/9 GR	-	1	319	-	-	-	609	-	-	11	940
1/10 GR	44	30	13	311	436	24	26	36	-	14	934
2/10 GR	24	44	27	310	383	56	11	-	-	67	922
*BEE, N	2	-	-	-	-	-	-	-	-	-	2

1936	MAGAR	GURUNG	THAKUR	LIMBU	RAI	SUNWAR	CHHETRI	DURA	RANABHAT	OTHER GURKHA	TOTAL
1/1 GR	523	362	5	2	1	-	19	-	-	16	928
2/1 GR	523	336	14	3	2	-	21	-	-	20	919
1/2 GR	442	432	25	2	-	-	-	-	-	12	913
2/2 GR	496	379	8	-	-	-	17	-	-	22	922
1/3 GR	466	433	10	1	-	-	6	-	-	11	927
2/3 GR	488	400	14	3	1	-	9	-	-	12	927
1/4 GR	477	389	8	-	1	1	7	-	-	17	900
2/4 GR	495	389	10	-	-	1	2	-	-	19	916
1/5 RGR	369	478	16	-	3	-	10	-	-	27	903
2/5 RGR	467	400	16	1	3	2	6	-	-	33	928
1/6 GR	535	358	1	2	4	-	7	-	-	15	922
2/6 GR	478	405	19	-	2	-	3	-	-	8	915
1/7 GR	20	24	-	358	412	91	6	-	-	15	926
2/7 GR	31	19	3	333	481	24	10	-	-	17	918
1/8 GR	566	347	16	-	3	-	5	-	-	12	949
2/8 GR	542	345	11	1	2	-	11	-	-	21	933
1/9 GR	7	1	307	-	-	-	587	-	-	9	911
2/9 GR	-	1	299	-	-	-	593	-	-	12	905
1/10 GR	37	29	8	344	430	26	30	-	-	47	951
2/10 GR	24	42	18	329	390	61	16	-	-	53	933
*BEE, N	1	-	-	-	-	-	-	-	-	-	1

*British Envoy's Escort Nepal

1937	MAGAR	GURUNG	THAKUR	LIMBU	RAI	SUNWAR	CHHETRI	DURA	RANABHAT	OTHER GURKHA	TOTAL
1/1 GR	501	370	2	2	1	-	18	-	-	17	911
2/1 GR	513	345	12	2	2	-	21	-	-	29	924
1/2 GR	446	431	23	2	-	-	-	-	-	13	915
2/2 GR	516	372	11	-	-	-	16	-	-	14	929
1/3 GR	462	442	10	1	-	-	5	-	-	8	928
2/3 GR	480	399	16	2	1	1	7	-	-	12	918
1/4 GR	489	399	8	-	3	1	7	-	-	16	923
2/4 GR	471	396	7	-	-	3	4	-	-	20	901
1/5 RGR	377	485	16	-	1	-	10	-	-	25	914
2/5 RGR	464	418	17	1	3	2	6	-	-	32	943
1/6 GR	527	363	1	1	4	-	7	-	-	14	917
2/6 GR	486	375	21	-	2	-	2	-	-	4	890
1/7 GR	21	29	-	373	430	75	5	-	-	15	948
2/7 GR	30	20	1	358	474	30	9	-	-	16	938
1/8 GR	528	345	13	-	4	-	5	-	-	11	906
2/8 GR	539	339	10	1	2	-	8	-	-	21	920
1/9 GR	7	2	313	-	-	-	608	-	-	8	938
2/9 GR	-	1	313	-	-	-	600	-	-	11	925
1/10 GR	40	24	12	335	405	21	28	-	-	48	913
2/10 GR	33	35	5	329	406	50	21	-	-	57	936
*BEE, N	1	1	-	-	-	-	-	-	-	-	2

1938	MAGAR	GURUNG	THAKUR	LIMBU	RAI	SUNWAR	CHHETRI	DURA	RANABHAT	LAMA	OTHER GURKHA	TOTAL
1/1 GR	527	354	2	2	2	1	16	-	-	1	17	922
2/1 GR	534	349	12	3	2	-	25	-	-	-	19	944
1/2 GR	423	449	19	1	-	-	2	-	-	-	10	904
2/2 GR	531	355	16	-	1	-	13	-	-	8	12	936
1/3 GR	498	419	20	1	-	-	1	-	-	-	7	946
2/3 GR	468	415	7	3	1	1	9	-	-	1	14	919
1/4 GR	485	399	6	-	1	-	6	-	-	-	16	913
2/4 GR	470	410	12	-	-	1	2	-	-	-	18	913
1/5 RGR	381	492	16	-	1	-	6	-	-	-	23	919
2/5 RGR	455	422	15	2	3	2	6	-	-	8	26	939
1/6 GR	527	369	1	1	2	-	8	-	-	1	16	925
2/6 GR	383	497	16	-	2	-	1	-	-	-	3	902
1/7 GR	22	28	-	348	398	68	5	-	-	8	7	884
2/7 GR	25	19	2	337	461	28	9	-	-	2	18	901
1/8 GR	568	339	19	-	4	-	4	-	-	8	8	950
2/8 GR	548	362	10	-	2	-	5	-	-	3	11	941
1/9 GR	8	2	313	-	-	-	618	-	-	-	8	949
2/9 GR	-	1	318	-	-	-	584	-	-	-	12	915
1/10 GR	44	26	9	334	421	20	29	-	-	33	8	924
2/10 GR	34	35	4	334	388	50	19	8	-	47	6	925
*BEE, N	1	-	-	1	-	-	-	-	-	-	-	2

*British Envoy's Escort Nepal

1939	MAGAR	GURUNG	THAKUR	LIMBU	RAI	SUNWAR	CHHETRI	DURA	RANABHAT	LAMA	OTHER GURKHA	TOTAL
1/1 GR	540	356	2	2	1	-	15	-	-	1	15	932
2/1 GR	530	329	9	3	1	-	17	-	-	-	35	924
1/2 GR	458	416	22	1	8	-	-	-	-	-	8	913
2/2 GR	545	345	17	-	1	-	12	-	-	8	10	938
1/3 GR	484	423	16	1	-	-	2	-	-	-	7	933
2/3 GR	451	427	6	4	1	1	8	-	-	-	28	926
1/4 GR	509	423	6	-	1	-	7	-	-	-	17	963
2/4 GR	472	421	12	-	-	1	1	-	-	-	18	925
1/5 RGR	368	512	15	-	1	-	9	-	-	-	23	928
2/5 RGR	440	425	15	2	1	2	3	-	-	7	26	921
1/6 GR	503	401	1	1	1	-	8	-	-	-	15	930
2/6 GR	497	381	17	-	2	-	2	-	-	-	3	902
1/7 GR	23	27	-	369	444	66	5	-	-	9	5	948
2/7 GR	24	20	1	352	473	30	7	-	-	8	12	927
1/8 GR	535	320	17	-	3	-	5	-	-	8	5	893
2/8 GR	532	358	8	-	2	-	6	2	-	3	8	919
1/9 GR	7	2	331	-	-	-	562	-	-	-	10	912
2/9 GR	-	1	312	-	-	-	621	-	-	-	12	946
1/10 GR	42	22	17	341	432	14	24	-	-	31	9	932
2/10 GR	32	32	4	336	378	48	22	-	-	40	13	905
*BEE, N	1	-	1	-	-	-	-	-	-	-	-	2

*British Envoy's Escort Nepal

The Burma Military Police units continued to have a large number of Gurkhas in the period 1921 to 1939. These are shown in the same manner as the regular regiments by separate classes/jats. The table which follows shows only the total number of Gurkhas in each unit, all of which had some non Gurkhas on their strengths. The Shwebo Battalion had no Gurkhas in 1921 and disappears from the list in 1922, presumably because it was disbanded or absorbed into another battalion. The Toungoo Battalion had no Gurkhas in 1923 to 1925 and is deleted in 1926. The Salween Battalion is shown in 1925 with no Gurkhas, and disappears in 1926. Likewise the Chindwin Battalion disappears in 1923. The Mandalay Battalion had no Gurkhas until 1932. The Myitkyina Battalion divided into an Eastern and Western Battalion in 1926 at which date the North West Border/North West Frontier Battalion ceased to be shown; perhaps it became part of the new divided Myitkyina Battalions. The Putao Battalion appears up to 1925 after which it disappears. The Chindwin Battalion appears up to 1922 and thereafter disappears. The Rangoon Battalion divides in 1932 into a 1st and 2nd Battalion. In 1936 Burma was separated from India but the troops in the new Burma Armed Forces continued to be shown in the Annual Class Returns. The Burma Military Police was divided in 1938 into Burma Military Police (Mandalay, 1st and 2nd Rangoon Battalion) and the remainder into the Burma Frontier Force.

GURKHAS IN BURMA MILITARY POLICE UNITS AS AT 1 JANUARY

	1921	1922	1923	1924	1925	1926	1927	1928	1929	1930
Bhamo	208	175	122	10	-	113	109	110	109	112
Putao	650	605	540	543	485	X	X	X	X	X
Chin Hills	349	237	210	229	200	217	217	213	221	232
Chindwin	362	314	X	X	X	X	X	X	X	X
Northern Shan States	354	308	224	225	211	205	222	217	216	222
Southern Shan States	803	661	588	557	414	436	430	435	437	470
Myitkyina	1473	1249	1031	1015	985	^{E}867	^{E}659	^{E}675	^{E}686	^{E}699
						^{W}433	^{W}645	^{W}539	^{W}564	^{W}563
Rangoon	371	429	425	381	318	193	220	216	378	344
Arakan Hill Tracts	159	151	158	160	162	160	148	92	X	X
Reserve Bn	453	369	216	117	222	207	220	321	329	336
Salween	X	X	57	61	-	X	X	X	X	X
NW Border	X	X	205	218	21	X	X	X	X	X
Mandalay	-	-	-	-	-	-	-	-	-	-

	1931	1932	1933	1934	1935	1936	1937	1938	1939
Bhamo	113	113	105	104	113	111	152	142	143
Putao	X	X	X	X	X	X	X	X	X
Chin Hills	232	217	212	252	241	247	229	213	159
Chindwin	X	X	X	X	X	X	X	X	X
Northern Shan States	231	229	226	223	229	225	459	447	404
Southern Shan States	452	534	531	522	510	481	508	454	362
Myitkyina	^{E}703	^{E}670	^{E}672	^{E}646	^{E}665	^{E}674	^{E}468	734	586
	^{W}539	^{W}541	^{W}570	^{W}564	^{W}540	^{W}578	^{W}273	-	-
Rangoon	349	1st109 2nd293	1st66 2nd197	1st185 2nd255	1st270 2nd239	1st261 2nd236	1st258 2nd149	1st243 2nd272	1st248 2nd250
Arakan Hill Tracts	X	X	X	X	X	X	X	X	X
Reserve Bn	338	339	487	465	467	494	518	501	481
Salween	X	X	X	X	X	X	X	X	X
NW Border NW Frontier	X	X	X	X	X	X	X	X	X
Mandalay	-	317	318	365	340	336	488	488	493

The Assam Rifles Battalions continued to enlist Gurkhas throughout the period 1921 to 1939. Every Battalion had large Gurkha numbers, but none were wholly Gurkha. The Annual Class Returns show each battalion with the same separate categories of classes/jats as for the rest of the Indian Army. The table which follows shows only the total number of Gurkhas. The Assam Rifles had five battalions up to 1933 when they reduced to four. The 1st Battalion is entered as the Lushai Hills Battalion up to 1932. The 2nd Battalion is entered as the Lakhimpur Battalion throughout the period, and the 3rd Battalion is likewise shown as Naga Hills Battalion throughout. The 4th Battalion is shown as Manipur Battalion from 1923 to 1925.

The table which follows also shows the Eastern Frontier Rifles, a Bengal Military Police battalion, which was originally called the Dacca Military Police. There were also three Military Police Companies (Bhagalpur, Ranchi and Arrah) shown in the same table, all under the same entry. The Bhagalpur and Arrah units had no Gurkhas so the table entry which follows is listed as Ranchi Military Police Company.

GURKHAS IN ASSAM RIFLES AS AT 1 JANUARY

	1921	1922	1923	1924	1925	1926	1927	1928	1929
1st Bn (Lushai Hills)	830	762	688	558	540	523	514	459	443
2nd Bn (Lakhimpur)	724	647	599	558	554	544	548	559	555
3rd Bn (Naga Hills)	608	592	567	507	492	472	464	463	427
4th Bn (Manipur)	680	614	554	545	507	481	502	547	533
5th Bn	547	552	525	500	493	559	553	550	572
Eastern Frontier Rifles	197	189	192	179	177	182	204	217	249
Ranchi Coy	213	217	245	246	231	220	219	220	213

	1930	1931	1932	1933	1934	1935	1936	1937	1938	1939
1st Bn (Lushai Hills)	470	443	472	493	498	535	547	529	541	545
2nd Bn (Lakhimpur)	607	615	595	1003	1005	933	938	1084	1084	1022
3rd Bn (Naga Hills)	438	423	415	454	458	467	462	500	513	526
4th Bn (Manipur)	535	548	504	539	555	551	552	590	528	551
5th Bn	547	560	502	-	-	-	-	-	-	-
Eastern Frontier Rifles	287	313	330	337	358	356	358	340	357	373
Ranchi Coy	214	219	213	210	208	212	222	220	209	220

The Annual Class Returns continued to show Gurkhas in many units of the Indian Army. Each unit entry is broken down by separate clans/jats, but in the table which follows only the Gurkha totals are shown. The Indian Army had a major reorganization in 1922 so these total are shown under the post 1922 titles. There continue to be some anomalies and perhaps misprints for instance in 1921 there are 72 Gurkhas shown in the 40th Cavalry, a war-raised regiment. There are no Gurkhas shown in this unit in the years before or after 1921. From the year 1938 onwards the 20th Burma Rifles entries are no longer shown since Burma was separated from India in 1936.

GURKHAS IN NON-GURKHA UNITS 1921–1939 AS AT 1 JANUARY

	1921	1922	1923	1924	1925	1926	1927	1928	1929	1930
19 Lancers	-	-	3	-	-	-	-	-	-	-
40 Cavalry	72	-	-	-	-	-	-	-	-	-
Arty Units	30	18	-	-	-	3	7	1	3	3
Engineer Units	47	-	-	-	-	32	43	32	33	-
Signals Units	122	177	179	167	149	139	104	85	69	58
MG Corps	2	-	-	-	-	-	-	-	-	-
Drivers Depot	2	-	-	-	-	-	-	-	-	-
1 Punjab	1	1	-	-	-	-	-	1	1	1
2 Punjab	-	-	-	-	-	-	-	-	-	-
4 Bombay Grenadiers	-	-	-	-	-	-	-	1	1	3
5 Mahratta LI	2	2	-	2	8	18	21	18	21	22
6 Rajputana Rifles	25	23	22	22	23	33	31	35	35	32
7 Rajput	5	4	4	2	3	4	4	4	4	4
8 Punjab	-	-	-	-	1	-	3	2	4	2
9 Jat	3	-	-	-	10	-	-	-	-	-
11 Sikh	-	1	-	3	3	2	1	1	1	1
12 Frontier Force Regt	4	-	-	-	-	-	-	-	-	-
13 Frontier Force Rifles	-	-	-	-	-	1	-	-	-	-
16 Punjab	-	-	-	2	1	1	1	1	-	-
17 Dogras	1	1	1	1	1	1	1	3	4	4
18 R Garhwal Rifles	22	-	-	15	24	31	32	29	26	31
19 Hyderabad	-	-	-	-	-	5	1	-	3	10
1st Kumaon Rifles	57	78	69	40	20	40	42	42	40	38
20th Burma Rifles	-	2	38	13	11	35	68	70	75	72
MT Units	-	72	61	48	47	36	36	26	22	25
Mule Corps	-	228	48	24	10	3	19	-	4	1
BullockCorps	-	13	3	6	7	6	6	15	3	-
Sikh Pioneers	-	1	-	-	-	-	-	-	-	-
Bombay Pioneers	1	2	4	2	-	1	-	-	-	-
15 Punjab	1	-	-	-	-	-	-	-	-	-
42 Deoli	1	-	-	-	-	-	-	-	-	-

	1931	1932	1933	1934	1935	1936	1937	1938	1939
19 Lancers	-	-	-	-	-	-	-	-	-
48 Cavalry	-	-	-	-	-	-	-	-	-
Arty Units	2	2	2	2	2	2	3	2	2
Engineer Units	-	-	-	13	9	8	4	4	4
Signals Units	51	46	31	24	21	16	8	1	-
MG Corps	-	-	-	-	-	-	-	-	-
Drivers Depot	-	-	-	-	-	-	-	-	-
1 Punjab	1	1	1	1	-	-	-	-	-
2 Punjab	-	-	-	-	-	-	1	-	-
4 Bombay Grenadiers	-	-	-	-	-	-	-	-	-
5 Mahratta	23	31	38	42	18	43	42	42	44
6 Rajputana Rifles	29	29	29	25	-	26	27	24	28
7 Rajput	5	3	4	4	4	4	4	4	4
8 Punjab	2	2	2	2	2	2	2	3	1
9 Jat	3	1	-	-	-	-	-	-	-
11 Sikh	1	1	1	1	1	1	1	1	1
12 Frontier Force Regt	-	-	-	-	-	-	-	-	-
13 Frontier Force Rifles	-	-	-	-	-	-	-	-	-
16 Punjab	-	-	-	-	-	-	-	-	-
17 Dogras	1	1	1	1	1	1	1	1	2
18 R Garhwal Rifles	25	24	19	16	14	11	12	11	11
19 Hyderabad	1	9	10	10	11	13	13	14	11
1st Kumaon Rifles	-	39	19	13	11	8	12	10	4
20th Burma Rifles	67	-	62	59	62	64	96	-	-
MT Units	26	30	24	20	21	14	8	5	9
Mule Corps	3	3	3	3	1	2	2	4	3
BullockCorps									
Sikh Pioneers	-	-	-	-	-	-	-	-	-
Bombay Pioneers	-	-	-	-	-	-	-	-	-
15 Punjab									
42 Deoli	-	-	-	-	-	-	-	-	-

The Forces of the Indian Princely States changed their designation in 1920 from Imperial Service Troops to Indian States Forces. Throughout the period 1920 to 1939 they continued to recruit a number of Gurkhas. Under their agreements with the Government of India, these States were supposed to recruit within their own boundaries (with some exceptions). It is not known where they recruited their Gurkha soldiers. They did not come through the Gurkha Brigade recruiting organization. It is possible that some might have been ex-servicemen; others could have been India domiciled.

The States Forces of Kashmir continued to have a large number of Gurkhas, mainly in the 2nd and 3rd Kashmir Rifles. The annual total in these two units was between 600 and 800 Gurkhas. They were a number also enlisted in other Kashmir units.

Rampur had a Gurkha Company in 1924 and this grew in strength to become a battalion in 1933 with a total of 150 Gurkhas. It continued to have a high Gurkha content up to 1939.

Baria Ranjit Infantry and Rajpipla Infantry had some 30 to 60 Gurkhas throughout most of this period. Benares 1st Infantry and Alirajpur Infantry also had a good Gurkha cohort from 1925 onwards. Tripura Bir and Bikram units had 30 to 70 Gurkhas from 1931 onwards. Lunwada State Rifles had 45 to 55 in the period 1933 to 1936. Jaipur Sawai Man Guard had over 20 from 1935 onwards. Mewar Bhupal and Sajjan Infantry had 80 to 100 from 1935 onwards. Bhawalpur 2nd Haroon Infantry had 40 plus from 1937 onwards. The Sirmoor Sappers and Miners had a good Gurkha content throughout.

In the Annual Class Returns all the State Forces entries for Gurkhas are shown in the same categories as for the regular units. All classes are represented but the great majority are Magar/Gurung and Rai/Limbu and other jats. In the table which follows only the total numbers are shown.

GURKHAS IN INDIAN STATES FORCES 1921–1939 AS AT JANUARY

	1921	1922	1923	1924	1925	1926	1927	1928	1929	1930
Sirmoor S & M	44	103	100	84	104	95	95	92	87	89
HQ Sirmoor State Forces	-	-	-	-	-	12	12	14	15	12
Sirmoor Band	-	-	-	-	-	-	-	-	-	-
Rampur Inf Gurkha Inf	-	-	-	32	35	145	117	30	30	30
Rampur 2nd Inf	-	-	-	-	-	-	-	-	-	-
Alirajpur Partap Inf	-	-	-	-	37	-	23	23	-	19
1st Jaipur Inf	-	-	-	-	-	-	1	1	1	3
Jaipur Sawai Man Guard	-	-	-	-	-	-	-	-	-	-
Jaipur IS Transport Corps	11	11	11	-	-	-	-	-	-	-
Jaipur Pony Transport Corps	-	-	-	-	-	3	1	-	-	-
Jaipur State Transport	-	-	-	-	-	-	-	-	-	-
Tehri Garhwal Inf	-	-	-	-	-	2	3	-	10	14
Tehri Garhwal S & M	-	-	-	-	-	-	-	-	-	-
Tehri Garhwal Narendra Pioneers	-	-	-	-	-	-	-	3	3	29
Mysore Lancers	-	-	-	-	-	-	-	-	-	-
1st Mysore Infantry	-	-	-	-	-	-	-	-	-	-
2nd Mysore Infantry	-	-	-	-	-	-	-	-	-	-
1st Tripura Bir Ciy	-	-	-	-	-	-	-	-	-	-
2nd Tripura Bikram Coy										
Tripura Bir Bikram Manikya Infantry	-	-	-	-	-	-	-	-	-	-
Patiala 1st Infantry	-	-	-	-	-	-	-	-	-	-
Patiala 2nd Infantry	-	-	-	-	-	-	-	-	1	-
Patiala 4th Infantry	-	-	-	-	-	-	-	38	-	-

	1931	1932	1933	1934	1935	1936	1937	1938	1939
Sirmoor S & M	106	93	102	95	74	72	70	65	65
HQ Sirmoor State Forces	17	16	17	19	18	16	4	3	3
Sirmoor Band	-	-	-	-	-	-	16	14	16
Rampur Inf Gurkha Infantry	29	-	-	-	-	-	-	-	-
Rampur 2nd Infantry	-	119	151	150	150	86	125	119	112
Alirajpur Partap Infantry	21	1	5	12	11	25	22	28	33
1st Jaipur Infantry	3	3	-	4	4	4	-	5	4
Jaipur Sawai Man Guard	-	-	-	-	22	9	39	40	39
Jaipur IS Transport Corps	-	-	-	-	-	-	-	-	-
Jaipur Pony Transport Corps	-	-	-	-	-	-	-	-	-
Jaipur State Transport	-	1	1	1	-	-	-	-	-
Tehri Garhwal Infantry	18	16	2	3	4	8	6	4	9
Tehri Garhwal S & M	-	-	-	1	1	1	1	1	1
Tehri Garhwal Narendra Pioneers	2	2	2	-	-	-	1	2	2
Mysore Lancers	-	-	-	1	1	1	1	1	1
1st Mysore Inf	-	-	1	2	-	-	-	-	-
2nd Mysore Inf	-	-	1	-	-	-	-	-	-
1st Tripura Bir Ciy	28	28	28	36	33	33	30	33	-
2nd Tripura Bikram Coy	-	-	-	66	72	75	83	67	-
Tripura Bir Bikram Manikya Infantry	-	-	-	-	-	-	-	-	95
Patiala 1st Infantry	-	19	-	-	-	-	-	-	-
Patiala 2nd Infantry	-	-	-	-	-	-	-	-	-
Patiala 4th Infantry	-	-	-	-	-	-	-	-	-

	1921	1922	1923	1924	1925	1926	1927	1928	1929	1930
Jodhpur Sardar Infantry	-	-	-	-	-	-	-	2	-	-
Jodhpur Band	-	-	-	-	-	-	-	-	3	3
Kotah 1st Umed Infantry	-	-	-	-	-	-	-	-	-	-
1st Travancore Nayar Inf	-	-	-	-	-	-	-	-	-	-
2nd Travancore Nayar Inf	-	-	-	-	-	-	-	-	-	-
Bhopal Sultania Pioneers	-	-	1	5	6	15	19	16	-	-
Bhopal Sultania Infantry	-	-	-	-	-	-	-	-	-	11
Bhopal Training Company	-	-	-	-	-	-	-	-	-	-
Bhopal Gohar-i-Taj Own Coy	-	-	-	-	-	-	-	-	-	-
Indore Holkar Coy	-	1	-	-	-	-	-	-	-	-
Indore Holkar Transport Corps	-	-	-	2	2	-	-	-	-	-
Lunwada State Rifles	-	-	-	-	-	-	-	-	-	-
Panna State Infantry	-	-	-	-	-	-	-	-	-	-
Suket State Infantry	-	-	-	-	-	-	-	-	-	-
Udaipur Mewar Infantry	-	-	-	-	-	-	-	-	-	-
Mewar Bhupal Infantry	-	-	-	-	-	-	-	-	-	-
Mewar Sajjan Infantry	-	-	-	-	-	-	-	-	-	-
Mewar Training Company	-	-	-	-	-	-	-	-	-	-
Bikaner Camel Corps	-	-	-	-	-	-	-	-	-	-
Bikaner Band	-	-	-	-	2	3	4	4	4	4

	1931	1932	1933	1934	1935	1936	1937	1938	1939
Jodhpur Sardar Inf	-	-	-	-	-	-	-	-	-
Jodhpur Band	6	5	5	8	7	5	5	5	7
Kotah 1st Umed Infantry	12	12	11	10	10	2	2	3	2
1st Travancore Nayar Inf	-	-	-	-	-	-	1	1	-
2nd Travancore Nayar Inf	-	-	-	-	-	-	-	1	1
Bhopal Sultania Pioneers	-	-	-	-	-		-	-	-
Bhopal Sultania Infantry	9	6	7	7	4	-	5	5	3
Bhopal Training Company	-	-	-	8	13	-	13	-	-
Bhopal Gohar-i-Taj Own Coy	-	1	-	-	-	-	-	1	-
Indore Holkar Coy	-	-	-	-	-	-	-	-	-
Indore Holkar Transport Corps	-	-	-	-	-	-	-	-	-
Lunwada State Rifles	-	-	52	56	46	48	52	-	-
Panna State Inf	-	-	1	1	1	1	1	3	4
Suket State Inf	-	-	13	9	9	10	9	10	12
Udaipur Mewar Infantry	-	-	-	45	-	12	51	-	-
Mewar Bhupal Infantry	-	-	-	-	47	42	-	55	49
Mewar Sajjan Infantry	-	-	-	-	40	54	-	48	55
Mewar Trg Company	-	-	-	-	-	-	-	10	12
Bikaner Camel Corps	-	-	-	-	-	3	-	-	-
Bikaner Band	4	4	5	5	3	-	2	2	4

	1921	1922	1923	1924	1925	1926	1927	1928	1929	1930
2nd Baroda Infantry	-	-	-	-	-	-	-	-	-	-
Porbandar Infantry	-	-	-	-	-	-	-	-	-	4
1st Gwalior Infantry	-	-	-	-	-	-	-	-	-	18
2nd Gwalior Infantry	-	-	-	-	-	-	-	1	-	-
4th Gwalior Infantry	9	2	1	1	1	2	2	2	2	36
7th Gwalior Training Battalion	-	-	-	-	-	-	4	-	-	-
Gwalior S & M	-	-	-	-	-	-	-	-	-	-
Nawanagar State Infantry	-	-	2	-	-	-	-	-	-	-
Idar Sir Pratap Infantry	-	-	-	-	-	-	-	-	-	-
Mandi Joginder Infantry	-	-	-	3	4	4	3	1	1	1
Mandi Guard Platoon	-	-	-	-	-	-	-	-	-	-
Mandi Palace Guard	-	-	-	-	-	-	-	-	-	-
Baria Subhag Cavalry	-	-	-	-	-	-	-	-	-	1
Bara Ranjit Inf	-	-	-	40	48	51	45	52	58	60
Dhrangadhra Inf	-	-	-	3	8	11	8	16	33	22
Dhrangadhra Makhwan Inf	-	-	-	-	-	-	-	-	-	-
Nabha 1st Akal Infantry	-	-	-	-	-	-	-	-	2	-
Jind Infantry	-	-	-	-	-	-	-	-	-	-
Bharatpur Jaswant Inf	-	-	-	-	-	1	1	1	1	1
Bharatpur 2nd Haroon Inf	-	-	-	-	-	-	-	-	-	-
Chamba Infantry	-	-	-	-	5	4	3	2	1	1

	1931	1932	1933	1934	1935	1936	1937	1938	1939
2nd Baroda Infantry	-	-	-	-	-	-	-	32	33
Porbandar Infantry	4	4	3	3	3	2	2	1	1
1st Gwalior Infantry	-	-	-	-	-	-	-	-	-
2nd Gwalior Infantry	-	-	30	-	1	-	2	2	2
4th Gwalior Infantry	56	32	-	-	-	-	-	-	-
7th Gwalior Training Battalion	-	-	-	-	-	-	-	-	-
Gwalior S & M	-	-	-	1	1	1	-	-	-
Nawanagar State Infantry	-	-	-	-	-	-	-	1	3
Idar Sir Pratap Infantry	-	-	-	-	-	-	-	1	3
Mandi Joginder Infantry	1	-	-	-	-	-	-	-	-
Mandi Guard Platoon	-	1	1	1	1	-	-	-	-
Mandi Palace Guard	-	-	-	-	-	1	-	-	-
Baria Subhag Cavalry	1	1	1	1	1	1	1	1	1
Baria Ranjit Infantry	60	61	62	62	62	61	62	61	64
Dhangadhra Infantry	17	8	-	-	-	-	-	-	-
Dhrangadhra Makhwan Inf	-	-	2	2	1	1	-	-	-
Nabha 1st Akal Infantry	-	-	-	-	-	-	-	-	-
Jind Infantry	-	-	-	-	-	1	-	-	-
Bharatpur Jaswant Inf	-	3	3	2	1	2	1	1	1
Bharatpur 2nd Haroon Inf	-	-	-	-	-	-	41	52	105
Chamba Infantry	1	1	1	1	1	1	1	1	1

	1921	1922	1923	1924	1925	1926	1927	1928	1929	1930
Rajpipla Infantry	-	-	-	-	66	45	40	-	37	38
Benares 1st Infantry	-	-	-	-	33	28	22	19	15	13
1st Kashmir Rifles	87	35	25	1	-	-	-	-	-	-
2nd Kashmir Rifles	237	236	256	396	386	393	374	407	399	404
3rd Kashmir Rifles	396	423	394	409	381	408	407	424	412	438
4th Kashmir Rifles	-	-	43	32	-	-	-	-	-	-
5th Kashmir Infantry	-	-	-	-	-	-	-	18	-	-
6th Kashmir Pioneers	-	-	-	1	1	1	-	-	5	3
Kashmir Training School	-	-	-	-	-	2	4	-	-	-
Kashmir Training Battalion	-	-	-	-	-	-	-	-	-	-
Kashmir Temple Guard	-	-	-	-	15	15	18	17	16	15
Jammu Temple Guard	-	-	-	-	-	-	-	10	17	19

	1931	1932	1933	1934	1935	1936	1937	1938	1939
Rajpipla Infantry	36	37	34	37	36	36	33	37	37
Benares 1st Infantry	13	12	12	13	12	12	12	12	9
1st Kashmir Rifles	-	-	-	-	-	-	-	-	-
2nd Kashmir Rifles	371	354	375	355	371	365	384	393	384
3rd Kashmir Rifles	380	378	361	378	376	344	364	366	362
4th Kashmir Rifles	-	-	-	-	-	-	-	-	2
5th Kashmir Infantry	-	-	-	-	-	-	-	-	-
6th Kashmir Pioneers	2	4	-	-	-	-	-	-	-
Kashmir Training School	-	-	2	2	1	1	2	-	-
Kashmir Training Battalion	-	-	46	49	23	66	55	36	20
Kashmir Temple Guard	18	9	-	-	-	-	-	-	-
Jammu Temple Guarrd	2	2	-	-	-	-	-	-	-

The totals shown in the various abstracts, including Gurkhas in Indian States Forces, for the period 1921 to 1939 are given in the next table.

ABSTRACT OF TOTAL GURKHAS AS AT 1 JANUARY

JANUARY	INDIAN ARMY	INDIAN STATES FORCES	MILITARY POLICE	TOTAL
1921	28333	784	8980	38097
1922	20360	854	8071	29285
1923	18985	822	7146	26953
1924	18483	997	6609	26089
1925	18574	1135	6012	25721
1926	18528	1267	5812	25607
1927	18474	1209	5874	25557
1928	18872	1179	5833	25884
1929	19007	1162	5932	26101
1930	18958	1261	6076	26295
1931	19028	1236	6078	26342
1932	18703	1215	6393	26311
1933	18767	1360	6420	26547
1934	18725	1444	6663	26832
1935	18702	1463	6698	26863
1936	18670	1422	6722	26814
1937	18677	1550	6759	26986
1938	18601	1524	6726	26851
1939	18846	1555	6363	26764

This table shows that there was a rapid decrease in overall Gurkha strengths from the high point in 1919 at 68903 to under half that number (29285) in 1922. There is little record of what happened to the 39,000 Gurkhas who left the service in that three year period. The total Gurkha strengths then level out in 1923 and remain somewhere between 25,000 and 27,000 for the whole period up to 1939.

The Digest of Services of the 2nd Battalion 2nd Gurkha Rifles throws some light on the demobilization process. On 1 January 1919 the entry reads "After this date demobilization was pushed on. The Battalion whose strength was 1543 all ranks was required to be reduced to 918. Owing to heavy sickness this would not leave Field Service Strength of fit men. The point was referred but orders were received to complete demobilization as ordered." It is assumed that similar orders were issued across the whole Indian Army.

A further entry in the same Digest of Services in the following year (1920) referred to the disbandment of the 3rd Battalion 2nd Gurkha Rifles. This stated that "On August 15th the 3rd Battalion of the regiment was disbanded [actual operative date was 3 October 1920], in accordance with the policy in force at Army Headquarters. Six Gurkha Officers, and 157 other ranks were transferred to the 2nd Battalion, some went to 1st Battalion, and the rest were discharged .... "This summary discharge was a great blow to many men, and deprived the Regiment of some splendid youngsters, who were very keen indeed, and were coming on excellently. Many of them left expressing their intention of returning and re-enlisting again next year, in one of the old Battalions of the Regiment".

SECOND WORLD WAR

Again, during the Second World War, all regiments were authorised to raise 3rd and later 4th Battalions. The 1st, 2nd and 9th Gurkha Rifles which lost battalions in Singapore in 1942 were authorised to raise a 5th Battalion. Again the 2nd Battalion of the 7th Gurkha Rifles was re-raised after being captured at Tobruk.

A number of other units came into being. There were the Gurkha elements of the Indian Airborne forces. The 25th and 26th Gurkha Rifles were raised as garrison battalions, taking soldiers from all regiments. There were training battalions (14th, 29th, 38th, 56th and 710th) in the Siwaliks, composed of men from each of two regiments to train for the Burma Campaign. They took their titles from the amalgamated number of the parent regiments, thus 14th was from 1st and 4th Gurkha Rifles. Large Regimental Centres were created which included their own training battalions as well as administrative sub-units.

In the various documents assessing the contribution of the Indian Army during the Second World War the recruitable population for Gurkhas was given as 280,000, and the pre-War total serving was given as 18,000. The total recruited up to the end of 1944 was 94,960, giving a grand total of 112,960 enrolled Gurkhas although the Recruiting Officer gave a rounded up total of 114,000 for the whole of the war.

The recruiting of Dotiyals from the Far West of Nepal for medical and labour units was also organised by the recruiting staffs. These were non-military personnel.

However as in all previous records there are slightly different figures given in different documents. The Journal of the Gurkha Recruiting Depots and Record Offices 1939–47 gives a breakdown of the "various tribes enlisted during the War". This gives:

	Western	Eastern	Total
Magars	34,854	3,023	37,877
Gurungs	15,996	2,729	18,725
Chhetris	13,302	4,186	17,488
Rais	49	12,965	13,014
Limbus	3	7,243	7,246
Tamangs	924	5,042	5,966
Thakurs	3,142	80	3,222
Sunwars		1,413	1,413

In addition several thousand 'others' were enlisted in which were included Newars, Dotiyals and other stop-gaps. If we include the several thousand 'others' the total recruited is 104,951.

The Annual Class Returns continued up to 1 January 1942. The same categories of clan/jats continued to be used including Dura and Ranabhatt. Very few of these two jats are recorded in the Gurkha Brigade units, although the 5th Royal Gurkha Rifles showed some in the 1941 return and in 1942 they listed 73 Duras at the Regimental Centre.

The 1940 Return still shows the pre-War two battalion structure for each Gurkha Regiment. By 1941 new entries for Regimental Centres and 3rd Battalions are shown.

In 1942 4th Battalions are added.

The custom in all these returns is to give the full regimental title. For some unexplained reason the 4th Gurkha Rifles are not listed as Prince of Wales's Own until the last entry in 1942.

The first set of tables show the strengths as at 1 January for Gurkha Regiments in 1940, 1941 and 1942.

GURKHA STRENGTHS IN GURKHA UNITS 1940–1942
AS AT 1 JANUARY

1940	MAGAR	GURUNG	THAKUR	LIMBU	RAI	SUNWAR	CHHETRI	DURA	RANABHATT	LAMA	OTHER GURKHA	TOTAL
1/1 GR	543	348	2	1	2	-	13	-	-	1	12	922
2/1 GR	507	374	10	3	1	-	12	-	-	-	28	935
1/2 GR	433	450	2	1	8	-	19	-	-	-	8	921
2/2 GR	530	345	16	-	1	-	14	-	-	8	10	924
1/3 GR	480	423	14	1	-	-	5	-	-	-	10	933
2/3 GR	447	436	11	3	-	1	3	-	-	-	12	913
1/4 GR	477	411	5	-	-	-	6	-	-	-	16	915
2/4 GR	472	419	11	-	-	1	2	-	-	-	14	919
1/5 RGR	381	496	16	-	1	-	7	-	-	1	26	928
2/5 RGR	429	446	11	2	1	2	4	-	-	7	25	927
1/6 GR	487	409	1	1	2	-	10	-	-	-	14	924
2/6 GR	480	415	12	-	1	-	1	-	-	-	7	916
1/7 GR	20	28	-	380	455	64	4	-	-	8	4	963
2/7 GR	23	19	1	367	503	30	9	-	-	5	7	964
1/8 GR	516	337	17	-	3	-	6	-	-	7	5	891
2/8 GR	539	365	8	-	2	-	4	-	-	3	10	931
1/9 GR	5	2	328	2	-	-	615	-	-	-	10	962
2/9 GR	-	1	315	-	-	-	599	-	-	-	12	927
1/10 GR	37	18	17	358	403	13	19	-	-	28	10	903
2/10 GR	41	37	-	365	387	53	23	-	-	43	13	962

1941	MAGAR	GURUNG	THAKUR	LIMBU	RAI	SUNWAR	CHHETRI	DURA	RANABHATT	LAMA	OTHER GURKHA	TOTAL
1/1 GR	398	250	2	2	1	-	7	-	-	-	7	667
2/1 GR	354	259	9	2	1	10	5	-	-	-	8	648
3/1 GR	524	267	1	29	57	1	12	-	-	-	7	898
1 GRRC	1041	543	10	-	1	-	18	-	-	1	27	1641
1/2 GR	320	321	13	-	11	-	-	-	-	-	4	669
2/2 GR	379	251	14	-	1	-	11	-	-	5	2	663
3/2 GR	520	367	5	-	-	-	8	-	-	-	2	902
2 GRRC	693	446	5	26	29	-	11	-	-	1	10	1221
1/3 GR	662	527	14	1	1	1	4	-	-	-	8	1218
2/3 GR	298	270	3	3	-	-	3	-	-	-	10	587
3/3 GR	576	307	4	1	-	1	1	-	-	-	9	899
3 GRRC	682	474	5	-	-	-	1	-	-	-	5	1167
1/4 GR	316	267	4	-	-	-	4	-	-	-	10	601
2/4 GR	333	276	4	-	-	3	1	-	-	-	7	624
3/4 GR	549	337	8	-	2	-	-	-	-	-	8	904
4 GRRC	1019	476	8	1	1	1	-	-	-	1	9	1516
1/5 RGR	284	324	13	-	1	-	6	-	-	3	26	657
2/5 RGR	332	324	10	1	1	2	2	6	9	3	7	697
3/5 RGR	472	405	9	1	2	-	7	1	1	5	1	904
5 RGRRC	707	575	22	-	1	1	6	4	2	6	-	1324
1/6 GR	361	264	-	1	1	-	14	-	-	-	15	656
2/6 GR	351	244	11	-	-	-	3	-	-	-	4	613
3/6 GR	553	322	6	-	-	-	-	-	-	-	3	884
6 GRRC	670	424	1	-	2	-	1	-	-	-	3	1101
1/7 GR	11	21	-	266	314	41	1	-	-	5	3	662
2/7 GR	15	14	-	247	326	24	6	-	-	10	5	647
3/7 GR	34	36	-	284	463	46	3	-	-	22	5	893
7 GRRC	98	96	1	506	893	129	6	-	-	67	1	1797
1/8 GR	370	236	12	-	1	-	4	-	-	3	6	632
2/8 GR	396	263	7	-	2	1	4	-	-	2	9	684
3/8 GR	587	292	6	1	1	-	4	-	-	7	6	904
8 GRRC	1080	534	12	2	4	-	22	-	-	8	6	1668
1/9 GR	8	1	210	1	-	-	466	-	-	-	8	694
2/9 GR	-	1	240	-	-	-	410	-	-	-	9	660
3/9 GR	-	-	245	-	-	-	644	-	-	1	5	895
9 GRRC	5	6	424	1	1	-	1358	-	-	1	4	1800
1/10 GR	29	10	14	245	278	14	11	-	-	19	8	628
2/10 GR	32	26	-	260	264	39	19	10	-	30	4	684
3/10 GR	34	34	-	299	452	13	7	-	5	57	-	901
10 GRRC	36	33	-	451	617	64	2	-	-	71	18	1292

1942	MAGAR	GURUNG	THAKUR	LIMBU	RAI	SUNWAR	CHHETRI	DURA	RANABHATT	LAMA	OTHER GURKHA	TOTAL
1/1 GR	614	337	5	1	1	-	4	-	-	-	11	973
2/1 GR	565	350	9	1	2	-	3	-	-	-	18	948
3/1 GR	380	213	1	32	42	1	12	-	-	-	12	693
4/1 GR	408	243	10	41	32	1	13	-	-	1	27	776
1 GRRC	1053	583	117	65	36	-	232		-	44	273	2403
1/2 GR	446	404	6	24	29	-	3	-	-	4	5	921
2/2 GR	688	399	10	14	55	7	10	-	-	16	9	1208
3/2 GR	390	240	4	1	4	-	10	-	-	5	10	664
4/2 GR	378	188	10	8	41	1	10	-	-	2	10	648
2 GRRC	1225	704	58	45	87	-	189	-	-	31	132	2471
1/3 GR	414	342	9	7	23	2	6	-	-	6	10	819
2/3 GR	519	370	3	2	-	-	11	-	-	-	18	923
3/3 GR	525	250	-	11	13	-	1	-	-	-	45	845
4/3 GR	385	207	5	9	63	6	8	1	-	3	11	698
3 GRRC	1326	762	49	37	36	3	108	-	-	43	25	2389
1/4 GR	488	318	5	-	-	-	6	-	-	-	10	827
2/4 GR	545	356	5	1	-	-	1	1	-	-	10	919
3/4 GR	505	269	9	-	3	-	-	-	-	1	10	797
4/4GR	464	240	3	5	50	5	9	-	-	-	25	801
4 GRRC	1269	749	57	40	54	1	112	-	-	1	168	2451
1/5 RGR	406	460	19	-	3	2	4	-	-	5	8	907
2/5 RGR	438	389	11	21	30	2	3	-	-	4	18	916
3/5 RGR	477	372	10	1	4	-	-	-	-	-	18	882
4/5 RGR	457	406	18	4	5	-	5	-	-	15	2	912
5 RGRRC	1202	658	70	17	23	4	96	73	-	42	42	2227
1/6 GR	546	305	1	15	9	-	11	-	-	-	19	906
2/6 GR	534	353	7	-	3	-	-	-	-	-	4	901
3/6 GR	460	235	3	15	9	-	2	-	-	9	4	737
4/6 GR	542	272	1	3	1	-	6	-	-	-	10	835
6 GRRC	1502	696	39	29	32	-	14	-	-	3	160	2475
1/7 GR	33	32	-	352	443	44	9	-	-	35	7	955
2/7 GR	15	20	1	363	460	45	3	-	1	20	4	932
3/7 GR	39	37	-	249	458	48	5	-	-	48	10	894
4/7 GR	48	31	1	118	451	58	2	-	-	32	16	757
7 GRRC	51	81	1	650	1092	116	15	2	1	287	37	2333
1/8 GR	490	275	11	10	13	1	2	-	-	1	6	809
2/8 GR	568	343	8	-	4	1	9	-	-	3	4	940
3/8 GR	575	247	2	2	6	-	3	-	-	8	9	852
4/8 GR	548	202	5	11	9	-	15	-	-	10	9	809
8 GRRC	1416	715	61	38	46	1	81	-	-	52	81	2491
1/9 GR	5	1	254	-	1	-	676	-	-	-	7	944
2/9 GR	2	-	280	2	-	-	643	-	-	1	14	942
3/9 GR	2	-	186	-	2	-	555	-	-	-	8	753
4/9 GR	1	-	155	1	-	-	474	-	-	-	4	635
9 GRRC	9	5	345	1	-	10	2186	-	-	1	4	2561
1/10 GR	27	11	10	304	337	16	10	-	-	21	14	750
2/10 GR	38	38	-	331	388	42	22	-	-	49	14	922
3/10 GR	34	37	-	280	404	51	7	-	-	76	10	899
4/10 GR	34	33	-	240	470	54	12	-	-	82	16	941
10 GRRC	62	60	-	505	1130	124	19	-	-	359	24	2283

The Burma Frontier Force and Burma Military Police continued to be shown in 1940 and 1941 but were omitted from the 1942 returns. The Assam Rifles had four battalions up to 1941 when a 5th Battalion was re-raised. The Eastern Frontier Rifles (Bengal Battalion) and Ranchi Military Police Company continued to recruit Gurkhas. From 1941 the Ranchi Company is listed as Bihar Military Police.

GURKHAS IN BURMA MILITARY POLICE AND BURMA FRONTIER FORCE UNITS AS AT 1 JANUARY

Burma Frontier Force	1940	1941
Bhamo Battalion	140	161
Chin Hills Battalion	160	168
Lashio Battalion	409	439
South Shan States Battalion	505	370
Myitkina Battalion	516	576
Reserve Battalion	441	414
Kokine Battalion	-	206
Burma Military Police Mandalay Battalion	520	206
1st Rangoon Battalion	225	270
2nd Rangoon Battalion	253	291

GURKHAS IN ASSAM RIFLES AND BENGAL AND BIHAR MILITARY POLICE AS AT 1 JANUARY

Assam Rifles	1940	1941	1942
1st Assam Rifles	538	522	496
2nd Assam Rifles (Lakhimpur)	1138	1190	676
3rd Assam Rifles (Naga Hills)	537	493	497
4th Assam Rifles	587	545	541
5th Assam Rifles	-	-	636
Bengal M P Eastern Frontier Rifles	369	380	373
Bihar M P Ranchi MP Company	218	222	219

In the old Burma Army, apart from the Military Police and Frontier Force battalions already mentioned, there were a number of Gurkhas.

The 7th Battalion The Burma Rifles raised in 1940 from Burma Police and Burma Military Police had Gurkhas as well as Burmans, Karens and Kumaonis. There were also in Burma in the period between 1940-42, six Garrison Companies which enlisted Kachins, Chins, Karens, Burmese and Gurkhas.

Following the fall of Burma to the Japanese in 1942, the surviving military forces of Burma re-grouped in India and a new regiment was formed, The Burma Regiment, from nationals, domiciles and Gurkhas who had served in the Burma Military Forces. The Burmese and indigenous tribes were concentrated in the surviving 2nd Battalion, Burma Rifles. All the Burmese Army units were based in Hoshiarpur, Central India.

The new Regiment consisted, on raising, of the following:

1st Battalion
2nd Battalion [not to be confused with the 2nd Battalion, Burma Rifles,
the sole surviving Battalion of that Regiment]
3rd Battalion
4th Battalion
5th Battalion
6th Battalion
7th Battalion (Reconnaissance)
10th Battalion (Training)
25th Battalion (Garrison)
26th Battalion (Garrison)
Chin Hills Battalion [not to be confused with the Chin Levies/Rifles.
This was the surviving Battalion of The Burma Frontier Force]
1st Reinforcement Battalion
2nd Reinforcement Battalion.

The two garrison battalions were probably raised from the 2nd to 7th Burma Garrison Companies and were originally designated as 1st and 2nd Garrison Battalions. They were later re-designated as 25th and 26th. Gurkhas, Punjabi Muslims, Kumaonis, Sikhs and other Indians from the erstwhile Burma Rifles, Military Police and Frontier Force were enlisted. The 1st Battalion, for example, had Gurkhas, Kumaonis, Punjabi Muslims and Sikhs. The 2nd (all Gurkha from 1947) and 4th Battalions were mainly Gurkha units. The Chin Hills Battalion had Gurkhas, Kumaonis and Chins.

After the war the new State of Burma had no requirement for Indian nationals in its Army and most of the Burma Regiment battalions were demobilised. The Burmese Army retained the two Gurkha battalions (2nd and 4th).

The Annual Class Returns continue to show a number of Gurkhas serving in non-Gurkha units. Again these are shown in the same categories as for the Gurkha Brigade units. They have small numbers of Western jats and very few Eastern jats. The Engineer Survey Depot and Training units had 140 Gurkhas in 1942 and No 18 Indian Garrison Company was largely an all Gurkha unit with 220 to 240 Gurkhas in 1940 to 1942.

GURKHAS IN REGULAR UNITS 1940-1942
AS AT 1 JANUARY

	1940	1941	1942
RA Training Centre	1	1	-
4th Anti-Tank Regiment	-	-	2
5th Anti Tank Regiment	-	-	1
Bengal S & M	8	-	-
Engineer Depot (Survey Depot & Training Units)	-	10	140
Indian Signals	-	29	3
1st Punjab Regiment	-	1	-
5th Mahratta L I	52	51	47
6th Rajputana Rifles	26	25	24
7th Rajput Regiment	4	7	7
8th Punjab Regiment	2	-	-
9th Jat Regiment	-	-	4
10th Baluch Regiment	-	-	1
11th Sikh Regiment	1	-	-
18th Royal Garhwal Rifles	10	9	10
19th Hyderabad Regiment	14	30	41
1st Kumaon Rifles	8	8	8
1st Bihar Regiment	-	-	2
No 5 Garrison Company	-	-	1
No 18 Garrison Gompany	240	238	225
RIASC Units	8	35	135
IAOC Units	-	-	81
Auxiliary Pioneer Units	-	-	102

Another return, dated 1 January 1945, gave an interesting breakdown of Gurkhas then serving in all branches of the Indian Army and this shows a remarkable number serving outside the infantry. The breakdown was:

Armoured Corps	5
Artillery	9
Engineers	696
Signals	9
RIASC	319
IAMC	872
IAOC	97
IEME	274
Indian Pioneer Corps	1177
Miscellaneous Corps	453
Infantry	<u>65210</u>
Total in Army	<u>69121</u>

The Indian State Forces continued to enlist Gurkhas in a number of units. Again they are all shown in the same categories as the regular units. The totals in the various units for 1940 to 1942 are shown in the next table. Again the Kashmir Rifles have a large proportion of Gurkhas, but there are substantial numbers in the Bhawalpur, Rampur, Baria, Sirmoor and Mewar units.

GURKHAS IN INDIAN STATES FORCES
AS AT 1 JANUARY 1940-1942

	1940	1941	1942
Sirmoor S & M	59	36	63
Tehri-Garhwal S & M	1	1	1
Suket Laksman S & M	-	17	17
Faridkot S &M	-	1	-
Bikaner Ganga Risala	-	3	-
Tehri-Garhwal Pioneers	-	7	5
Kashmir MT Troop	1	1	1
Alwar Pratap Paltan	-	1	-
Alirajpur Pratap Infantry	25	-	-
Baria Ranjit Infantry	66	89	97
Baroda 1st Infantry	8	9	6
Baroda 2nd Infantry	33	30	28
Benares 1st Infantry	9	25	22
Benares Training Company	-	-	12
Bharatpur Jaswant Infantry	3	1	1
Bharatpur 2nd Harroon Infantry & Training Company	97	106	109
Bhopal Sultania Infantry	2	1	2
Bikaner State Band	3	-	-
Chamba Infantry	1	1	-
Dholpur Narsingh Infantry	1	1	1
Faridkot State Band	1	2	3
Gwalior 2nd Infantry	2	2	1

Gwalior 7th Training Battalion	-	1	-
Idar Sir Pratap Infantry	4	6	2
Jaipur 1st Infantry	1	1	2
Jaipur 2nd Infantry	3	3	3
Jaipur Sawai Man Guard	9	-	1
Jaipur Training School	-	9	-
Jodhpur Military Band	7	-	-
Jodhpur Training Company	-	7	7

	1940	1941	1942
Jammu & Kashmir 2nd Rifles	358	348	373
Jammu & Kashmir 3rd Rifles	340	306	308
Jammu & Kashmir Training Battalion.	18	167	331
Kashmir Fort Guard	-	2	-
Kotah 1st Umed Infantry	2	2	2
Mewar Bhupal Infantry	51	84	88
Mewar Sajjan Infantry	50	27	16
Mewar Bhupal Training Company.	10	4	7
Mysore 2nd Infantry	-	-	2
Nawanagar Shatrushalya Infantry.	1	1	-
Panna State Infantry	4	3	33
Porbandar State Infantry	1	1	1
Rajpipla Infantry	32	38	17
Rampur 2nd Infantry	111	149	156
HQ Sirmoor State Forces	2	43	-
Sirmoor Band	15	17	17
Suket State Infantry	10	-	-
Tehri-Garhwal Infantry Company	8	-	-
Travancore 2nd Nayar Infantry.	1	-	-
Tripura 1st Bir Bikram	91	86	18

None of the Indian States' Forces units were 100% Gurkha, although it has been stated that the Holkar Saluting Battery of Indore State in Central India was composed of Gurkhas. This unit does not appear in the Annual Class Returns.

Some examples of the class composition of selected Indian States' Forces units which had a good Gurkha content are given in the next table. One unit which does not appear in the 1942 Returns is the 3rd Tripura Rifles. They were stated to have enlisted Gurkhas. This unit was absorbed into the Assam Rifles in 1948.

Alirajpur Pratrap Infantry	Reorganised 1924 (of Alirajpur,Central India)	Rajputs, Bhils, Mohamedans and Gurkhas
Baria Ranjit Infantry	Raised 1909 (of Baria,Gujerat Circle)	Gurkhas, Rajputs, Bhils
Mewar Bhupal Infantry	Raised 1932 (of Mewar,Rajputana)	Rajputs, Gujars, Bhils, Jats and Gurkhas (one platoon)
Mewar Sajjan Infantry	Raised 1 July 1932 (of Mewar,Rajputana)	Rajputs, Mohamedans, Bhils, Brahmins and Gurkhas (one platoon)
2nd Bahawalpur Light Infantry (Haroon Battalion)	Raised 1827 (of Bahawalpur)	Punjabi Muslims (Locals), Jats and Gurkhas
Rajpipla State Infantry	Raised 20 April 1923 (of Rajpipla, Rajputana)	Gurkhas, Mohamedans and Rajputs
2nd Rampur (Murtaza) Infantry	Raised 1896 which in 1925 became part of 2nd Rampur (Murtaza) Infantry of Rampur, United Provinces)	Rohilla Pathans, Hindus and Gurkhas
Sirmoor Sappers and Miners	Raised 15 March 1890 (of Sirmoor, United Provinces)	Sirmooris and Gurkhas
Suket Lakshman Infantry (later Sappers and Miners)	(of Suket, Punjab)	Dogras, Sikhs and Gurkhas
1st Tripura (Bir Bikram) Manikya Rifles	Raised as 1st Company 1926-27 and 2nd Company 1928-29 and became 1st Tripura Bir and 2nd Tripura Bikram Companies Amalgamated 1938	Thakurs, Tripuras, Gurkhas, Bengali Hindus and Muslims

The totals shown in the various abstracts including Gurkhas in Indian States Forces, in the period 1940 to 1942 are given in the next table:

ABSTRACT OF TOTAL GURKHAS AS AT 1 JANUARY

JANUARY	INDIAN ARMY	INDIAN STATES FORCES	MILITARY POLICE	TOTAL
1940	19168	1472	6556	27196
1941	37776	1639	6770	46185
1942	59489	1753	3439	64681

The Burma Frontier Force and Burma Military Police units are omitted from the 1942 return. These would have added a further 3000+ to the totals, which show a doubling in total Gurkha strength in the two years between 1940 and 1942.

Gurkhas also served in the Indian Hospital Corps and the Army Bearer Corps. In 1942 the Police in Assam raised a special police force from domiciled Gurkhas at a strength of around 1000. They were employed to patrol the railway line and came under command of the Indian Infantry Battalion on railway protection. There were some Gurkhas serving in the Royal Indian Navy and the Royal Indian Air Force.

Many other Gurkhas found other employment in British Service. Both the Calcutta Armed Police and the Chittagong Armed Police enlisted Gurkhas. The Armed Branch of the Assam Police had a number of Gurkhas including buglers and pipers.

As already noted the Annual Class Returns continued up to 1 January 1942. Thereafter the breakdown by class or caste was discontinued and only a summary of total strengths as at 1 January was recorded. There is some difficulty in interpreting these figures. Each year they include "Boys" who are stated to be recruits who have not yet reached enlistment age. In one year (1945) the number of recruits is stated to include 6240 reinforcements. In 1943 the total is stated to include Parachute Battalion, Record Office and Duty Platoon but not "units overseas or which are ineffective". In 1944 the notes state "includes the Gurkha Rifles, the Gurkha Garrison Rifles, Parachute Battalions, Training Units etc." For 1945 and 1946 the Titles state "in SEA [South East Asia] and India Commands". And for 1947 this title states "in Indian Armed Forces and British Forces in India Command". All entries are as at 1 January except the last entry which was as at 1 July 1947.

ABSTRACT OF TOTAL GURKHAS AS AT 1 JANUARY

	GURKHA OFFICERS	OTHER RANKS	RECRUITS	BOYS
1943	1023	33724	20965	1123
1944	1530	46334	27661	2211
1945	1740	62292	19493	2784
1946	1971	62044	4446	2142
1947	1416	40812	2722	509

ABSTRACT OF TOTAL GURKHAS AS AT 1 JULY

1947	1056	27821	1609	452

The Journal of the Recruiting Depots and Record Offices 1939–1947 gives some interesting figures for number of Gurkhas Released up to 1 January 1947. Separate entries are given for the Depots at Kunraghat [near Gorakpur] and Ghoom [near Darjeeling]. The entry for IPR is 'Indian Parachute Regiment'.

GURKHAS RELEASED UP TO 1 JANUARY 1947

	Kunraghat	Ghoom	Total
1 GR	6645	597	7242
2 GR	5936	502	6438
3 GR	5781	512	6293
4 GR	5888	630	6518
5 RGR	5167	504	5671
6 GR	5987	472	6459
7 GR	2859	2276	5135
8 GR	5137	531	5668
9 GR	5726	942	6668
10 GR	3967	3188	7155
25 GR	275 }		
26 GR	1152 }	318	2959
IPR	1039 }		
Misc	175 }		
Total	55734	10472	66206

The same journal gives a table of casualties recorded in the Second World War:

GURKHA CASUALTIES DURING SECOND WORLD WAR

Unit	Killed	Died of Wounds	Died of Disease	Accidental Deaths	Total Deaths	Wounded	Missing	P.O.D.	Injured	Total
1 GR	272	79	167	-	518	910	123	12	24	1,587
2 GR	443	60	204	115	822	817	2	32	50	1,723
3 GR	424	111	148		683	1,770	93	35	-	2,581
4 GR	407	73	259	8	747	1,466	88	4	61	2,366
5 RGR	616	155	177	21	969	2,005	403	119	31	3,527
6 GR	406	121	190	35	752	1,492	16	-	50	2,310
7 GR	436	96	182	17	731	1,272	266	49	-	2,318
8 GR	414	114	118	33	679	1,275	27	-	65	2,046
9 GR	299	64	173	19	555	1,114	321	12	-	2,002
10 GR	513	130	252	74	969	1,958	102	3	38	3,070
25 GR	8	2	17	6	33	-	-	-	-	33
26 GR	-	-	3	1	4	-	-	-	-	4
I.P.R.	62	6	3	6	77	3	-	-	-	80
Total	4,300	1,011	1,893	335	7,539	14,082	1,441	266	319	23,647

This table can be compared with another summary from official records in the United Kingdom and in India compiled by Ashok Nath in the 1990s. These give casualty numbers for the ten numbered Gurkha Regiments divided into three theatres Burma, Far East, and Middle East. There is no separate record for India/North West Frontier or for Europe, although the latter are almost certainly covered by Middle East which is assumed to include Italy and Greece as well as North Africa and other countries of the Middle East. These Casualty figures are divided into Killed, Died or Wounded and it is not possible to reconcile the two tables. The wounded figures are in particular difficult. Reporting of "wounded" depended on whether the wounded soldier was able to remain on duty or not.

ASHOK NATH'S SUMMARY

1939 to 1945			BURMA				FAR EAST				MIDDLE EAST			
			BRITISH OFFICERS	GURKHA OFFICERS	GURKHA OTHER RANKS	NON COMBATANTS	BRITISH OFFICERS	GURKHA OFFICERS	GURKHA OTHER RANKS	NON COMBATANTS	BRITISH OFFICERS	GURKHA OFFICERS	GURKHA OTHER RANKS	NON COMBATANTS
1 GR	Killed		15	2	255	3	3	1	35	-	-	1	-	-
	Died		3	3	118	-	-	-	182	-	-	-	11	-
	Wounded		21	24	809	11	1	3	18	-	-	4	-	-
2 GR	Killed		4	-	59	1	4	-	31	4	4	5	154	1
	Died		3	-	225	9	3	4	88	6	3	5	131	6
	Wounded		6	8	270	2	1	3	67	6	17	19	430	4
3 GR	Killed		12	7	274	1	1	1	12	-	2	2	108	4
	Died		6	5	236	12	-	-	16	-	-	3	58	2
	Wounded		14	26	991	6	-	2	31	-	8	19	389	5
4 GR	Killed		16	12	249	-	-	-	-	-	5	6	153	-
	Died		3	2	49	2	-	-	2	-	2	2	48	-
	Wounded		26	23	909	8	-	-	6	-	7	17	415	5
5 RGR	Killed		14	14	399	4	-	1	1	-	4	3	187	2
	Died		3	9	83	18	1	-	1	-	2	3	60	1
	Wounded		35	40	234	4	-	1	38	-	16	16	645	4
6 GR	Killed		12	10	290	-	-	-	-	-	1	4	96	2
	Died		7	4	3	5	-	-	-	-	2	2	39	2
	Wounded		19	30	991	9	-	-	-	-	10	11	395	4
7 GR	Killed		12	10	256	5	-	-	-	-	4	7	149	2
	Died		5	3	366	18	-	-	3	-	1	3	74	7
	Wounded		22	14	615	6	-	-	-	-	15	14	395	16
8 GR	Killed		15	7	263	1	-	1	11	-	-	3	138	-
	Died		5	5	119	5	-	-	13	-	2	2	82	3
	Wounded		21	25	805	11	-	1	18	-	13	19	435	2
9 GR	Killed		4	2	57	-	4	-	20	-	3	2	196	-
	Died		1	1	63	3	3	5	130	1	3	5	61	1
	Wounded		8	4	225	-	2	2	88	2	10	18	99	3
10 GR	Killed		9	10	352	1	-	-	15	-	3	3	165	1
	Died		4	-	279	13	2	1	16	-	-	1	49	2
	Wounded		24	37	1258	13	2	6	84	-	15	18	474	-

The Indian strengths during World War 2 are recorded on a board in the Imperial War Museum. This shows strengths as at:

	September 1939	September 1945
Combatants	189,000	1,876,999
Non-Combatants	41,000	622,910
Totals	230,000	2,499,909

Taking the combatant totals and comparing them against recorded Gurkha strengths at roughly the same dates (1939–26,764, 1945–85,309) it can be calculated that at the beginning of World War 2, Gurkhas provided 14% of the combatant strength of the Indian Army and 4.5% at the end of the War.

THE POST WAR PERIOD

In late 1944 a Committee was set up to examine the Organisation and Composition of the Indian Army after the war. [The Chairman was General Willcocks and one of the members was Brigadier Enoch Powell]. Their report was submitted in October 1945 and although never put into effect it contained proposals for a restructuring of the Gurkha Brigade. This concluded that there should be only sixteen regular Gurkha battalions, of which twelve should be active at any one time and the other four should be stationed at regimental centres. All Nepal leave would be carried out by sending the whole of the regimental centre battalion on block leave.

The organisation and Class composition proposed was to be:

Group Centre	Regiments	Class Composition
14th	1st and 4th	2/3 Magar, Gurung
		1/3 Limbu, Rai, Sunwar
29th	2nd and 9th	Thakur, Chhetri
38th	3rd and 8th	2/3 Magar, Gurung
		1/3 Limbu, Rai, Sunwar
56th	5th and 6th	2/3 Magar, Gurung
		1/3 Limbu, Rai, Sunwar

The 7th and 10th being junior by nearly half a century to the remainder were to be disbanded and the Eastern Nepal classes distributed across all the other regiments except the 2nd and 9th, which would become Thakur Chhetri regiments.

In addition, each regiment would have a Boys Company of approximately fifty boys per battalion.

In the reorganisation of the parachute formation, the proposed 4th Parachute Battalion would be composed of one company from each of the Gurkha regimental groups.

None of the above plans were put into effect and in the period between the end of the Second World War and Independence and Partition, most of the war-raised battalions were disbanded. The 2nd, 6th, 7th and 10th Gurkha Rifles were chosen to transfer to the British Army with their original two regular battalions each. Any of their war-raised battalions still existing went over to join the other regiments remaining in the new Indian Army. Thus the 4th/2nd became the 5th/8th and the 3rd/6th became the 5th/5th. The new Indian Army incidentally retained all the war-raised battalions which had not been disbanded and have since raised many more. They recreated a new 11th Gurkha Rifles to absorb the non-optees of 7th and 10th Gurkha Rifles.

THE PERIOD FROM 1948 ONWARDS

Soon after the four regiments (2nd, 6th, 7th and 10th) came over to the British Army on 1 January 1948, it was decided to form a Division of Gurkhas and plans were made to recruit or convert soldiers for the new arms or corps necessary. Between 1 January 1948 and 23 September 1948, all four regiments were officially part of The Gurkha Regiment (Reference number 100/INDIA/3757), although in fact they kept their old titles. The title was changed to The Brigade of Gurkhas on 23 September 1948 under Army Order No 79 of 1948. The 7th Gurkha Rifles were converted to Artillery from June 1948 to December 1949. Engineers and Signals were raised and gradually brought up to regimental strength. Recruits were enlisted in 1950 to join Gurkha Ordnance, EME and Catering units, although these were never formed. Gurkha Military Police was raised and served from 1949 to 1965. Gurkha Army Service Corps, later to become The Queen's Own Gurkha Logistic Regiment, was raised in 1958. Gurkha Army Medical Corps was due to be raised in 1961, but this never occurred. A Boys Company served from 1948 to 1968. The Gurkha Independent Parachute Company, formed by secondment of men from the regiments, served from 1963 to 1971.

Although commanded by British Officers, there were other Gurkha units raised during this period, which do not form part of The British Armed Forces. The Gurkha Contingent of the Singapore Police raised in 1949 still exists under the Republic of Singapore, commanded by British Officers on contract. There were also some 400 prison guards enlisted in the Republic of Singapore, but in 1981 these were absorbed into the Gurkha Contingent of the Singapore Police. The British Embassies in Saigon, Bangkok and Kabul, amongst others, have or had Gurkha Guards, recruited usually from ex-service Gurkhas. A security force of ex-service Gurkhas was raised in Brunei in the early 1970s, and became the Gurkha Reserve Unit in 1981.

Various changes of title took place in the Brigade of Gurkhas as reflected in the lineage lists.

By the mid 1960s, during the Confrontation campaign in Malaysia, the maximum authorised strength of The Brigade of Gurkhas rose to around 14,400. In the late 1960s a rundown was ordered, reducing the overall strength by the early 1970s to around 8,000.

All the 2nd Battalions were due to disappear, by amalgamation with their 1st Battalions. This process was halted just before the process was completed and the 2nd Gurkha Rifles retained two battalions for a further 23 years. There was a temporary expansion of strength between 1981 and 1986, when the 2nd Battalion, 7th Gurkha Rifles was re-raised.

In 1992 a further rundown was ordered, reducing the overall strengths to around 4,000. The five infantry battalions were reduced progressively to only two, plus some extra semi-independent companies.

On 1 July 1994, the four numbered regiments (2nd, 6th, 7th and 10th Gurkha Rifles) were amalgamated in one Regiment - designated The Royal Gurkha Rifles. The remaining Gurkha Corps continued to serve, each at about one squadron strength.

The four infantry Battalions were reduced to three in 1994 and then to two in 1996. Their strength varied over the next decade. Their fourth rifle companies were reduced in order to conform to all other British Infantry establishments. However, the two battalions of The Royal Gurkha Rifles had to provide extra Companies as Demonstration Company at the Royal Military Academy Sandhurst and Demonstration Companies at the Infantry school in Brecon and the Training Wing at Catterick. In 2008 further reinforcement companies were authorized without raising a new battalion, and these were attached to understrength UK Infantry Battalions.

Meanwhile the Gurkha Corps units had all expanded to two squadrons and in some cases three squadron strength.

In January 2009, there were new instructions issued to absorb and employ the extra Gurkha manpower which had been generated by the revised Gurkha Terms and Conditions of service. These new terms allowed all serving Gurkhas to transfer to a 22 year Open Engagement from the previous Gurkha Engagement of 15 years which had applied up to October 2007. By 2009 this surplus manpower had reached a total of 690 who were in excess of their original liability. This surplus manpower was used to create two additional Gurkha Reinforcement Companies, one with 1st Battalion The Mercian Regiment and the other with 1st Battalion The Yorkshire Regiment. Further surplus Gurkha manpower was permitted to transfer to the "Wider Army". Initially about 300 Gurkha officers and soldiers opted for this course.

A further consequence of the revised Gurkha Terms and Conditions of Service in 2009 was to transfer all the enlisted Gurkha clerks into a new unit. Each regiment or corps had originally had their own clerks. In earlier times these were mainly Indian civilian clerks, always known as writers. These civilian clerks continued to serve, after transfer to the British Army, until the late 1950's. Most of the uniformed Gurkha clerks were recruited from the Darjeeling area of India, where education opportunities were much better than in the recruiting areas in Nepal. After 1970 the clerk recruiting policy was changed and only those domiciled in Nepal were enlisted. After 1994 all Gurkha clerks were re-badged into The Royal Gurkha Rifles. On 30 June 2011 all serving Gurkha clerks were re-badged into the Gurkha Staff and Personnel Support Company.

The numbers recruited into the British Army since 1949 are given in the next table. The highest number recruited in any one year was 1562 in 1961; and the lowest number was 1 in 1977.

GURKHAS RECRUITED INTO THE BRITISH ARMY FROM 1949

YEAR	RECRUITS	YEAR	RECRUITS
1949	1405	1981	840
1950	525	1982	486
1951	531	1983	490
1952	1104	1984	498
1953	594	1985	482
1954	545	1986	300
1955	1045	1987	226
1956	823	1988	212
1957	1018	1989	276
1958	1198	1990	303
1959	1236	1991	120
1960	1386	1992	153
1961	1562	1993	153
1962	1042	1994	153
1963	448	1995	153
1964	967	1996	160
1965	936	1997	160
1966	763	1998	181
1967	402	1999	230
1968	403	2000	229
1969	365	2001	230
1970	304	2002	230
1971	207	2003	230
1972	178	2004	230
1973	279	2005	230
1974	318	2006	230
1975	325	2007	230
1976	299	2008	230
1977	1	2009	230
1978	393	2010	176
1979	1030	2011	176
1980	919	2012	176

GURKHA TOTALS IN BRITISH SERVICE

It is not possible to calculate accurately the number of Gurkhas who have served the Crown since 1814. It is however possible to give some figures for the 20th Century, starting with the First World War.

Assuming the highest case figures, and ignoring possible double-counting, the First World War totals can be shown to be:

	Serving in 1914	Enlisted 1914 - 1919	Totals in Service 1914 - 1919	Serving in 1919
Gurkhas in Named Gurkha units	18156	60822	78978	55377
Gurkhas in other Indian Army units. a. Infantry b. Non-Infantry	53 7	n.k.	n.k.	1020 1082
Gurkhas in Military Police units	5540	-	-	9700
Gurkhas in Indian States units	1013	-	-	910

These produce totals for the First World War of:

a. Directly employed by the Crown   90780
    (plus wartime enlistments into Military Police
    and other units with transfers to Gurkha units excluded).

b. Numbers serving in 1919   67179

c. Indian States units   approx   1000

d. Units of Royal Nepal Army serving in India   15778

The estimates for the Second World War can be shown to be:

	Serving in 1939	Enlisted 1939 - 1945	Totals in Service 1939 - 1945	Serving in 1945
Gurkhas in Named Gurkha units	18722	104951	123673	86308
Gurkhas in other Indian Army units.	124	n.k.	n.k.	5210
Gurkhas in Military Police units	6363	approx 3000	approx 9000	approx 6000
Gurkhas in Indian States units	1555	n.k.	n.k.	1753

These produce totals for Second World War of:

a   Directly employed by the Crown   approx 137,883

b. Numbers serving in 1945   approx 97,518

c. Indian States' units   1,753

d. Units of Royal Nepal Army serving   6,50
    in India and Burma

Taking the totals for both World Wars

a. Directly employed by the Crown   228,663

b. Allied Forces   25,031

Since 1949 and up to 2008 Gurkhas who have
enlisted in British Service number   38,767

GURKHA CASUALTIES IN BRITISH SERVICE

The figures are difficult to extract from the various records which exist and even the ones which have been published have not always been clearly defined.

Before the First World War there do not appear to be any official figures. The First World War figures are stated to be "over 20,000" Casualties which are believed to include killed in action, died of wounds, wounded and missing. The Commonwealth War Graves Commission has recorded two figures 6342 or 6168. These refer to recorded graves. The difference in these figures is almost certainly because one includes followers who would be listed under the regiment with which they served.

For the Second World War a more accurate table has been recorded (see page 116). Although, the published figure of "Casualties" has been stated to be 23,655; it can be seen that these include missing and injured as well as killed in action, died of wounds or diseases and accidental deaths. The Commonwealth War Graves Commission again records two figures, 9056 or 8816.

There were believed to be about 300 Casualties in Post Second World War operations in French Indo-China and the Dutch East Indies between 1945 and 1947. In the British Army since 1948 and up to 2000 there were 269 Gurkhas killed in action and others accidentally killed and died of disease. There is no record of the total of wounded.

.

PART 2

LINEAGES LISTS OF
GURKHA REGIMENTS AND UNITS

1st KING GEORGE V'S OWN GURKHA RIFLES
(THE MALAUN REGIMENT)

Raised at Subathu

24 April	1815	1st NUSSEREE BATTALION	(GGO of 24 April 1815)
6 May	1823	6th, 1st NUSSERI (GORKA) BATTALION	(GOCC unnumbered of 6 May covering GOGG No 8 of 2 May 1823)
March	1824	6th, 1st NUSSERI BATTALION	(Bengal Army list of 31 March 1824)
1 December	1826	4th, 1st NUSSERI BATTALION	(GGO No 231 of 5 October 1826)
1 February	1830	4th NUSSEREE BATTALION	(GGO No 251 of 4 December 1829)
	1845	4th NUSSEREE (RIFLE) BATTALION	
27 February	1850	66th, or GOORKA, REGIMENT, OF NATIVE INFANTRY	(GOCC Unnumbered of 27 February 1850
January	1851	66th REGIMENT OF NATIVE INFANTRY (GOORKAS)	(Bengal Army List of 7 January 1851)
October	1857	66th or GOORKA REGIMENT	(Bengal Army List of October 1857)
5 November	1858	66th or GOORKA LIGHT INFANTRY	(Bengal Army List of 1 July 1859) (GOCC of 5 November 1858)
May	1861	11th REGIMENT, NATIVE INFANTRY	(GGO No 400 of 3 May 1861)
29 October	1861	1st GOORKHA REGIMENT	(GGO No 990 of 29 October 1861)
12 April	1886	1st GOORKHA LIGHT INFANTRY	(GO No 25 of 12 April 1886)
20 February	1891	1st GURKHA (RIFLE) REGIMENT	(GO No 175 of 20 February 1891)
13 September	1901		1st GURKHA RIFLES (GGO No 837 of 13 September 1901)

1st KING GEORGE V'S OWN GURKHA RIFLES
(THE MALAUN REGIMENT) (Continued)

2 October	1903	1st GURKHA RIFLES (THE MALAUN REGIMENT)	(IAO No 181 of 2 October 1903)
1 January	1906	1st PRINCE OF WALES'S OWN GURKHA RIFLES (THE MALAUN REGIMENT)	(G of I of 1 January 1906; IAO No 56 of 29 January 1906)
2 December	1910	1st KING GEORGE'S OWN GURKHA RIFLES (THE MALAUN REGIMENT)	(G of I No 981 of 3 December 1910; IAO No 19 of 9 January 1911)
8 May	1937	1st KING GEORGE V'S OWN GURKHA RIFLES (THE MALAUN REGIMENT)	(G of I No 344 of 8 May 1937)

Into captivity in Singapore .

24/25 August	1946		Reconstituted from 3rd Battalion (IAO No 1387 of 1946)
13 June	1917	3rd Battalion.	Raised (AD letter 8668 of 12 June 1917 also AD letter 15157)
31 March	1921		Disbanded
1 October	1940		Re-raised
24/25 August	1946		Disbanded at midnight and reconstituted as 2nd Battalion (IAO No 1387 of 1946)
15 March	1941	4th Battalion.	Raised at Dharmsala
30 November	1946		Disbanded
1 June	1942	5th Battalion.	Raised at Dharmsala
30 October	1946		Disbanded

1st KING GEORGE V'S OWN GURKHA RIFLES
(THE MALAUN REGIMENT) (Continued)

15 August	1947	1st KING GEORGE V'S OWN GURKHA RIFLES (THE MALAUN REGIMENT)
10 February	1949	1st KING GEORGE V'S OWN GORKHA RIFLES (THE MALAUN REGIMENT)
26 January	1950	1st GORKHA RIFLES (THE MALAUN REGIMENT)

		1st Battalion)	
		)	Direct descent from above
		2nd Battalion)	
21 December	1959	3rd Battalion	Re-raised at Clement Town
1 January	1963	4th Battalion	Re-raised at Arbala
1 January	1965	5th Battalion	Re-raised at Sabathu

2nd KING EDWARD VII'S OWN GURKHA RIFLES (THE SIRMOOR RIFLES)

Raised at Nahan, Sirmoor

24 April	1815	SIRMOOR BATTALION	(GCO of 24 April 1815)
6 May	1823	8th SIRMOOR (GORKHA) BATTALION	(GOCC unnumbered of 6 May 1823 covering GOGG No 8 of 2 May 1823)
March	1824	8th SIRMOOR BATTALION	(Bengal Army List of 31 March 1823)
1 December	1826	6th SIRMOOR BATTALION	(GGO No 231 of 5 October 1826)
	1845	6th SIRMOOR (RIFLE) BATTALION	
1 March	1850	SIRMOOR (RIFLE) BATTALION	(GGO No 173 of 22 March 1850)
April	1852	SIRMOOR BATTALION	(Bengal Army List of April 1852)
4 September	1858	SIRMOOR RIFLE REGIMENT	(GOCC No 379 of 4 September 1858)
3 May	1861	17th REGIMENT, NATIVE INFANTRY	(GGO No 400 of 3 May 1861)
29 October	1861	2nd GOORKHA (THE SIRMOOR RIFLES) REGIMENT	(GGO No 990 of 29 October 1861)
14 March	1876	2nd (PRINCE OF WALES' OWN) GOORKHA REGIMENT (THE SIRMOOR RIFLES)	(GGO No 266 of 1876)
12 April	1886	2nd (PRINCE OF WALES'S OWN) GOORKHA REGIMENT (THE SIRMOOR RIFLES)	(GO No 25 of 12 April 1886)
20 February	1891	2nd (PRINCE OF WALES' OWN) GURKHA (RIFLE) REGIMENT (THE SIRMOOR RIFLES)	(GO No 175 of 20 February 1891)
13 September	1901	2nd (PRINCE OF WALES' OWN) GURKHA (RIFLE) REGIMENT (THE SIRMOOR RIFLES)	(GGO No 937 of 13 September 1901)
	1901	2nd GURKHA RIFLES (PRINCE OF WALES' OWN) (THE SIRMOOR RIFLES)	
2 October	1903	2nd PRINCE OF WALES' OWN GURKHA RIFLES (THE SIRMOOR RIFLES)	(IAO No 181 of 2 October 1903)

2nd KING EDWARD VII'S OWN GURKHA RIFLES
(THE SIRMOOR RIFLES) (Continued)

1 January	1906	2nd KING EDWARD'S OWN GURKHA RIFLES (THE SIRMOOR RIFLES)	(G of I of 1 January 1906; IAO No 56 of 29 January 1906)
27 June	1936	2nd KING EDWARD VII'S OWN GURKHA RIFLES (THE SIRMOOR RIFLES)	(G of I of 27 June 1936)
1 January	1948	2nd KING EDWARD VII'S OWN GURKHA RIFLES (THE SIRMOOR RIFLES) THE GURKHA REGIMENT	(AO No 147 of 30 December 1947)
23 September	1948	2nd KING EDWARD VII'S OWN GURKHA RIFLES (THE SIRMOOR RIFLES) THE BRIGADE OF GURKHAS	(AO No 79 of 23 September 1948)
1 January	1950	2nd KING EDWARD VII'S OWN GURKHA RIFLES (THE SIRMOOR RIFLES)	(AO No 135 of November 1949)
1 July	1994	Amalgamated to form part of THE ROYAL GURKHA RIFLES	Royal Warrant of 24 March 1994; D/PS(A) 1104/10/1/PS 12(A) dated 15 September 1992)

---

14 September	1992	1st Battalion	Title first used in 1886 when 2nd Battalion raised Amalgamated with 2nd Battalion in Hong Kong (D/DASD/8/4/28/5 ASD 1 dated 18 October 1991)
1886		2nd Battalion	Raised from 1st Battalion at Dehra Dun (GO of 6 February 1886)
15 February 14/15 May	1942 1946		Into captivity in Singapore . Reconstituted from 3rd Battalion (IAO No 1255 of 1946)
14 September	1992		Amalgamated with 1st Battalion in Hong Kong (D/DASD/8/4/28/5 ASD 1 dated 18 October 1991)
12 June	1917	3rd Battalion	Raised at Dehra Dun (AD letter 8668 of 12 June 1917. Also AD letter 15157)

2nd KING EDWARD VII'S OWN GURKHA RIFLES
(THE SIRMOOR RIFLES) (Continued)

3 October	1920		Disbanded
October	1940		Re-raised at Dehra Dun
14/15 May	1946		Disbanded and reconstituted with 2nd Battalion at Santa Cruz Bombay at midnight (IAO No 1255 of 1946)
3 March	1941	4th Battalion	Raised at Dehra Dun
1 January	1948		Became 5th Battalion, 8th GURKHA RIFLES
18 March	1942	5th Battalion	Raised at Dehra Dun.
January	1947		Disbanded in Dehra Dun

3rd QUEEN ALEXANDRA'S OWN GURKHA RIFLES

Raised at Hawalbagh, near Almora

24 April	1815	KEMAOON BATTALION	(GGO of 24 April 1815)
	1816	KEMAOON PROVINCIAL BATTALION	
6 May	1823	9th KEMAOON BATTALION	(GOCC unnumbered of 6 May 1823 covering GGO No 8 of 2 May 1823)
1 December	1826	7th KEMAOON BATTALION	(GGO No 231 of 5 October 1826)
1 March	1850	KEMAOON BATTALION	(GGO No 173 of March 1850)
3 May	1861	18th REGIMENT, NATIVE INFANTRY	(GGO No 400 of 3 May 1861)
29 October	1861	3rd GOORKHA (THE KEMAOON REGIMENT)	(GGO No 990 of 29 October 1861)
	1864	3rd (THE KUMAON) GOORKHA REGIMENT	
		3rd GOORKHA REGIMENT	
20 February	1891	3rd GURKHA (RIFLE) REGIMENT	(GO No 175 of 20 February 1891)
13 September	1901	3rd GURKHA RIFLES	(GGO No 837 of 13 September 1901)
22 February	1907	3rd THE QUEEN'S OWN GURKHA RIFLES	(LG of 22 February 1907. Also IAO No 241 republishing G of I notification of 19 April 1907)
6 April	1908	3rd QUEEN ALEXANDRA'S OWN GURKHA RIFLES	(IAO No 195 of 6 April 1908)

		1st Battalion	Title first used in 1887 when 2nd Battalion raised
April	1881	2nd Battalion	Raised at Almora (Special IAO 23 March 1887 Originally to be Garhwalis from all Gurkha Rgts In June 1887, to be half Gurkhas and half Garhwalis (GOCC 20 June 1887). Transferred to become 39th (THE GARHWALI) REGIMENT OF BENGAL INFANTRY in 1891. Redesignated 39th (THE GARHWAL) Rgt OF BENGAL INFANTRY in 1892
	1891	New 2nd Battalion	Raised at Lansdowne

3rd QUEEN ALEXANDRA'S OWN GURKHA RIFLES (Continued)

3 February	1917	3rd Battalion	Raised in Egypt (AD letter 2265 of 15 February 1917)
September	1920	Disbanded	
1 October	1940	Re-raised	
1 October	1916	4th Battalion	Raised at Rawalpindi as 1st Reserve Battalion, Gurkha Rifles. Companies came from 2nd Battalion 2nd KEO Gurkha Rifles and 1st Battalons 3rd QAO Gurkha Rifles, 5th Gurkha Rifles and 6th Gurkha Rifles (AD letter 19853 of 2 October 1916)
9 June	1917		Became 4th Battalion at Kohat (Army Department letter No 47874-1 AD of 30 May 1917)
16 March	1922		Disbanded at Abbottabad
15 March	1941		Re-raised at Ghangora (Dehra Dun)
30 April	1947		Disbanded at Dehra Dun

Note: From 1816 until February 1839, the Regiment came under the Civil Department

---

15 August	1947	3rd QUEEN ALEXANDRA'S OWN GURKHA RIFLES
10 February	1949	3rd QUEEN ALEXANDRA'S OWN GORKHA RIFLES
26 January	1950	3rd GORKHA RIFLES

		1st Battalion)	
		2nd Battalion)	Direct descent
		3rd Battalion)	from above
20 February	1962	4th Battalion	Re-raised at Dehra Dun
1 October	1963	5th Battalion	Raised at Dehra Dun

4th PRINCE OF WALES'S OWN GURKHA RIFLES

Raised at Pithoragarh

1 July	1857	EXTRA GOORKHA REGIMENT	(GOCC of 15 March 1858)
3 May	1861	19th REGIMENT, NATIVE INFANTRY	(GGO No 400 of 3 May 1861)
29 October	1861	4th GOORKHA REGIMENT	(GGO No 990 of 29 October 1861)
20 February	1891	4th GURKHA (RIFLE) REGIMENT	(GO No 175 of 20 February 1891)
13 September	1901	4th GURKHA RIFLES	(GGO No 837 of 13 September 1901)
13 August	1924	4th PRINCE OF WALES'S OWN GURKHA RIFLES	(IAO No 702 of 1924 - A/26757/AG9)

		1st Battalion	Title first used in 1886 when 2nd Battalion raised
10 April	1886	2nd Battalion	Raised from 1st Battalion at Bakloh (Special IAO 10 April 1886)
1 October	1940	3rd Battalion	Raised at Bakloh
5 March	1941	4th Battalion	Raised at Bakloh
18 October	1946	Disbanded at Bakloh	

Note: The 3rd Battalion should have been raised from the 1st Reserve Battalion in October 1916 but because of a clerical error this was converted into the 4th Battalion, 3rd QUEEN ALEXANDRA'S OWN GURKHA RIFLES: thus no 3rd Battalion existed in the 1914-18 War.

---

15 August	1947	4th PRINCE OF WALES'S OWN GURKHA RIFLES
10 February	1949	4th PRINCE OF WALES'S OWN GORKHA RIFLES
20 January	1950	4th GORKHA RIFLES

Direct descent from above. Handed over to India

1st Battalion		31 December 1947 at Amritsar
2nd Battalion		31 December 1947 at Amritsar
3rd Battalion		27 March 1948 at Barrackpore
1 March	1962	4th Battalion

1 March	1962	4th Battalion	Re-raised at Amballa

4th PRINCE OF WALES'S OWN GURKHA RIFLES (Continued)

1 January	1963	5th Battalion	Raised at Bakloh
September	1970	6th Battalion	Raised

5th ROYAL GURKHA RIFLES (FRONTIER FORCE)

Raised at Abbottabad, by transfers of men borne as Gurkhas on the rolls of 4th REGIMENT SEIKH INFANTRY, CORPS OF GUIDES INFANTRY, 24th REGIMENT of PUNJAB INFANTRY and 5th PUNJAUB POLICE BATTALION

22 May	1858	25th PUNJAB INFANTRY or HUZARA GOORKHA BATTALION	(Bengal GO No 984 of 25 June 1858 confirming Chief Commissioner of Punjaub Order No 443 of 22 May 1858)
	1861	7th REGIMENT OF INFANTRY (or HAZARA GOORKHA BATTALION), PUNJAUB IRREGULAR FORCE	
29 October	1861	5th GOORKHA REGIMENT (THE HAZARA GOORKHA BATTALION) ATTACHED TO THE PUNJAUB IRREGULAR FORCE	(GGO No 990 of 29 October 1861)
	1886	5th GOORKHA REGIMENT, THE HAZARA GOORKHA BATTALION	
December	1887	5th GOORKHA REGIMENT	
December	1891	5th GURKHA (RIFLE) REGIMENT	(GO No 175 of 20 February 1891)
13 September	1901	5th GURKHA RIFLES	(GGO No 837 of 13 September 1901)
2 October	1903	5th GURKHA RIFLES (FRONTIER FORCE)	(IAO No 181 of 2 October 1903)
15 February	1921	5th ROYAL GURKHA RIFLES (FRONTIER FORCE)	(IAO No 821 of 26 July 1921)

		1st Battalion	Title first used in 1886 when 2nd Battalion raised
20 October	1886	2nd Battalion	Raised at Abbottabad (Special IAO of 1 Oct 1886). Raised from 1st Battalion and 42nd, 43rd and 44th Regiments Goorkha (Light) Infantry; not more than 100 volunteers per regiment. (GOCC 20 October 1886)

5th ROYAL GURKHA RIFLES (FRONTIER FORCE) (Continued)

28 November 1916		3rd Battalion	Raised at Ferozepore, as 2nd Reserve Battalion, Gurkha Rifles. Companies came from 1st Battalions, 4th Gurkha Rifles and 9th Gurkha Rifles and 2nd Battalions, 1st KGO Gurkha Rifles and 10th Gurkha Rifles. (AD ltr 13999 of 1 December 1916) Became 3rd Battalion on 29 May 1917. Subsidiary Title Frontier Force added 9 October 1917.
July	1921		Disbanded
1 October	1940		Re-raised
15 March	1941	4th Battalion	Raised
December	1946		Disbanded

---

15 August	1947	5th ROYAL GURKHA RIFLES (FRONTIER FORCE)
10 February	1949	5th ROYAL GORKHA RIFLES (FRONTIER FORCE)
26 January	1950	5th GORKHA RIFLES (FRONTIER FORCE)

		1st Battalion)	
		2nd Battalion)	Direct descent from above
		3rd Battalion)	
1 January	1963	4th Battalion	Re-raised at Dehra Dun
1 January	1948	5th Battalion	3rd Battalion, 6th GURKHA RIFLES became 5th Battalion (Chindits) 5th ROYAL GURKHA RIFLES (FRONTIER FORCE)

	1948	6th Battalion	Raised 1948 primarily from men of 6th GURKHA RIFLES who opted for service with India

---

6th QUEEN ELIZABETH'S OWN GURKHA RIFLES

Raised at Chaubiaganj, Cuttack

17 May	1817	THE CUTTACK LEGION	(GOCC of 16 May 1817)
September	1822	RUNGPORE LOCAL BATTALION	(Bengal Army List of 30 September 1822, GOCC of 14 February and 15 March 1823)
28 March	1823	RUNGPOOR LIGHT INFANTRY	(Bengal Army List of April 1823, GOGG of 29 March 1823)
6 May	1823	10th RUNGPOOR LIGHT INFANTRY	(GOCC unnumbered of 6 May 1823 covering GOGG No 8 of 2 May 1823)
1 December	1826	8th RUNGPOOR LIGHT INFANTRY	(GGO No 231 of 5 October 1826)
16 May	1828	8th RUNGPORE LIGHT INFANTRY	(GOCC No 104 of 16 May 1828)
1 November	1828	8th ASSAM LIGHT INFANTRY	(Government letter No. 334 of 20 June 1828)
9 August	1844	8th 1st ASSAM LIGHT INFANTRY BATTALION	(GGO No 234 of 1844)
1 March	1850	1st ASSAM LIGHT INFANTRY BATTALION	
3 May	1861	46th (1st ASSAM) LIGHT INFANTRY	(GGO No 400 of 3 May 1861)
29 October	1861	42nd (ASSAM) LIGHT INFANTRY	(GGO No 990 of 29 October 1861)
	1864	42nd (ASSAM) REGIMENT OF BENGAL NATIVE (LIGHT) INFANTRY	(Indian Army List of 1865)
January	1885	42nd (ASSAM) REGIMENT OF BENGAL (LIGHT) INFANTRY	
June	1886	42nd REGIMENT, GOORKHA (LIGHT) INFANTRY	
	1889	42nd (GOORKHA) REGIMENT OF BENGAL (LIGHT) INFANTRY	
20 February	1891	42nd GURKHA (RIFLE) REGIMENT OF BENGAL INFANTRY	(GO No 175 of 20 February 1891)

6th QUEEN ELIZABETH'S OWN GURKHA RIFLES (Continued)

13 September	1901	42nd GURKHA RIFLES	(GGO No 837 of 13 September 1901)
2 October	1903	6th GURKHA RIFLES	(IAO No 181 of 2 October 1903)
1 January	1948	6th GURKHA RIFLES, THE GURKHA REGIMENT	(AO No 147 of 30 December 1947)
23 September	1948	6th GURKHA RIFLES, THE BRIGADE OF GURKHAS	(AO No 79 of 23 September 1948)
1 January	1950	6th GURKHA RIFLES	(AO No 135 of November 1949)
1 January	1959	6th QUEEN ELIZABETH'S OWN GURKHA RIFLES	(LG of 1 January 1959 and AO No 1 of 1959)
1 July	1994	Amalgamated to form part of THE ROYAL GURKHA RIFLES	(Royal Warrant of 24 March 1994; D PS(A)/104/10/1/PS12(A) dated 15 September 1992)

―――――――――――――

		1st Battalion	Title first used in 1904 when 2nd Battalion raised
5 November	1904	2nd Battalion	Raised 1904 at Abbottabad from nucleus of 1st Battalion (IAO No 790 of 1904)
16 June	1969		Amalgamated with 1st Battalion in Hong Kong
5 February	1917	3rd Battalion	Raised at Rawalpindi as 3rd Reserve Battalion, Gurkha Rifles (AD letter 2384 of 7 Feb 1917). Drafts came from 1st and 2nd Battalions of 2nd KEO Gurkha Rifles, 4th Gurkha Rifles, 9th Gurkha Rifles and 10th Gurkha Rifles and from 2nd Battalion 6th Gurkha Rifles. Later in 1917 became 3rd Battalion
1 February	1921		Disbanded
1 October	1940		Re-raised
1 January	1948		Became 5th Battalion (Chindits), 5th ROYAL GURKHA RIFLES (FRONTIER FORCE)
15 March	1941	4th Battalion	Raised
28 February	1947		Disbanded

―――――――――――――

6th QUEEN ELIZABETH'S OWN GURKHA RIFLES (Continued)

Note: 2nd Battalion was raised to replace 65th CARNATIC LIGHT INFANTRY, whose men were mustered out. Inherited the funds, Mess and band property, but not the battle honours or regimental precedence

This Regiment was formerly

1759	6th BATTALION COAST SEPOYS
1769	6th CARNATIC BATTALION
1770	5th CARNATIC BATTALION
1784	5th MADRAS BATTALION
1796	1st Battalion, 5th REGIMENT MADRAS NATIVE INFANTRY
1824	5th REGIMENT MADRAS NATIVE INFANTRY
1885	5th REGIMENT MADRAS INFANTRY
1901	5th MADRAS INFANTRY
1903	65th CARNATIC LIGHT INFANTRY

Battle Honours: Carnatic, Sholinghur, Mysore, Pegu, Burma 1885-87

———————————————————

7th DUKE OF EDINBURGH'S OWN GURKHA RIFLES

1st Battalion raised at Thayetmyo from nucleus of men from 10th GURKHA RIFLES, BURMA MILITARY POLICE and other Gurkha units.

16 May	1902	8th GURKHA RIFLES	(GOCC No 252 dated 12 April 1902)
13 July	1903	2nd Battalion, 10th GURKHA RIFLES	(Indian Army Circulars Clause 20 of 1903 and GGO No 127 of 13 July 1903)
18 July	1907	Split into two wings to form two battalions, one retaining this name; the other unnamed.	
18 July	1907	1st Battalion, 7th GURKHA RIFLES	(IAO No 483 of 27 September 1907)

		2nd Battalion	
18 July	1907	A new battalion raised at Quetta but unnamed, from a wing of 2nd Battalion, 10th GURKHA RIFLES	(IAO No 342 of 18 July 1907)
27 September 1907		2nd Battalion, 7th GURKHA RIFLES	(IAO No 483 of 27 September 1907)

---

1 January	1948	7th GURKHA RIFLES, THE GURKHA REGIMENT	(AO No 147 of 30 December 1947)
23 September 1948		7th GURKHA RIFLES, THE BRIGADE OF GURKHAS	(AO No 79 of 23 September 1948)
1 January	1950	7th GURKHA RIFLES	(AO No 135 of November 1949)
1 January	1959	7th DUKE OF EDINBURGH'S OWN GURKHA RIFLES	(LG of 1 January 1959 and AO No 1 of 1959)
1 July	1994	Amalgamated to form part of THE ROYAL GURKHA RIFLES	(Royal Warrant of 24 March 1994; /PS(A)104/10/ PS12 (A) dated 15 September 1992)

		1st Battalion	Title first used in 1907 when 2nd Battalion raised.
February	1942		Amalgamated with 3rd Battalion, after severe losses at Sittang, being only 300 men strong

7th DUKE OF EDINBURGH'S OWN GURKHA RIFLES (Continued)

May	1942		Reformed
	1907	2nd Battalion	Raised
	1916		Re-raised after the fall of Kut and captivity
	1942		Re-raised after the fall of Tobruk and captivity
1 August	1970		Amalgamated with 1st Battalion in Hong Kong
1 May	1981		Re-raised 1 May 1981 in Hong Kong as GURKHA REINFORCEMENT BATTALION (D/DINF/54/1C (Inf 1a) of 8 July 1981)
19 October	1981		Retitled as 2nd Battalion (D/DASD/8/11/3 (ASD 1a) of September 1981)
23 October	1986		Disbanded in Hong Kong (DInf/54/1/D (Inf) dated 14 August 1986)
June	1917	3rd Battalion	Raised (AD ltr 8688 of 12 June 1917. Also AD ltr 15157)
March	1921		Disbanded
1 October	1940		Re-raised
February	1942		Amalgamated with 1st Battalion after severe losses at Sittang, being only 170 men strong
May	1942		Reformed
4 August	1943		Became 154 (GURKHA) PARACHUTE BATTALION
November	1945		Redesignated 3rd GURKHA BATTALION, INDIAN PARACHUTE REGIMENT
26 October	1946		Reverted to regimental title
November	1946		Disbanded
15 March	1941	4th Battalion	Raised
30 May	1947		Disbanded

Note: 1. Between June 1948 and December 1949, the 1st and 2nd Battalions served respectively as 101st and 102nd Field Regiments, ROYAL ARTILLERY (7th GURKHA RIFLES) without alteration to their gazetted title

---

7th DUKE OF EDINBURGH'S OWN GURKHA RIFLES (Continued)

Note: 2. The 8th GURKHA RIFLES were raised to replace 8th MADRAS INFANTRY, whose men were mustered out. Inherited the funds, Mess and band property, but not battle honours or precedence

This Regiment was formerly:

1761	9th COAST SEPOYS
1769	9th CARNATIC BATTALION
1771	8th MADRAS BATTALION
1796	1st Battalion, 8th REGIMENT MADRAS NATIVE INFANTRY
1824	8th REGIMENT MADRAS NATIVE INFANTRY
1885	8th REGIMENT MADRAS INFANTRY
1901	8th MADRAS INFANTRY

Battle honours: Carnatic, Sholinghur, Seringapatam, Assaye. On Colours and appointments "The Elephant"

8th GURKHA RIFLES

1st Battalion raised at Sylhet

19 February	1824	16th or SYLHET LOCAL BATTALION	(GGO No 64 of November 1824)
1 December	1826	11th or SYLHET LOCAL BATTALION	(GGO No 231 of 5 October 1826)
27 April	1827	11th or SYLHET LIGHT INFANTRY	(Bengal General Orders of 27 April 1827 and Bengal Army List of 1 July 1827)
3 May	1861	48th (SYLHET) LIGHT INFANTRY	(GGO No 400 of 3 May 1861)
29 October	1861	44th (SYLHET) LIGHT INFANTRY	(GGO No 990 of 29 October 1861)
	1864	44th (SYLHET) LIGHT INFANTRY	(Indian Army List of 1865)
January	1885	44th (SYLHET) REGIMENT OF BENGAL (LIGHT) INFANTRY	
June	1886	44th REGIMENT GOORKHA (LIGHT) INFANTRY	
	1889	44th (GOORKHA) REGIMENT OF BENGAL (LIGHT) INFANTRY	
20 February	1891	44th GURKHA (RIFLE) REGIMENT OF BENGAL INFANTRY	(GO No 175 of 20 February 1891)
13 September	1901	44th GURKHA RIFLES	(GGO No 837 of 13 September 1901)
2 October	1903	8th GURKHA RIFLES	(AO No 181 of 2 October 1903)
27 September	1907	Became 1st Battalion, 8th GURKHA RIFLES	(IAO No 483 of 27 September 1907)

2nd Battalion raised at Gauhati from two companies of ASSAM LIGHT INFANTRY (see 6th QUEEN ELIZABETH'S OWN GURKHA RIFLES)

13 April	1835	ASSAM SEBUNDY CORPS	(GGO No 98 of 13 April 1835)
27 August	1839	THE LOWER ASSAM SEBUNDY CORPS	(GOCC No 140 of 21 August 1839)
5 November	1839	1st ASSAM SEBUNDY CORPS	(GOCC No 187 of 23 October 1839)

8th GURKHA RIFLES (Continued)

	1844	1st ASSAM SEBUNDY REGIMENT	
9 August	1844	2nd ASSAM LIGHT INFANTRY BATTALION	(GOGG No 234 of 9 August 1844)
3 May	1861	47th (2nd ASSAM) LIGHT INFANTRY	(GGO No 400 of 3 May 1961)
29 October	1861	43rd (ASSAM) LIGHT INFANTRY	(GGO No 990 of 29 October 1861)
	1864	43rd (ASSAM) REGIMENT OF BENGAL NATIVE (LIGHT) INFANTRY	(Indian Army List of 1865)
January	1885	43rd (ASSAM) REGIMENT OF BENGAL (LIGHT) INFANTRY	
June	1886	43rd REGIMENT GOORKHA (LIGHT) INFANTRY	
	1889	43rd (GOORKHA) REGIMENT OF BENGAL (LIGHT) INFANTRY	
20 February	1891	43rd GURKHA (RIFLE) REGIMENT OF BENGAL INFANTRY	(GO No 175 of 20 February 1891)
13 September	1901	43rd GURKHA RIFLES	(GGO No 837 of 13 September 1901)
2 October	1903	7th GURKHA RIFLES	(IAO No 181 of 2 October 1903)
27 September	1907	Became 2nd Battalion, 8th GURKHA RIFLES	(IAO No 483 of 27 September 1907)

		1st Battalion	Direct descent from 16th or SYLHET LOCAL BATTALION
		2nd Battalion	Direct descent from ASSAM SEBUNDY CORPS
June	1917	3rd Battalion	Raised at Lansdowne (AD letter 8668 of 12 June 1917. Also AD letter 15157).
15 June	1921		Disbanded (IAO No 325 of 3 May 1921).
October	1940		Re-raised
April	1946		Disbanded

8th GURKHA RIFLES (Continued)

15 March	1941	4th Battalion	Raised
	1944	88th INFANTRY COMPANY, 8th GURKHA RIFLES	Formed Redesignated No 1 (8th GURKHA RIFLES) Infantry Company
	1947		Disbanded

Note: The 2nd Battalion between 1835 and 1850 although shown amongst the local battalions between the 8th and 9th was never given a local battalion precedence

---

15 August	1947	8th GURKHA RIFLES	
10 February	1949	8th GORKHA RIFLES	
		1st Battalion) 2nd Battalion) 4th Battalion)	Direct descent from above
1 January	1963	3rd Battalion	Re-raised at Dehra Dun
1 January	1948	5th Battalion 4th Battalion, 2nd KING EDWARD VII'S OWN GURKHA RIFLES (THE SIRMOOR RIFLES) transferrred to 8th GURKHA RIFLES	
17 February	1948	and redesignated 5th Battalion	

---

4 February	1948	6th Battalion	Raised at Dehra Dun
2 April	1981	1st Battalion Redesignated as 3rd Battalion MECHANISED INFANTRY REGIMENT (1st/8th GORKHA RIFLES)	

9th GURKHA RIFLES

Raised at Fatehgarh

	1817	FATEHGARH LEVY	
	1818	MYNPOORY LEVY	
June	1823	1st Battalion, 32nd REGIMENT OF BENGAL NATIVE INFANTRY	(GGO No 65 of June 1823)
May	1824	63rd REGIMENT OF BENGAL NATIVE INFANTRY	(GGO No of 20 May 1824)
3 May	1861	9th REGIMENT OF BENGAL NATIVE INFANTRY	(GGO No 400 of 3 May 1861)
January	1885	9th REGIMENT OF BENGAL INFANTRY	
15 April	1893	9th GURKHA (RIFLE) REGIMENT OF BENGAL INFANTRY	(GOCC No 39 of 15 April 1893)
13 September	1901	9th GURKHA RIFLES	(GGO No 837 of 13 September 1901)

		1st Battalion	Title first used in 1904 when 2nd Battalion raised
1904		2nd Battalion	Raised from 1st Battalion at Dehra Dun (IAO No 800 of 1904)
15 February	1942		In captivity in Singapore
31 May/1 June	1946		Reconstituted from 5th Battalion at Wana (IAO No 1255 of 1946)
June 1917		3rd Battalion	Raised (AD letter 8668 of 12 June 1917. Also AD letter 15157)
28 February	1921	Disbanded	
1 October	1940	Re-raised	
1 November	1940	4th Battalion	Raised at Dehra Dun.
10 March	1947	Disbanded	
15 July	1942	5th Battalion	Raised at Dehra Dun.

9th GURKHA RIFLES (Continued)

31 May/1 June 1946		Disbanded at Wana and reconstituted as 2nd Battalion (IAO No 1225 of 1946)

---

15 August	1947	9th GURKHA RIFLES
10 February	1949	9th GORKHA RIFLES

	1st Battalion)	
	2nd Battalion)	Direct descent from above
	3rd Battalion)	
9 September 1961	4th Battalion	Re-raised at Dehra Dun
1 January 1963	5th Battalion	Re-raised at Dehra Dun

Note: 2nd Battalion was raised from a nucleus of men of 1st Battalion, to replace the 71st COORG RIFLES, whose men were mustered out. This Regiment was formerly

1767	15th COAST SEPOYS
1769	12th CARNATIC BATTALION
1770	11th CARNATIC BATTALION
1784	11th MADRAS BATTALION
1796	2nd Battalion, 9th REGIMENT OF MADRAS NATIVE INFANTRY
1824	11th REGIMENT OF MADRAS NATIVE INFANTRY
1885	11th REGIMENT OF MADRAS INFANTRY
1902	11th COORG INFANTRY
1903	71st COORG RIFLES

Battle Honour: Seringapatam

10th PRINCESS MARY'S OWN GURKHA RIFLES

Personnel of the KUBO VALLEY MILITARY POLICE BATTALION, were drafted in to replace the personnel of the 10th REGIMENT MADRAS INFANTRY, whose soldiers were mustered out.

May	1887	KUBO VALLEY MILITARY POLICE BATTALION	(GOCC of 9 April 1887)
1 May	1890	10th (BURMA) REGIMENT OF MADRAS INFANTRY	(GGO No 231 of 14 March 1890 under GGO No 176 of 24 March 1890. Also GGO No 251 dated 21 March 1890 under GGO No 194 of 1 April 1890)
[6 June	1890	1st REGIMENT OF BURMA INFANTRY	(GGO No 505 of 6 June 1890) (Title later rescinded)
7 April	1891	10th REGIMENT (1st BURMA BATTALION) OF MADRAS INFANTRY	(GGO No 196 of 7 April 1891; GGO No 276 of 20 March 1891)
9 February	1892	10th REGIMENT (1st BURMA RIFLES) OF MADRAS INFANTRY	(GGO No 98 of 9 February 1892)
3 May	1895	10th REGIMENT (1st BURMA GURKHA RIFLES) MADRAS INFANTRY	(GGO No 462 of 3 May 1895)
14 September	1901	10th GURKHA RIFLES	(GGO No 837 of 14 September 1901)
1 January	1948	10th GURKHA RIFLES, THE GURKHA REGIMENT	(AO No 147 of 30 December 1947)
23 September	1948	10th GURKHA RIFLES, THE BRIGADE OF GURKHAS	(AO No 69 of 23 September 1948)
1 January	1950	10th PRINCESS MARY'S OWN GURKHA RIFLES	(AO No 135 of November 1949)
1 July	1994	Amalgamated to form part of THE ROYAL GURKHA RIFLES	(Royal Warrant of 24 March 1994; D/PS(A)1104/10/1/PS12 (A) dated 15 September 1992)

July	1903	1st Battalion	Title first used when 2nd Battalion raised
13 July	1903	2nd Battalion	Redesignated from 8th GURKHA RIFLES (Indian Army Circular 1903 Clause 20 and GGO No 127 of 13 July 1903)

10th PRINCESS MARY'S OWN GURKHA RIFLES (Continued)

27 September 1907			Became 7th GURKHA RIFLES on 27 September 1907 (see 7th GURKHA RIFLES) (IAO No 483 of 27 September 1907) Having previously split into two wings and formed another battalion (IAO No 342 of 18 July 1907)
September	1908	New 2nd Battalion	Raised at Dehra Dun (Special IAO of 18 September 1908)
September	1969		Amalgamated with 1st Battalion as 10th PRINCESS MARY'S OWN GURKHA RIFLES in Penang
10 October	1940	3rd Battalion	Raised at Dehra Dun.
30 April	1947		Disbanded
15 March	1941	4th Battalion	Raised Abbottabad
January	1946		Disbanded

Note 1: The KUBO VALLEY MILITARY POLICE BATTALION was raised in May 1887 under GOCC of 9 April 1987. The men were mainly Gurkhas. The personnel of this unit were drafted into the 10th REGIMENT MADRAS INFANTRY in May 1890; the existing personnel of which being mustered out

Note 2: Under Madras GO No 194 of 1 April 1890, covering GO No 251 of 21 March 1890, the Regiment was allotted the number and place in the Madras line of the old 10th REGIMENT MADRAS INFANTRY whose men were mustered out. The funds, colours, Mess and Band property were transferred to the new Regiment. This Regiment was formerly

1766	14th BATTALION OF SEPOYS, MADRAS NATIVE INFANTRY	(6 June 1766)
1767	THE AMBOOR BATTALION, MADRAS NATIVE INFANTRY	(16 December 1767)
1769	11th CARNATIC BATTALION, MADRAS NATIVE INFANTRY	
1770	10th CARNATIC BATTALION, MADRAS NATIVE INFANTRY	
1784	10th MADRAS BATTALION, MADRAS NATIVE INFANTRY	
1796	1st BATTALION, 10th REGIMENT MADRAS NATIVE INFANTRY	
1824	10th REGIMENT, MADRAS NATIVE INFANTRY	
1885	10th REGIMENT, MADRAS INFANTRY	(1 January 1885)

Battle Honours: Amboor (and Rock Fort), Assaye (and Elephant), Ava, Carnatic, Mysore,   Burma 1885-7

Note 3: The title 1st REGIMENT OF BURMA INFANTRY was promulgated under GGO 305 of 6 June 1890 without consultation with the Madras Government or the Secretary of State for India. It was countermanded by the Secretary of State. (IOR L/MIL/7/7045 & 7048)

10th PRINCESS MARY'S OWN GURKHA RIFLES (Continued)

Note 4:   When the 2nd Battalion was finally raised in 1908 it took the place of the 77th MOPLAH RIFLES whose men were mustered out. The Mess, band property and funds were transferred to the new battalion.

This Regiment was formerly:

1777	17th CARNATIC BATTALION
1784	17th MADRAS BATTALION
1796	2nd Battalion, 1st REGIMENT MADRAS NATIVE INFANTRY
1806	Disbanded
1807	Reformed as 2nd Battalion 24th REGIMENT MADRAS NATIVE INFANTRY
1818	Original title restored as 2nd Battalion, 1st REGIMENT MADRAS NATIVE INFANTRY
1824	17th REGIMENT MADRAS NATIVE INFANTRY
1885	17th REGIMENT MADRAS INFANTRY
1902	1st MOPLAH RIFLES
1903	77th MOPLAH RIFLES
1907	Disbanded

Battle Honours: Carnatic, Sholinghur, Nagpore, Burma 1885-7

Note 5:   The date of grant for the title "Princess Mary's Own" was noted in a letter dated 30 January 1949 in which the King gave approval to the Regiment being renamed 10th (PRINCESS MARY's OWN) GURKHA RIFLES. The Army Order promulgating this did not appear until November 1949 and the new title did not include the brackets. The effective date appears to be 1 January 1950

Note 6:   In 1988 the Regiment was granted the battle honours of the 10th REGIMENT MADRAS INFANTRY (See Note 2 above), but not the precedence of this Regiment

---

11th GURKHA RIFLES (1918-1922)

1st BATTALION

18 May	1918	Raised at Kut by transfer of one company each from 1st and 2nd Battalions of 5th GURKHA RIFLES (FRONTIER FORCE) and 6th GURKHA RIFLES	
20 July	1921	Disbanded at Abbottabad: men going to 2nd Battalion 5th GURKHA RIFLES (FRONTIER FORCE)	(Special IAO No 32-S of 3 May 1921)

2nd BATTALION

24 May	1918	Raised at Baghdad by transfer of one company each from 1st Battalions of 2nd KING EDWARD'S OWN GURKHA RIFLES (THE SIRMOOR RIFLES), 3rd QUEEN ALEXANDRA'S OWN GURKHA RIFLES, 7th GURKHA RIFLES and 2nd Battalion, 4th GURKHA RIFLES	
15 July	1921	Disbanded at Abbottabad; men going to 2nd Battalion, 4th GURKHA RIFLES and 1st Battalion, 7th GURKHA RIFLES	(Special IAO No 35-S of 31 May 1921)

3rd BATTALION

25 May	1918	Raised at Baghdad by transfer of one company each from 2nd Battalion 9th GURKHA RIFLES and 1st Battalion 10th GURKHA RIFLES and one company each from 1st and 2nd Battalions of 39th GARHWAL RIFLES. Received drafts from 1st Battalions of 7th GURKHA RIFLES and 9th GURKHA RIFLES and 2nd Battalion 10th GURKHA RIFLES to replace Garhwalis transferred out	
12 March	1922	Disbanded at Abbottabad: men going to 2nd Battalion, 5th GURKHA RIFLES (FRONTIER FORCE), 1st Battalion, 7th GURKHA RIFLES and 10th GURKHA RIFLES	(Special IAO No 95 of 1 February 1922)

11th GURKHA RIFLES (1918-1922) (Continued)

4th BATTALION

24 May	1918	Raised in Palestine from one company each from 1st Battalion, 1st KING GEORGE'S OWN GURKHA RIFLES, 2nd and 3rd Battalions, 3rd QUEEN ALEXANDRA'S OWN GURKHA RIFLES and 2nd Battalion, 7th GURKHA RIFLES
Late	1919	Disbanded in India, having sent drafts to reinforce 1st, 2nd and 3rd Battalions

---

THE ROYAL GURKHA RIFLES

Formed by amalgamation of 2nd KING EDWARD VII'S OWN GURKHA RIFLES (THE SIRMOOR RIFLES), 6th QUEEN ELIZABETH'S OWN GURKHA RIFLES, 7th DUKE OF EDINBURGH'S OWN GURKHA RIFLES, and 10th PRINCESS MARY'S OWN GURKHA RIFLES on 1 July 1994

1 July	1994	THE ROYAL GURKHA RIFLES	(Royal Warrant of 2 March 1994; D/PS(A)104/10/1/PS1Z2(A) dated 15 September 1992)
		_____	
1 July	1994	1st Battalion	Formed by amalgamation of 2nd KING EDWARD VII'S OWN GURKHA RIFLES (THE SIRMOOR RIFLES) with 6th QUEEN ELIZABETH'S OWN GURKHA RIFLES in Hong Kong
1 July	1994	2nd Battalion	Formed on 7th DUKE OF EDINBURGH'S OWN GURKHA RIFLES in Seria, Brunei
November	1996		Amalgamated with 3rd Battalion in Seria, Brunei
1 July	1994	3rd Battalion	Formed on 10th PRINCESS MARY'S OWN GURKHA RIFLES in Church Crookham
November	1996		Amalgamated with 2nd Battalion in Seria, Brunei

THE QUEEN'S GURKHA ENGINEERS

Raised at Kluang, Johore, Malaya

September	1948	Cadres from Gurkha Rifle Regiments formed in Kluang
December	1948	Unofficial title in use being ROYAL ENGINEERS GURKHA Gurkha Training Squadron Engineer Training Centre formed
1 October	1949	67 Gurkha Field Squadron Royal Engineers (RE) raised at Kluang
1 April	1950	68 Gurkha Field Squadron RE raised at Kluang
13 April	1951	RHQ 50 Field Engineer Regiment RE raised in Hong Kong to command 67 Gurkha Field Squadron RE and 68 Gurkha Field Squadron RE (and also 75 Malay Field Squadron and 76 Malay Field Park Squadron in Kluang)
5 April	1952	RHQ 50 Field Engineer Regiment RE established
14 September	1954	Known unofficially as GURKHA ROYAL ENGINEERS (AO No 102 of 1955)
25 July	1955	Title changed to 50 Field Engineer Regiment RE
28 September	1955	GURKHA ENGINEERS Established as a separate Corps within the Brigade of Gurkhas
1 July	1956	50 Field Engineer Regiment redesignated 50 (Gurkha) Field Engineer Regiment (The Malay Squadrons formed into 51 Field Engineer Regiment)
2 April	1960	70 Field Park Squadron raised at Sungei Besi Reorganised as The Gurkha Engineers comprising: HQ The Gurkha Engineers HQ Squadron 67 Gurkha Field Squadron 68 Gurkha Field Squadron 70 Gurkha Field Park Squadron
20 March	1961	67 Gurkha Field Squadron retitled 67 Gurkha Inependent Field Squadron 68 Gurkha Field Squadron retitled 68 Gurkha Independent Field Squadron
1 April	1961	Cadre of 69 Gurkha Field Squadron raised

THE QUEEN'S GURKHA ENGINEERS (continued)

January	1962	Functions of Gurkha Training Squadron Engineer Training Centre absorbed by HQ Squadron and 70 Park Training Squadron	
April	1962	69 Gurkha Field Squadron formed	
1 April	1966	Reorganised as: HQ and Training Establishment comprising: 70 Park Training Squadron and HQ Squadron 67 Gurkha Independent Field Squadron 68 Gurkha Independent Field Squadron 69 Gurkha Independent Field Squadron	
June	1966	70 Park Training Squadron and HQ Squadron amalgamated as 70 Park Training Squadron.	
1 January	1968	70 Park Training Squadron re-designated 70 Support Training Squadron	
17 August	1968	69 Gurkha Independent Field Squadron Field Squadron disbanded	(FE 363702 SD 3 dated 9 July 1968)
1 April	1970	67 Gurkha Independent Field Squadron retitled 67 Gurkha Field Squadron 68 Gurkha Independent Field Squadron retitled 68 Gurkha Field Squadron	(HK 160 G SD dated 12 May 1970)
8 May	1970	HQ and Training Establishments reorganised and re-designated as follows:	
1 June	1970	70 Training Squadron The Gurkha Engineers in Singapore and	
31 July	1970	Regimental Headquarters The Gurkha Engineers	(FE 32020 SD dated 8 May 1970)
31 July	1971	70 Training Squadron disbanded	(FE 320302 dated 5 April 1971)
31 December	1975 1975	HQ Squadron formed at Sham Shui Po, Hong Kong and A/57/Engrs/6985	(HK 500G SD dated 8 December (ASD 2) dated 14 November 1975)
21 April	1977	QUEEN'S GURKHA ENGINEERS	(SARO No 196 dated 25 April 1977)
2 June	1977	THE QUEEN'S GURKHA ENGINEERS	(ARO No 246 dated 2 June 1977 and DCI (General) 174/1977; & Royal Warrant 27 September 1977)

THE QUEEN'S GURKHA ENGINEERS (continued)

25 May	1978	HQ Squadron re-designated as Support Squadron The Queen's Gurkha Engineers	(LBC 191345Z May 1978 from EinC)
1 March	1981	69 Gurkha Independent Field Squadron The Queen's Gurkha Engineers re-raised in Hong Kong for service in the United Kingdom	(D/DASD/50/1M (ASD 2e) dated 19 December 1980)
6 August	1982	Support Squadron re-designated as 70 Squadron The Queen's Gurkha Engineers	(D/EinC/1/83/1 dated 17 June 1982)
1 April	1993	69 Gurkha Independent Field Squadron, re-designated 69 Gurkha Field Squadron and incorporated into 36 Engineer Regiment at Kitchener Barracks, Chatham	
18 December	1993	70 Squadron The Queen's Gurkha Engineers disbanded in Hong Kong	
31 December	1996	67 Gurkha Independent Field Squadron The Queen's Gurkha Engineers disbanded in Hong Kong.	(HK 11252/2J3 OAD dated 14 December 1996)
April	2003	70 Squadron The Queen's Gurkha Engineers re-raised, fully manned and incorporated into 36 Engineer Regiment	

QUEEN'S GURKHA SIGNALS

Raised in Kuala Lumpur, Malaya

October	1948	Small cadre attached to Malaya District Signal Regiment under establishment X Infantry Brigade Signal Squadron to begin raising Gurkha Signals Training Wing
November	1948	First cadre of Gurkha instructors posted in. Two establishments written: Gurkha Signals Training Wing Independent Brigade Signal Squadron ROYAL SIGNALS GURKHA
1 May	1949	110 Gurkha transferees and recruits posted in. Above establishments approved. Gurkha Signals Training and Holding Wing formed
August	1950	Gurkha Independent Brigade Signal Squadron formed.
Early	1951	Establishments written for: Regimental HQ and HQ 1 Squadron 17 Gurkha Division Signal Regiment 3 Squadron 17 Gurkha Division Signal Regiment 48 Gurkha Independent Brigade Signal Squadron
November	1951	K Troop of 3 Squadron formed and joined 63 Gurkha Infantry Brigade
May	1952	I Troop of 3 Squadron formed and reorganised as a Squadron and joined 26 Gurkha Infantry Brigade 48 Gurkha Independent Brigade Signal Squadron reorganised as J Troop
October	1952	L Troop of 3 Squadron formed and joined 99 Gurkha Infantry Brigade
December	1952	3 Squadron and 26 Gurkha Infantry Brigade Signal Squadron fully established
April	1953	1 Squadron 17 Gurkha Division Signal Regiment formed

QUEEN'S GURKHA SIGNALS (continued)

October 1953 17 Gurkha Division Signal
Regiment fully established with
Regimental HQ
Royal Signals Gurkha
26 Gurkha Infantry Brigade
Signal Squadron
1 Squadron
3 Squadron
Signal Training Squadron

23 September 1954 GURKHA ROYAL SIGNALS

Early 1955 26 Gurkha Infantry Brigade Signal
Squadron redesignated
48 Gurkha Infantry Brigade Signal Squadron

28 September 1955 GURKHA SIGNALS   (AO No 102 of 1955)

GURKHA ROYAL SIGNALS
incorporated into the Brigade
of Gurkhas and titled GURKHA SIGNAL

1957 HQ Squadron 17 Gurkha
Infantry Division
Signal Regiment

1 September 1959 New Establishment introduced:

17 Gurkha Division Signal Regiment
became 17 Gurkha Signal Regiment
48 Gurkha Infantry Brigade Signal
Squadron became 246 Gurkha
Signal Squadron (Airportable)
K Troop became 247 Gurkha
Signal Squadron (Airportable) with
63 Gurkha Infantry Brigad
L Troop became 248 Gurkha Signal Squadron (Airportable)
with 99 Gurkha Infantry Brigade
Signal Training Squadron became
250 Gurkha Signal Squadron
J Troop disbanded

1961 17 Gurkha Signal Regiment ceased
to function as a Divisional Signal Regiment.

Units of Gurkha Signals reorganised as:
The Gurkha Signal Regiment
1 Squadron (Depot)
2 Squadron (formerly 250 Squadron)
3 Squadron (Lines of Communication)
246 (Gurkha) Signal Squadron
247 (Gurkha) Signal Squadron
248 (Gurkha) Signal Squadron.

QUEEN'S GURKHA SIGNALS (continued)

	1962	The Gurkha Signal Regiment redesignated as 17 Gurkha Signal Regiment	
	1967	247 (Gurkha) Signal Squadron disbanded 248 (Gurkha) Signal Squadron reorganised and became 99 Gurkha Infantry Brigade HQ and Signal Squadron 246 (Gurkha) Signal Squadron reorganised and became 48 Gurkha Infantry Brigade HQ and Signal Squadron	
1 February	1970	99 Gurkha Infantry Brigade disbanded in Singapore and Squadron became 248 Gurkha Signal Squadron in Hong Kong	
31 July	1971	17 Gurkha Signal Regiment disbanded in Singapore Gurkha Signals units comprised: HQ Gurkha Signals as part of 248 Gurkha Signal Squadron 248 Gurkha Signal Squadron 48 Gurkha Infantry Brigade HQ and Signal Squadron 526 Gurkha Infantry Battalion Signal Troop 531 Gurkha Infantry Battalion Signal Troop 534 Gurkha Infantry Battalion Signal Troop 541 Gurkha Infantry Battalion Signal Troop 581 Gurkha Infantry Battalion Signal Troop	
1 June	1976	Personnel from disbanded 27 Signal Regiment rebadged Gurkha Signals to form British Forces HQ and Signal Squadron	(Encl 1 to A/083/6638 (ASD 2) dated 25 May 1976)
15 December	1976	48 Gurkha Infantry Brigade HQ and Signal Squadron redesignated as Gurkha Field Force HQ and Signal Squadron	(EJ2 to D/DASD/105/ 109 (ASD 2) dated 21 September 1976)

QUEEN'S GURKHA SIGNALS (continued)

20 April	1977	GURKHA SIGNALS retitled QUEEN'S GURKHA SIGNALS	(Special ARO No 18 dated 25 April 1977; and DCI 174 dated 17 June 1977; and Royal Warrant dated 27 September 1977)
1 June	1977	British Forces HQ and Signal Squadron disbanded 248 Gurkha Signal Squadron re-designated Hong Kong Gurkha Signal Squadron	(ARO No.238 dated 26 May 1977)
16 May	1983	Queen's Gurkha Signals re-structured: Regimental HQ HQ Squadron Gurkha Field Force HQ and Signal Squadron re-designated 246 (Gurkha Field Force) Signal Squadron Hong Kong Gurkha Signal Squadron reorganized to form: 247 Gurkha Signal Squadron 248 Gurkha Signal Squadron	
	1986	246 (Gurkha Field Force) Signal Squadron re-designated 246 Gurkha Signal Squadron	
1 June	1990	250 Gurkha Signal Squadron raised in UK to form part of 30 Signal Regiment	
28 June	1994	246, 247 and 248 Gurkha Signal Squadrons amalgamated to form Hong Kong Gurkha Signal Squadron	
1 October	1994	HQ Squadron disbanded	
31 December	1994	Organised as: Regimental HQ Queen's Gurkha Signals Hong Kong Gurkha Signal Squadron 250 Gurkha Signal Squadron Brunei Signal Troop Nepal Signal Troop 526 Gurkha Infantry Battalion Signal Troop 531 Gurkha Infantry Battalion Signal Troop 581 Gurkha Infantry Battalion Signal Troop	
1 April	1996	Regimental HQ Queen's Gurkha Signals collocated with 30 Signal Regiment	

QUEEN'S GURKHA SIGNALS (continued)

November   1996   581 Gurkha Infantry Battalion Signal Troop
                        disbanded

30 June   1997   Hong Kong Gurkha Signal Squadron disbanded

3 December   2001   246 Gurkha Signal Squadron reformed as part
                        of 2 Signal Regiment

24 September   2004   248 Gurkha Signal Squadron reformed as part
                        of 21 Signal Regiment

_____

THE QUEEN'S OWN GURKHA LOGISTIC REGIMENT

Raised at Nee Soon, Singapore

1 July	1958	GURKHA ARMY SERVICE CORPS	(AO No 67 of 1958)
1 July	1958	Raising Cadres formed at Nee Soon for: 28 Company Gurkha Army Service Corps (Mechanical Transport) 30 Company Gurkha Army Service Corps Infantry Brigade Group)	(GHQ FARELF letter FE/58309 MP 2 (ORG) of 11 July 1958)
1 August	1958	Companies completed at Batu Pahat and Kluang respectively; operational 22 June 1959 and 15 June 1959 respectively	
1 July	1959	Raising Cadres formed at Nee Soon for: 31 Company Gurkha Army Service Corps (Infantry Brigade Group) 34 Company Gurkha Army Service Corps (Mechanical Transport)	(GHQ FARELF letter FE 58309 MP 2 (ORG) of 20 March 1959)
1 July	1960	HQ Gurkha Army Service Corps formed from HQ Royal Army Service Corps HQ 17 Gurkha Division at Kluang	(FE1278/4/61(P) (REGT))
1 August	1960	31 Company Gurkha Army Service Corps completed at Kluang	
1 September	1960	34 Company Gurkha Army Service Corps completed at Batu Pahat	
1 November	1965	THE GURKHA TRANSPORT REGIMENT Companies re-designated as Squadrons	(AO No 66 of 18 November 1965)
1 January	1969	30 Squadron, The Gurkha Transport Regiment disbanded 1968)	(HQ FARELF letter FE 363702 SD3 of 26 July

THE QUEEN'S OWN GURKHA LOGISTIC REGIMENT (Continued)

1 July	1970	34 Training Squadron, The Gurkha Regiment redesignated Gurkha All Arms Mechanical Transport Training Wing The Gurkha Transport Regiment	(HQ FARELF FE/321002 SD of 22 June 1970)
18 July	1971	Gurkha All Arms Mechanical Transport Training Wing The Gurkha Transport Regiment redesignated The Gurkha Mechanical Transport School and formed part of 31 Squadron The Gurkha Transport Squadron	(HQLF letter HK 170 GSD of 21 July 1971)
1 September	1976	29 Squadron Royal Corps of Transport and 415 Maritime Troop, Royal Corps of Transport included in Regimental establishment	
1 January	1978	HQ Squadron formed	
25 November	1990	28 (Ambulance) Squadron The Gurkha Transport Regiment formed Transport Regiment for for service in the Gulf War 1991 on Operation GRANBY	Composite squadron formed from 28 and 31 Squadrons The Gurkha
5 April	1991	28 (Ambulance) Squadron The Gurkha Transport Regiment disbanded	
3 June	1991	34 (United Nations Force in Cyprus (UNIFCYP)) Transport Squadron The Gurkha Transport Regiment formed squadron for a 6 month operational tour as part of the British Contingent UNFICYP	Composite squadron formed from squadrons of The Gurkha Transport Regiment as a roulement
15 February	1992	34 (UNIFCYP) Transport Squadron The Gurkha Transport Regiment disbanded	

30 August	1992	THE QUEEN'S OWN GURKHA TRANSPORT REGIMENT	(Royal Warrant dated 30 September 1992)

5 April 1993 28 and 31 Squadrons The Queen's Own Gurkha Transport Regiment designated 28 and 31 Transport Squadrons The Queen's Own Gurkha Transport Regiment

9 October 1993 The Gurkha Mechanical Transport School disbanded

1 November 1993 Gurkha Troop Army School of Mechanical Transport formed

20 November 1993 28 Transport Squadron The Queen's Own Gurkha Transport Regiment re-deployed to Roman Barracks Colchester under command 10 Transport Regiment The Royal Logistic Corps

31 March 1994 HQ Squadron The Queen's Own Gurkha Transport Regiment disbanded

8 April 1994 Hong Kong Logistic Support Regiment The Royal Logistic Corps formed taking 29 Transport Squadron The Royal Logistic Corps and 31 Transport Squadron The Queen's Own Gurkha Transport Regiment under local command

31 October 1994 31 Transport Squadron The Queen's Own Gurkha Transport Regiment disbanded. The Queen's Own Gurkha Transport Regiment Detachment Hong Kong formed

31 December 1994 Organised as: Regimental HQ The Queen's Own Gurkha Transport Regiment; 28 Transport Squadron (The Queen's Own Gurkha Transport Regiment) 10 Transport Regiment Royal Logistic Corps; and The Queen's Own Gurkha Transport Regiment Detachment Hong Kong Hong Kong Logistic Support Regiment The Royal Logistic Corps

1 January 1997 Hong Kong Logistic Support Regiment The Royal Logistic Corps disbanded and Hong Kong Logistic Support Squadron The Royal Logistic Corps formed

THE QUEEN'S OWN GURKHA LOGISTIC REGIMENT (continued)

30 June	1997	Hong Kong Logistic Support Squadron The Royal Logistic Corps and The Queen's Own Gurkha Transport Regiment Detachment Hong Kong disbanded	
5 April	2001	THE QUEEN'S OWN GURKHA LOGISTIC REGIMENT	(MOD letter D/DPS (A)/104/9 PS12(A) dated 9 October 2000)
5 April	2002	Gurkha chefs re-badged The Queen's Own Gurkha Logistic Regiment	
5 July	2002	94 Stores Squadron The Royal Logistic Corps designated 94 Stores Squadron The Queen's Own Logistic Regiment	
1 July	2005	1 Engineer Support Squadron The Royal Logistic Corps designated 1 Transport Squadron The Queen's Own Gurkha Logistic Regiment	(D/DGS/027313 (LIAB) dated 27 June 2005)
12 May	2006	10 Transport Regiment Royal Logistic Corps re-designated as 10 Transport Regiment The Queen's Own Gurkha Logistic Regiment	(D/DGS/02/3322 (LIAB) dated 3 April 2006)
6 October	2006	36 HQ Squadron The Royal Logistic Corps designated 36 HQ Squadron The Queen's Own Gurkha Logistic Regiment	(DRLC letter dated 27 October 2006)
1 April	2008	94 Stores Squadron The Queen's Own Logistic Regiment re-designated 94 Materiel Squadron The Queen's Own Logistic Regiment	
5 July	2008	10 Transport Regiment The Queen's Own Gurkha Logistic Regiment re-designated 10 The Queen's Own Gurkha Logistic Regiment	(DGS/03/1220/ Liab/GSO dated 24 October 2008)

GURKHA STAFF AND PERSONNEL SUPPORT COMPANY

Formed at Shorncliffe by re-badging Gurkha clerks from The Royal Gurkha Rifles.

30 June	2011	GURKHA STAFF AND PERSONNEL SUPPORT COMPANY	(LF-ORG Plans/4/12/3 dated 11 April 2011)

EASTERN OR RUNGPORE BATTALION (1813-1826)

4 September	1813	EASTERN OR RUNGPORE BATTALION RUNGPORE LOCAL BATTALION	(GOCC of 17 September 1813; GO of 6 May 1823)
3 April	1816	received two companies from GORAKHPORE HILL RANGERSApril 1816) (in exchange for natives of the plains)	(Bengal Military Consultations dated 3
31 March	1823	absorbed the men of the SYLHET SIBANDY CORPS which was dissolved	(GOCC of 17 February 1823)
1 April	1823	DINAGEPORE LOCAL BATTALION when name RUNGPORE was transferred to the CUTTACK LEGION (see 6th GURKHA RIFLES) DINAJPORE BATTALION	(GOCC of 17 February 1823; GOCC of 14 February 1823)
1 December	1826	disbanded	(GGO No 231 dated 29 September 1826)

WESTERN OR BETTIAH CORPS (1813-1826)

4 September	1813	WESTERN OR BETTIAH CORPS	(GOCC of 17 September 1813; GO of 6 May 1823)
January	1814	BETTIAH LOCAL BATTALION	
26 August	1814	CHAMPARUN LIGHT INFANTRY	(AG letter No 115 of 22 August 1814)
1 December	1826	disbanded	(GGO No 231 dated 29 September 1826)

2nd NUSSERI BATTALION (1815-1830)

Raised at Subathu

24 April	1815	2nd NUSSEREE BATTALION	(GGO of 24 April 1815)
31 January	1819	2nd NUSSEREE BATTALION	(Bengal Army List of 31 January 1819)
30 September	1822	2nd NUSSEREE BATTALION September 1822)	(Bengal Army List of 30
6 May	1823	7th, 2nd NUSSERI (GORKA) BATTALION	(GOCC unnumbered of 6 May 1823 covering GOGG No 8 of 2 May 1823)
March	1824	7th, 2nd NUSSERI BATTALION	(Bengal Army List of 31 March 1824)
1 December	1826	5th, 2nd NUSSERI BATTALION	(GGO No 231 of 5 October 1826)
1 February	1830	Reduced. All the soldiers who were natives of Nepal with over 6 years' service were drafted in equal proportions to the 1st NUSSERI and SIRMOOR BATTALIONS, the remainder having the option of transferring to the KEMAOON BATTALION, or taking their discharge. All were allowed to opt for service in Regiments of the line	(GGO No 251 of 4 December 1829)

GORAKHPORE HILL RANGERS (1815-1816)

Raised by the Rajah of Bootwal on the Gorrockpore (sic) frontier

16 April	1815	CORPS OF IRREGULARS designated GORAKHPORE HILL CORPS; later GORAKHPORE HILL RANGERS	(GO of 12 August 1815)
3 April	1816	reduced	(Bengal Military Consultations dated 3 April 1816)

two Companies sent to:
GORAKHPORE PROVINCIAL
BATTALION
one Company sent to:
CHAMPARUN LIGHT INFANTRY
two Companies sent to:
RUNGPORE BATTALION

There was also a unit called

20 January	1818	GHORUCKPORE LOCAL BATTALION	(GO of 6 May 1823)
	later	GHORUCKPORE LIGHT INFANTRY the dates of which are not known	

9th (HILL) COMPANY OF BENGAL PIONEERS (1815 – 1834)

Raised in 1815 to be composed of "Gorkhas and Kumaoonies"

14 July	1815	9th (HILL) COMPANY OF BENGAL PIONEERS	(GO of 14 July 1815)
		7th (HILL) COMPANY OF BENGAL PIONEERS	
February	1834	disbanded	

There was also a unit called 10th (HILL) COMPANY OF BENGAL PIONEERS later renumbered as 8th which also recruited Kumaonis and Gurkhas

---

SYLHET FRONTIER CORPS (1817-1823)

16 May	1817	SYLHET FRONTIER CORPS	(GOCC of 14 August 1817; and GO of 16 May 1823)
	1819	SYLHET SIBANDY CORPS	
31 March	1823	dissolved, being absorbed into RUNGPOOR LOCAL BATTALION	(GOCC of 17 February 1823)

4th REGIMENT OF INFANTRY, SHAH SHOOJA'S FORCE (1838-1841)

June	1838	4th (GOORKHA) REGIMENT OF INFANTRY, SHAH SHOOJA'S CONTINGENT
November	1841	Ceased to exist after the siege and withdrawal from Charikar, Afghanistan. Survivors, approximately 165, were drafted to 4th NUSSEREE and 6th SIRMOOR BATTALIONS

BROADFOOT'S SAPPERS, SHAH SHOOJA'S FORCE (1840-1843)

Raised in India in 1840 and included many Gurkhas and Hillmen

BROADFOOT'S SAPPERS, SHAH SHOOJA'S CONTINGENT

31 January	1843	Disbanded. 200 Gurkhas surviving in this Corps went to the 4th NUSSEREE, 6th SIRMOOR and 7th KEMAOON BATTALIONS. The remainder became 7th and 8th Companies BENGAL SAPPERS AND MINERS in March 1843

DARJEELING SEBUNDY CORPS (1838–1867)

Raised in Darjeeling from the border hills, and later included Gurkhas

21 July	1838	DARJEELING SEBUNDY CORPS (SAPPERS & MINERS) also known as "SIBUNDY SAPPERS"	(GGO No. 99 of 1838; GOPC of 2 July 1838; GOCC of 21 July 1838)
21 March	1867	reduced	

2nd ASSAM SEBUNDY CORPS (1839-1844)

Formed from drafts from the ASSAM LIGHT INFANTRY and the ASSAM SEBUNDY CORPS for civil duties in Upper Assam

August	1839	THE UPPER ASSAM SEBUNDY CORPS	(GOCC No 140 of 1839)
23 October	1839	2ND ASSAM SEBUNDY CORPS	(GOCC No 187 of 23 October 1839)
9 August	1844	Disbanded, men going to 8th, 1st, ASSAM LIGHT INFANTRY BATTALION August 1844)	(GOGG No 234 of 9 August 1844; GOCC of 24

NUSSEREE BATTALION (1850-1861)

Raised at Juttogh, Simla to replace 4th NUSSEREE (RIFLE) BATTALION when it was transferred to the line as 66th, or GOORKHA, REGIMENT OF NATIVE INFANTRY

27 February	1850	NUSSEREE (RIFLE) BATTALION	(GOCC Unnumbered of 27 February)
April	1852	NUSSEREE BATTALION	(Bengal Army List of April 1852)
3 May	1861	Broken up. Men dispersed to other Gurkha regiments	(GGO No 400 of 3 May 1861)

LANDOUR RANGERS (1858–1859)

Raised in 1858 as a Levy of Goorkhas, Sirmoorees and other hillmen. Establishment 5 Companies

8 June	1858	L'ESTRANGE'S GOORKHA LEVY	(GOCC OF 8 June 1858; Punjab Gazette No 6 of 28 September 1858; Punjab GO No 185 of 24 September 1858)
4 March	1859	CORPS OF LANDOUR RANGERS	(GGO No 286 of 4 March 1859)
30 June	1859	disbanded	(GOCC of 3 June 1859; GOCC of 24 August 1859)

7th GURKHA RIFLES (1903-1907)

2 October	1903	43rd GURKHA RIFLES became 7th GURKHA RIFLES	(IAO No 181 of 2 October 1903)
27 September 1907		Became 2nd Battalion 8th GURKHA RIFLES (See 8th GURKHA RIFLES)	(IAO No 483 of 27 September 1907)

8th GURKHA RIFLES (1902-1907)

16 May	1902	8th GURKHA RIFLES	(GOCC No 252 of 12 April 1902 and GO No 293 of 1902)
13 July	1903	Became 2nd Battalion 10th GURKHA RIFLES	(Indian Army Circulars 1903 Clause 20 and GGO No 127 of 13 July 1903)
18 July	1907	Divided into two battalions	(IAO No 342 of 18 July 1907).
27 September 1907		Became 1st and 2nd Battalions 7th GURKHA RIFLES (See 7th DUKE OF EDINBURGH'S OWN GURKHA RIFLES)	(IAO No 483 of 27 September 1907)

18th INDIAN GARRISON COMPANY (1940–1942)

This unit appears in the Annual Class returns for 1940, 1941 and 1942 with a Gurkha strength of 240, 238 and 225 for these three years. This Company was raised in 1939 and became 25th GURKHA RIFLES in late 1942 (see 25th GURKHA RIFLES). It was raised from old and wounded soldiers and from surplus recruits

---

153 (GURKHA) PARACHUTE BATTALION (1941-1947)

Formed at Delhi from volunteers from all Gurkha Regiments, the largest number coming from 2nd KING EDWARD VII'S OWN GURKHA RIFLES (THE SIRMOOR RIFLES)

October	1941	153 (GURKHA) PARACHUTE BATTALION
November	1945	2nd (GURKHA) Battalion, INDIAN PARACHUTE REGIMENT
November	1947	Disbanded

154 (GURKHA) PARACHUTE BATTALION (1943-1946)

May	1942	3rd Battalion, 7th GURKHA RIFLES
4 August	1943	Became 154 (GURKHA) PARACHUTE BATTALION
November	1945	3rd (GURKHA) Battalion, INDIAN PARACHUTE REGIMENT
26 October	1946	3rd Battalion, 7th GURKHA RIFLES
November	1946	Disbanded (See 7th DUKE OF EDINBURGH'S OWN GURKHA RIFLES)

5th/3rd GURKHA RIFLES (1942)

Formed when remnants of 1st Battalion, 3rd QUEEN ALEXANDRA'S OWN GURKHA RIFLES and 2nd Battalion, 5th ROYAL GURKHA RIFLES (FRONTIER FORCE) were amalgamated after severe losses, being respectively only 107 and 227 men strong after the Sittang battles

February	1942	Formed
May	1942	Broken up when original battalions were reconstituted

25th GURKHA RIFLES (1942-1946)

Raised at Jhelum, Punjab

	1939	18th GARRISON COMPANY
Late	1942	Converted to 25th GURKHA RIFLES
9 May	1946	Disbanded

Garrison Companies were formed from October 1939 onwards and by 1 January 1942 the 18th Company shows that there were 225 Gurkhas on strength. Raised from old and wounded soldiers and from surplus recruits for guard duties and as protection troops in Burma forward areas. Became the Garrison battalion to HQ 14th Army in 1944

26th GURKHA RIFLES (1943-1946)

Raised at Kala Base, North Punjab

November   1943   26th GURKHA RIFLES

15 May   1946   Disbanded at Abbottabad

Garrison battalion raised on a special establishment from old and wounded soldiers and from surplus recruits for guard duties and as protection troops in Burma forward area

---

14th GURKHA RIFLES (1943-1946)

Raised at Mohan, near Saharanpur

September   1943   14th GURKHA RIFLES

March   1946   Disbanded

Training Battalion for 1st KING GEORGE V'S OWN GURKHA RIFLES (THE MALAUN REGIMENT) and 4th PRINCE OF WALES'S OWN GURKHA RIFLES

29th GURKHA RIFLES (1943-1946)

Raised at Dehra Dun from Regimental Centres of 2nd and 9th GURKHA RIFLES

August   1943   29th GURKHA RIFLES

31 March   1946   Disbanded

Training Battalion for 2nd KING EDWARD VII'S OWN GURKHA RIFLES (THE SIRMOOR RIFLES) and 9th GURKHA RIFLES

38th GURKHA RIFLES (1943-1946)

Raised at Dehra Dun

15 August   1943   38th GURKHA RIFLES

31 March   1946   Disbanded at Dehra Dun   (Letter 6316/20/39 and Quetta
                                                       Org (c) dated 24 January 1946)

Training Battalion for 3rd QUEEN ALEXANDRA'S OWN GURKHA RIFLES and 8th GURKHA RIFLES

56th GURKHA RIFLES (1943-1946)

Raised at Abbottabad

August   1943   56th GURKHA RIFLES

March   1946   Disbanded

Training Battalion for 5th ROYAL GURKHA RIFLES (FRONTIER FORCE) and 6th GURKHA RIFLES

710th GURKHA RIFLES (1943-1946)

Raised at Alhilal in the Kangra Valley

15 August   1943   710th GURKHA RIFLES

24 January 1946   Disbanded at Palampur   (Letter 6316/20/39/
                                                     and Alhilal Org (c) dated 24 January 1946)

Training Battalion for 7th GURKHA RIFLES and 10th GURKHA RIFLES

BOYS COMPANY (1948-1968)

Formed at Sungei Patani, Kedah, Malaya

1 April   1948   BOYS TRAINING COMPANY
                      THE BRIGADE OF
                      GURKHAS BOYS
                      COMPANY

1 November 1968   Disbanded (HQ FARELF letter FE 363702 SD3 of 25 April 1968)

GURKHA MILITARY POLICE (1949-1970)

Raised in Malaya

1 July	1949	ROYAL MILITARY POLICE (GURKHA REGIMENT) A Gurkha Divisional Provost Company raised	(GHQ FARELF CR/ FARELF/2838/AG1 of 20 June 1949)
1 January	1957	GURKHA MILITARY POLICE Redesignated 17 Gurkha Divisional Provost Company	(FE 13209 MPZ 2 of 18 February 1957)
1 November	1958	A Gurkha Divisional Provost Company formed.	
1 January	1963	HQ and Training Establishment raised	(FE 25002 SD3 of 4 March 1963)
1 January	1965	Title and role changed to 5 (GURKHA) DOG COMPANY, GURKHA MILITARY POLICE	
1 October	1965	Title GURKHA MILITARY POLICE dropped and soldiers reverted to parent regiments. Corps disbanded	(Army Order No 50 of 16 September 1965)
1 January	1970	Company disbanded at Singapore	(FE 321902 SD3 of 18 December 1969)

ROYAL ARMY ORDNANCE CORPS (1950)

In 1950, 99 Gurkha recruits were enlisted but were posted to regiments after training. No establishment was published

---

ROYAL ELECTRICAL AND MECHANICAL ENGINEERS (1950)

In 1950, 48 Gurkha recruits were enlisted but were posted to regiments after training. No establishment was published

---

ARMY CATERING CORPS (1950-1951)

1 April	1950	Gurkha Training and Holding Wing, ARMY CATERING CORPS, raised. 275 recruits were enlisted and after one year's training were posted to regiments	(Estab FE 1016/1/49(S))
	1951	Disbanded	

THE STAFF BAND, THE BRIGADE OF GURKHAS

Raised at Sungei Patani, Kedah, Malaya

	1955	
15 May	1970	Amalgamated in Singapore with the Regimental Band of 2nd KING EDWARD VII'S OWN GURKHA RIFLES (THE SIRMOOR RIFLES), and rebadged as 2nd GURKHA RIFLES to form A MINOR STAFF BAND, THE BRIGADE OF GURKHAS (2nd KING EDWARD'S OWN GURKHA RIFLES REGIMENTAL BAND)
1 July	1994	Rebadged as part of THE ROYAL GURKHA RIFLES, with title BAND OF THE BRIGADE OF GURKHAS

ROYAL ARMY MEDICAL CORPS (1960)

In 1960, the training of Regimental Medical Assistants at the British Military Hospital Kinrara was started with a view to raising a Gurkha element of the ROYAL ARMY MEDICAL CORPS. The soldiers were posted back to their units after training

---

GURKHA INDEPENDENT PARACHUTE COMPANY (1961-1971)

Raised at Majedee Barracks, Johore Bahru in 1961 from a platoon of 1st Battalion, 10th PRINCESS MARY'S OWN GURKHA RIFLES and later from a platoon of 1st Battalion, 7th DUKE OF EDINBURGH'S OWN GURKHA RIFLES, and from 2nd Battalion, 10th PRINCESS MARY'S OWN GURKHA RIFLES

1 January	1963	GURKHA INDEPENDENT PARACHUTE COMPANY formed at Slim Barracks, Singapore under the sponsorship of 1st Battalion, 7th Duke of Edinburgh's Own Gurkha Rifles	
2 December	1971	Disbanded at Kota Tinggi, Johore	(HQLF Hong Kong 167 G SD dated 20 August 1971)

THE ASSAM RIFLES

Formed in 1917 from the Military Police Battalions in Assam and title granted in recognition of the reinforcements sent to the Gurkha battalions during 1914-1917. A total of 23 Gurkha officers and 3174 men volunteered to serve in regular battalions; 5 officers and 237 men were killed; 6 and 247 were wounded; 11 and 69 won honours

1st BATTALION ASSAM RIFLES (LUSHAI HILLS BATTALION)

(1)	1835	CACHAR LEVY raised. Strength 750. Recruited Bengalis
(2)	1838	JORHAT MILITIA raised. Recruited mostly Shans
(1) and (2) pre	1851	CACHAR LEVY and JORHAT MILITIA amalgamated as CACHAR LEVY or POLICE MILITIA
(3)	1850	KUKI LEVY formed. Strength 200 Kukis
(1) and (2)	1852	CACHAR LEVY (including old JORHAT MILITIA) split up, the larger portion becoming FRONTIER POLICE OF NOWGONG (see 3rd Battalion ASSAM RIFLES). The smaller portion became NORTH CACHAR HILLS FRONTIER POLICE
(4)	1860 became	BENGAL ARMED POLICE formed in Chittagong Hill Tracts. Strength 375, mostly Bengalis
	1866 Restyled	FRONTIER POLICE OF BENGAL. Bengalis replaced by Cacharis and Nepalese. Strength 550.
	1866	CHITTAGONG HILL TRACTS MILITARY FRONTIER FORCE; became
1 April	1891	SOUTH LUSHAI HILLS MILITARY POLICE BATTALION. Strength 540. Composition changed from Nepalese, Jaruas, Chakmas and Muslims to Gurkhas and Jaruas only
13 April	1898	Amalgamated with the NORTH LUSHAI HILLS MILITARY POLICE BATTALION when the South Lushai Hills became part of Assam, and renamed LUSHAI HILLS MILITARY POLICE
(1), (2) and (3)	1863 became	NORTH CACHAR HILLS FRONTIER POLICE and KUKI LEVY amalgamated. Strength 650. Designated CACHAR FRONTIER POLICE;
	1873	SURMA VALLEY FRONTIER POLICE. Kukis wasted out, being replaced by Gurkhas and Cacharis
	1883	SURMA VALLEY MILITARY POLICE BATTALION.
	1889	Strength given as 797

1st BATTALION ASSAM RIFLES (LUSHAI HILLS BATTALION) (Continued)

	1891	Major portion of SURMA VALLEY MILITARY POLICE at Aijal became NORTH LUSHAI MILITARY POLICE BATTALION. Composition Gurkhas and Jaruas. Remnant of SURMA VALLEY MILITARY POLICE reduced to 350 at Silchar
	1897	Strength given as 372. Incorporated into
	1903	DACCA MILITARY POLICE when East Bengal was transferred to Assam, less small detachment
	1913	Remnant 4 and 73 incorporated in DARRANG MILITARY POLICE BATTALION (See 4th Battalion ASSAM RIFLES)

---

(1), (2) and (3) 1891 NORTH LUSHAI HILLS MILITARY POLICE BATTALION raised at Aijal from SURMA VALLEY MILITARY POLICE. Strength 1000

(4) 13 April 1898 Amalgamated with SOUTH LUSHAI HILLS MILITARY POLICE BATTALION when South Lushai Hills became part of Assam, to become LUSHAI HILLS MILITARY POLICE BATTALION

---

(5) 1901 LUSHAI HILLS MILITARY POLICE BATTALION reduced in strength to 850

1905 Composition given as mostly Gurkhas with Garos, Rabhas, Meches and Cacharis

1912 Composition had become ¾ Gurkha, ¼ Jarua

1914 Strength given as 800. Raised to 1000. Became

September 1917 1st Battalion ASSAM RIFLES (LUSHAI HILLS BATTALION)

1925 Affiliated to 2nd Gurkha Group – 2nd King Edward's Own Gurkha Rifles (The Sirmoor Rifles) and 9th Gurkha Rifles   (AI (India) No 213 of 1925)

Notes:

1. Proposed in 1905 to amalgamate with LAKHIMPUR MILITARY POLICE BATTALION

2. Sent 8 and 817 reinforcements to Gurkha battalions 1914-1917

THE ASSAM RIFLES (Continued)

2nd BATTALION ASSAM RIFLES (LAKHIMPUR BATTALION)

1864	LAKHIMPUR ARMED POLICE BATTALION raised at Dibrugarh. Strength 500. Composed of Cacharis, Shans, and Nepalese transferred from NOWGONG FRONTIER POLICE (see 3rd Battalion ASSAM RIFLES) and Civil Police. Became
1873	LAKHIMPUR FRONTIER POLICE BATTALION. Became
1883	LAKHIMPUR MILITARY POLICE BATTALION. Received drafts from the GARO HILLS FRONTIER POLICE and NOWGONG FRONTIER POLICE (see 3rd Battalion ASSAM RIFLES). Strength 700 (retained title of FRONTIER POLICE in common use until 1888)
1889	Strength given as 819
1897	Strength given as 849
1905	Composition given as 78% Gurkha, the remainder being Garos, Rabhas, Meches and Kacharis. Strength 847
1910	Strength reduced to 673
1911	Strength raised to 850. Composed of 5 companies Gurkhas, 3 companies Jaruas
1912	Composition had become ¾ Gurkhas, ¼ Jaruas
1914	Strength given as 800. Raised to 1000. Became
September 1917	2nd Battalion ASSAM RIFLES (LAKHIMPUR BATTALION)
1925	Affiliated to 5th Gurkha Group - 7th Gurkha Rifles and 10th Gurkha Rifles (AI (India) No 213 of 1925)

Note: 1.   Sent 7 and 988 reinforcements to Gurkha battalions 1914-1917

3rd BATTALION ASSAM RIFLES (NAGA HILLS BATTALION)

(1)	1835	CACHAR LEVY raised. Strength 750. Recruited Bengalis

---

(2)	1838	JORHAT MILITIA raised. Recruited mostly Shans

---

(1) and (2) pre 1851   CACHAR LEVY and JORHAT MILITIA amalgamated as CACHAR LEVY or POLICE MILITIA

3rd BATTALION ASSAM RIFLES (NAGA HILLS BATTALION) (continued)

1852 CACHAR LEVY split up, the smaller portion becoming NORTH CACHAR HILLS FRONTIER POLICE (see 1st Battalion ASSAM RIFLES). The larger portion became NOWGONG FRONTIER POLICE. Became

1868 NAGA HILLS FRONTIER POLICE

1879 Detachment of 50 from GARO HILLS MILITARY POLICE transferred. Became

1883 NAGA HILLS MILITARY POLICE BATTALION

1889 Strength given as 671

1892 Composition given as 3 companies Gurkhas, 2 companies Jaruas, 1 company Dogras and Garhwalis

1897 Strength given as 672

1905 Strength given as 671

1906 Composition given as 4 companies Gurkhas, 3 companies Jaruas

1910 Strength given as 704

1912 Last Dogras served in 1912. Composition had become ¾ Gurkhas, ¼ Jaruas. Became

September 1917 3rd Battalion ASSAM RIFLES (NAGA HILLS BATTALION)

1925 Affiliated to 1st Gurkha Group - 1st King George's Own Gurkha Rifles (The Malaun Regiment) and 4th Prince of Wales's Own Gurkha Rifles (AI (India) No 213 of 1925)

Note: Sent 3 and 720 reinforcements to Gurkha battalions 1914-1917

THE ASSAM RIFLES (Continued)

4th BATTALION ASSAM RIFLES

(1)   1879   Armed Civil Police formed in Garo Hills. Strength 300. Composed chiefly of Nepalese and Cacharis. Became

     1883   GARO HILLS MILITARY POLICE BATTALION. Sikhs, Punjabis, Dogras and Muslims enlisted

     1889   Strength given as 243

     1897   Strength given as 202

     1903   Draft sent to DACCA MILITARY POLICE BATTALION when Assam took over East Bengal, which latter battalion had a strength of 784 in 1910

     1912   Composition had become ¾ Gurkhas, ¼ Jaruas

early   1913   Remaining 4 and 130 men transferred to the new battalion (see (3) below)

---

(2)   1905   Detachment of LAKHIMPUR MILITARY POLICE BATTALION stationed in Darrang at Dibrugarh

---

(3)   early   1913   Formed nucleus of NEW BATTALION.
Drafts coming from
LAKHIMPUR MILITARY POLICE - 95
LUSHAI HILLS MILITARY POLICE - 31
NAGA HILLS MILITARY POLICE - 60
to which were added last remnants of
SURMA VALLEY MILITARY POLICE - 4 and 73
GARO HILLS MILITARY POLICE - 4 and 130
Became

August   1913   DARRANG MILITARY POLICE BATTALION

     1915   Moved to Manipur State. Title of DARRANG dropped. Became

September   1917   4th Battalion ASSAM RIFLES.
Enlisted Gurkhas and Jaruas
Some Kukis enlisted after 1917

     1925   Affiliated to 4th Gurkha Group -   (AI (India) No 213
5th Royal Gurkha Rifles   of 1925)
(Frontier Force) and 6th Gurkha Rifles

Note: Sent 5 and 149 reinforcements to
Gurkha battalions 1914 -1917

THE ASSAM RIFLES (Continued)

5th BATTALION ASSAM RIFLES

Raised at Lokra, Tezpur District for duty on the Darrang and Kamrup Borders

10 June	1920	5th Battalion ASSAM RIFLES. Draft of 4 and 82 from 3rd Battalion and 1 and 40 from 4th Battalion. Remainder enlisted directly to make up strength of 12 and 498	
	1925	Affiliated to 3rd Gurkha Group - 3rd Queen Alexandra's Own Gurkha Rifles and 8th Gurkha Rifles	(AI (India) No 213 of 1925)
April	1932	Disbanded (as part of an economy drive; its personnel were transferred to 2nd Battalion to form a composite unit of 2 HQ platoons and 18 Service platoons)	
1 April	1942	Re-raised to act as a Training Battalion for the ASSAM RIFLES	

BATTALIONS RAISED SINCE 1947

6th Battalion Formed at Tripura in 1950 from TRIPURA RIFLES, Shillong, Mizoram

7th Battalion Raised at Jairampur North East Frontier Agency (NEFA) on 1 October 1952

8th Battalion Trensang, Nagaland

9th Battalion Kimmui, NEFA

10th Battalion	Mokokchung, Nagaland
11th Battalion	NEFA
12th Battalion	Nagaland
13th Battalion	Nagaland
14th Battalion	Nagaland
15th Battalion	Nagaland
16th Battalion	Nagaland

THE ASSAM RIFLES (Continued)

17th Battalion	Sikkim
18th Battalion	Lungleh, Mizoram
19th Battalion	Mizoram
20th Battalion	Manipur
21st Battalion	Manipur-Naga Border

BURMA MILITARY POLICE, BURMA FRONTIER FORCE AND THE BURMA REGIMENT (1886-1948)

In March 1886, two levies were raised in NORTH BURMA, each at a strength of 561 men. They recruited Punjabis, Hindustanis and Gurkhas. In 1886-1887 many more military police were raised for service in the frontier and tribal areas, and as Armed Police in settled districts. The units came to be known as THE BURMA MILITARY POLICE. The following battalions were found between 1886-1937 at various times:

October	1886 - January 1887	BURMA POLICE LEVY, CHINDWIN	
October	1886 - January 1887	BURMA POLICE LEVY, MANDALAY	
April	1887 - October 1889	KYAUKSE BATTALION	
April	1887 - 1892	PYINMANA BATTALION	
April	1887 - 1891	MYINGYAN BATTALION	
April	1887 - 1891	MINBU BATTALION	
April	1887 - 1891	SAGAIN BATTALION	
April	1887 - 1892 and 1901 - 1921)	SHWEBO BATTALION	(Shwebo)
April	1887 - April 1942	MANDALAY BATTALION	
April	1887 - July 1888	PAGAN BATTALION	
April	1887 - January 1889	TAUNGDWINGYI BATTALION	
April	1887 - January 1889) and 1901 - 1924)	CHINDWIN BATTALION	(Monwya)
April	1887 - 1893	YEU BATTALION	
July	1887 - 1897	KATHA BATTALION	
July	1887 - 1896	YAMETHIN BATTALION	
July	1887 - July 1888	RAILWAY POLICE LEVY, later BATTALION	
October	1887 - 1890	MEIKTILA BATTALION	
October	1887 - July 1889	MYADAUNG BATTALION	
October	1887 - April 1888	AVA BATTALION	
May	1887 - May 1890	KUBO VALLEY BATTALION (see 10th PRINCESS MARY'S OWN GURKHA RIFLES)	
January	1888 - 1914	RUBY MINES BATTALION	(Mogok)
April	1888 - April 1889	ALON BATTALION	
October	1888 - July 1889) and 1893 - April 1942)	BHAMO BATTALION	(Bhamo)
October	1888 - 1894	PAKKOKU BATTALION	
April	1889 - 1914	MAGWE BATTALION	(Thayetmyo, Pakkoku)
April	1889 - 1890	CHIN FRONTIER LEVY, later BATTALION	
April	1889 - July 1889	MOUNGWA BATTALION	
April	1889 - July 1889	KALEWA BATTALION	
July	1889 1898	MOGAUNG LEVY, later BATTALION	(Bhamo)
July	1889 - 1890	SHAN STATES LEVY	
July	1889 - 1900	UPPER CHINDWIN BATTALION	
July	1889 - 1900	LOWER CHINDWIN BATTALION	
July	1889 - 1890	KINDAI BATTALION	
	1890 -	MONWYA BATTALION	
	1891 - 1892	UPPER BURMA RESERVE BATTALION	
	1893 - 1894	TOUNGOO-KAREN BATTALION	(Toungoo)
	1895 - 1900	KAREN BATTALION	(Toungoo)
	1894 - April 1926	MYITKINA BATTALION	(Myitkyina)

BURMA MILITARY POLICE, BURMA FRONTIER FORCE
AND THE BURMA REGIMENT (1886-1948) (Continued)

1894 -1899	LASHIO BATTALION	(Lashio)
1892 - April 1942	RESERVE BATTALION	(Pyawbwe)
1895 - 1897	NORTH CHIN HILLS BATTALION	
1893 - April 1942	RANGOON BATTALION	(Rangoon)
	(later 1st and 2nd)	
1894 - 1897	SOUTHERN DIVISION BATTALION	
1895 - 1897	EASTERN DIVISION BATTALION	(Yamethin)
1897 - April 1942	CHIN HILLS BATTALION	(Falam, Tiddim)
1898 - April 1942	NORTHERN SHAN STATES BATTALION	(Lashio)
1900 - 1925	TOUNGOO BATTALION	(Toungoo)
1904 - 1940	SOUTHERN SHAN STATES BATTALION	
		(Taunggyi)
1914 - 1924	PUTAO BATTALION	(Putao, Fort Hertz)
1922 - 1925	NORTH WEST BORDER	(Monwya, Shwebo)
	BATTALION	
1926 - 1937	EASTERN BATTALION	(Myitkina)
1926 - 1937	WESTERN BATTALION	(Myitkina)
1937	On the Separation of Burma from India	
	THE BURMA MILITARY POLICE was	
	split into:	
	THE BURMA FRONTIER FORCE	
	consisting of	
	SOUTHERN SHAN STATES BATTALION	(Taunggyi)
	NORTHERN SHAN STATES BATTALION	(Lashio)
	MYITKYINA BATTALION	(Myitkyina)
	BHAMO BATTALION	(Bhamo)
	CHIN HILLS BATTALION	(Falam)
	RESERVE BATTALION	(Pyawabwe)
October 1940	KOKINE BATTALION	(Rangoon)
	who policed the frontier and tribal areas	
	under Army Officers seconded, and	
	THE BURMA MILITARY POLICE	
	consisting of	
	1st RANGOON BATTALION	
	2nd RANGOON BATTALION	
	MANDALAY BATTALION	
	who acted as Armed Police in the settled	
	districts	

BURMA MILITARY POLICE, BURMA FRONTIER FORCE
AND THE BURMA REGIMENT (1886-1948) (Continued)

December 1941- April 1942
During the Burma campaign the following units
of THE BURMA FRONTIER FORCE and THE
BURMA MILITARY POLICE FORCE were
found in the Order of Battle of the British Forces:

THE BURMA FRONTIER FORCE
BHAMO BATTALION
MYITKYINA BATTALION
CHIN HILLS BATTALION
NORTHERN SHAN STATES BATTALION
KOKINE BATTALION
RESERVE BATTALION
Independent Columns, F 1, 2, 3, 4, 5 and 6 MOUNTED INFANTRY DETACHMENT
and
THE BURMA MILITARY POLICE
consisting of
RANGOON BATTALION

April 1942 In this month the Armed Forces of Burma, including THE BURMA FRONTIER FORCE and the BURMA MILITARY POLICE, disintegrated as all men who wished to leave were allowed to do so. The bulk of the men of non-Burmese races, mainly Sikhs, Punjabi Mussalmans and Gurkhas continued the retreat into India and it was decided to reform them into:

30 September1942 THE BURMA REGIMENT
Initially battalions were supposed to be as follows, although it is doubtful whether these were al
formed:
1st Battalion - Sikhs and
Punjabi Mussalmans
       2nd Battalion) All Sikhs,
       3rd Battalion) Punjabi
       4th Battalion) Mussalmans and
       5th Battalion) Gurkhas. 4th
       6th Battalion) Battalion having 50% Gurkhas.

Early 1943 Only two battalions remained
       1st Battalion Sikhs and Punjabi Mussalmans only
       4th Battalion All Gurkhas
               remaining men including many
               Gurkhas were transferred to the
               BURMA INTELLIGENCE
               CORPS and used on attachment to other forces

1948 Regiment passed to new
Burma Army on independence

THE BURMA RIFLES (1915-1942)

Formed from the battalions of the 70th BURMA RIFLES, and from 85th BURMAN RIFLES as 20th BURMA RIFLES. The original battalions were composed of Chins, Kachins and Karens only, with some Gurkhas. Later battalions, up to the 6th, included Burmese

1ST BATTALION

10 November 1915		Two Companies, the BURMA PIONEERS	
19 September 1917		70th BURMA RIFLES	(Army Department letter No 14891 dated 4 October 1917)
22 December	1917	1st Battalion, 70th BURMA RIFLES	
	1922	1st Battalion, 20th BURMA RIFLES	
April	1937	1st Battalion, THE BURMA RIFLES	

2ND BATTALION

22 December	1917	2nd Battalion, 70th BURMA RIFLES	
	1922	2nd Battalion, 20th BURMA RIFLES	
April	1937	2nd Battalion, THE BURMA RIFLES	

3RD BATTALION

June	1917	BURMA POLICE Battalion became 85th BURMAN INFANTRY	(Army Department letter No 13901 dated 15 September 1917)
	1918	85th BURMAN RIFLES	
	1918	CHIN-KACHIN Battalion, composed of one Chin and three Kachin companies. The battalion was split in 1922 to form:	
14 February	1922	3rd Battalion, 70th KACHIN RIFLES)	(GO 117 dated February 1922)
14 February	1922	4th Battalion, 70th CHIN RIFLES)	
	1923	3rd Battalion, 20th BURMA RIFLES (KACHIN)	
April	1937	3rd Battalion, THE BURMA RIFLES	

THE BURMA RIFLES (1915-1942) (Continued)

4TH BATTALION

14 February	1922	Formed from CHIN-KACHIN Battalion, (see 3rd Battalion) as 4th Battalion, 70th CHIN RIFLES	(GO 117 dated 17 February 1922)
	1923	4th Battalion, 20th BURMA RIFLES (CHIN)	
	?	Disbanded	

4TH BATTALION

	1918	5th Battalion, 70th BURMA RIFLES
	1922	10th Battalion, 20th BURMA RIFLES
April	1937	4th Battalion, THE BURMA RIFLES

5TH BATTALION

1 April	1940	5th Battalion, THE BURMA RIFLES

6TH BATTALION

15 February	1940	6th Battalion, THE BURMA RIFLES

7TH BATTALION

1 November	1940	7th (Burma Police) Battalion, THE BURMA RIFLES raised at Mandalay from a nucleus of men of the BURMA POLICE and the BURMA MILITARY POLICE. Class composition was Burmans, Karens, Kumaonis and Gurkhas

8TH BATTALION

1 October	1940	8th (Frontier Force) Battalion, THE BURMA RIFLES composed of Sikhs and Punjabi Mussalmans serving with the BURMA FRONTIER FORCE

9TH BATTALION

24 July	1941	9th (Reserve) Battalion, THE BURMA RIFLES

10TH BATTALION

1 July	1941	10th (Training) Battalion, THE BURMA RIFLES

11TH BATTALION

	1922	11th (Territorial) Battalion, 20th BURMA RIFLES
April	1937	11th Battalion, THE BURMA RIFLES

THE BURMA RIFLES (1915-1942) (Continued)

12TH BATTALION
1 October   1939   12th (Lower Burma) Battalion,
                     THE BURMA RIFLES

13TH BATTALION
1 December 1939   13th (Shan States) Battalion,
                     THE BURMA RIFLES

14TH BATTALION
15 May   1941   14th (Shan States) Battalion,
                     THE BURMA RIFLES
April   1942   THE BURMA RIFLES disintegrated at the
                     conclusion of the first Burma Campaign.
                     Men returning to India were taken into
                     THE BURMA REGIMENT
                     THE BURMA INTELLIGENCE CORPS
                     The majority of the Gurkhas ended up in
                     the 4th Battalion THE BURMA REGIMENT

———————————————

JAMMU AND KASHMIR UNITS

2nd JAMMU AND KASHMIR RIFLES

25 April	1869	Raised at Jammu as THE BODYGUARD REGIMENT containing some Gurkhas	
1 January	1890	Became Imperial Service Troops. Reorganised on a 7 company basis. Gurkha content increased. Became 2nd KASHMIR RIFLES	
From	1912-1921	Composition 1 company Hindu Dogras, 4 companies Gurkhas, 3 companies Muslim Dogras	
January	1912	2nd KASHMIR RIFLES (THE BODYGUARD REGIMENT)	(Indian States Forces Army List January 1912)
January	1918	1st Battalion and 2nd Battalion shown.	
July	1921	Reduced to one battalion. Reorganised on 4 company basis. Composition 2 companies Gurkhas, 2 companies Muslim Dogras	
April	1923	Reorganised as Indian States Forces on Indian Army Establishment	
January	1924	2nd KASHMIR BODYGUARD RIFLE BATTALION	(Indian State Forces Army List January 1924)
January	1930	2nd JAMMU AND KASHMIR RIFLES	(Indian State Forces Army List January 1930)
March	1932	Reorganised on Indian Army Establishment	
January	1936	2nd JAMMU AND KASHMIR RIFLES (THE BODYGUARD REGIMENT)	(Indian States Forces Army List January 1936)
July	1940	2nd JAMMU AND KASHMIR RIFLES	(Indian States Forces Army List July 1940)
January	1948	Composition changed to half Gurkhas and half Hindu Dogras	

JAMMU AND KASHMIR UNITS (Continued)

Circa	1957	Integrated into the Indian Army, as 2nd (RIFLE) BATTALION JAMMU AND KASHMIR REGIMENT	
February	1963	2nd JAMMU AND KASHMIR RIFLES	

3rd JAMMU AND KASHMIR RIFLES

15 April	1856	Raised at Jammu as RAGHUNATH BATTALION, containing some Gurkhas	
1 January	1890	Became Imperial Service Troops	
	1896	3rd KASHMIR RIFLES. Gurkha content increased	
By January	1912	Composition 4 companies Hindu Dogras, 4 companies Gurkhas	
January	1917	3rd KASHMIR RIFLES (RAGHUNATH REGIMENT)	(Indian States Forces Army List January 1917)
July	1921	Reorganised on 4 company basis. Composition 2 companies Gurkhas, 2 companies Hindu Dogras	
January	1924	3rd KASHMIR RAGHUNATH BATTALION	(Indian States Forces Army List January 1924
January	1925	3rd KASHMIR RAGHUNATH RIFLE BATTALION	(Indian States Forces Army List January 1925)
January	1930	3rd JAMMU AND KASHMIR RIFLES	(Indian States Forces Army List January 1930)
March	1932	Reorganised on Indian Army Establishment	
January	1936	3rd JAMMU AND KASHMIR RIFLES (RAGHUNATH REGIMENT)	(Indian States Forces Army List January 1936)
July	1940	3rd JAMMU AND KASHMIR RIFLES	(Indian States Forces Army List July 1940)

JAMMU AND KASHMIR UNITS (Continued)

January	1957	Integrated into the Indian Army, as 3rd (RIFLE) BATTALION, JAMMU AND KASHMIR REGIMENT
February	1960	3rd JAMMU AND KASHMIR RIFLES

4th JAMMU AND KASHMIR RIFLES

	1837	Raised in Jammu as No 8 FATEH SHIBJI REGIMENT. Became No 7 KASHMIR INFANTRY (FATEH SHIBJI)
	1890	Became Imperial Service Troops, having 2 companies each of Dogras, Jammu Muslims and Gurkhas
by	1921	Became a Reserve Battalion composed of half Hindu Dogras and half Mohammedan Dogras, on amalgamation with No 9 KASHMIR INFANTRY RUDDHBAR SHIB NATH (Raised 1858)

5th JAMMU AND KASHMIR RIFLES

	1849	Raised in Jammu, from descendants of the original Gurkha invaders of the Dogra areas of Jammu and Kashmir at the end of the 18th century, as No 3 KASHMIR RIFLES (SURAJ GOORKHA BATTALION). Composed mainly of Gurkhas
	1890	Became an all Dogra unit
March	1921	Reorganised as first line Reserve Troops on an 8 company basis and became 6th KASHMIR RESERVE RIFLE BATTALION (THE SURAJ GURKHA RIFLES REGIMENT)
March	1923	Reorganised as Indian States Forces on Indian Army Establishment. Reduced to 4 companies. Composition 2 companies Hindu Dogras, 2 companies Muslim Dogras

JAMMU AND KASHMIR UNITS (Continued)

January	1924	5th KASHMIR (LIGHT) INFANTRY BATTALION	(Indian States Forces Army List January 1924)
January	1925	Became an all Hindu Dogra unit	
January	1930	5th JAMMU AND KASHMIR LIGHT INFANTRY BATTALION	(Indian States Forces Army List January 1930)
March	1932	Reorganised on Indian Army Establishment	
January	1936	5th JAMMU AND KASHMIR LIGHT INFANTRY BATTALION (THE SURAJ GURKHA RIFLE REGIMENT)	(Indian States Forces Army List January 1936)
July	1940	5th JAMMU AND KASHMIR LIGHT INFANTRY BATTALION	(Indian States Forces Army List January 1940)
January	1946	5th JAMMU AND KASHMIR LIGHT INFANTRY	(Indian States Army Army List January 1946)
	1951	Disbanded	
September	1961	Re-raised with 1 company Gurkhas, remainder being Hindu Dogras as 5th BATTALION, JAMMU AND KASHMIR REGIMENT	
February	1963	5th JAMMU AND KASHMIR RIFLES	

7th JAMMU AND KASHMIR RIFLES

9 March	1932	Raised at Jammu and organised on Indian Army Establishment	
	1945	Disbanded	
May	1947	Re-raised with 2 companies of Gurkhas and 1 company of Kangra Rajputs	
January	1957	Integrated into Indian Army, as 7th BATTALION, JAMMU AND KASHMIR REGIMENT	
February	1963	7th JAMMU AND KASHMIR RIFLES	

JAMMU AND KASHMIR UNITS (Continued)

JAMMU AND KASHMIR TRAINING BATTALION

1939   Contained a proportion of all
classes including Gurkhas

11th GORKHA RIFLES

Raised at Palampur as a new regiment from the 3,398 officers and men of 7th GURKHA RIFLES and 10th GURKHA RIFLES who opted for service in India.

18 December 1947	INDIAN GURKHA DETACHMENT, redesignated as
1 January 1948	11th GURKHA RIFLES REGIMENTAL CENTRE
1 January 1948	11th GURKHA RIFLES
10 February 1949	11th GORKHA RIFLES

1 September 1960	1st Battalion	Raised at Clement Town
11 January 1963	2nd Battalion	Raised at Clement Town
1 January 1948	3rd Battalion	Raised at Santa Cruz, Bombay
1 January 1948	4th Battalion Re-raised	Raised at Palampur. Disbanded 31 January 1951.
8 May 1952	5th Battalion	Raised at Palampur
2 October 1962	6th Battalion	Raised at Clement Town
1 January 1965	7th Battalion	Raised at Clement Town
1 October 1960	107th Battalion (Territorial Army)	Raised at Darjeeling Kataphar West Bengal

11th Gorkha Rifles Regimental Centre locations and dates

25 December	1952 Clement Town
16 May	1968 Ghanghora
31 January	1976 Jalapahar
6 July	1983 Lucknow

THE GURKHA MUSEUM PUBLICATIONS

Publications issued so far:

Number	Title
1.	The Story of Gurkha VCs. ISBN 978-1-908487-33-9 November 2012. 96 pages + cover
2.	The Lineages and Composition of Gurkha Regiments in British Service. ISBN 978-1-908487-41-4 March 1978, Revised editions May 1982,. September 1984, May 1997, March 2010. Third edition February 2013
3.	Campaign and Service Medals Awarded to Gurkha Regiments in British Service. March 1978. Revised editions July 1985, February 1987, April 1987, September 1991 and November 1996. 19 pages + Cover
4.	Bibliography of Gurkha Regiments and Related Subjects. April 1980. Revised editions, April 1982, July 1985 and April 1987. Second edition May 1994. Third edition January 2006. 136 Pages + Cover
5.	Recipes From the Brigade of Gurkhas. October 1991. Revised edition March 1994. Reset and reprinted August 1998. 38 Pages + Cover
6.	Insignia of The 1st King George V's Own Gurkha Rifles (The Malaun Regiment). January 1987, Revised editions August 1988, August 1989, June 1996, May 2000 and May 2002. 53 Pages + Cover
7.	Insignia of The 8th Gurkha Rifles. November 1996. Revised editions February 1998, May 2000 and May 2002. 57 Pages + Cover
8.	Insignia of The 6th Queen Elizabeth's Own Gurkha Rifles. December 1997. Revised editions May 2000 and May 2002. 66 Pages + Cover
9.	Insignia of The 2nd King Edward VII's Own Gurkha Rifles (The Sirmoor Rifles). July 1998. Revised editions January 1999 and August 2007. 99 Pages + Cover
10.	Insignia of The 7th Duke of Edinburgh's Own Gurkha Rifles. March 2000. Revised edition May 2002. 90 Pages + Cover
11.	Insignia of The 9th Gurkha Rifles. August 2000. Revised editions February 2001 and May 2002. 46 Pages + Cover
12.	Insignia of The 10th Princess Mary's Own Gurkha Rifles. March 2006. 100 pages + Cover
13.	Insignia of The 3rd Queen Alexandra's Own Gurkha Rifles. August 2002. Revised edition August 2007. 62 Pages + Cover
14.	Insignia of The 4th Prince of Wales's Own Gurkha Rifles. January 2006. 61 Pages + Cover
15.	Insignia of The 5th Royal Gurkha Rifles (Frontier Force). March 2006. 56 Pages + Cover
16.	Insignia of Gurkha Units in the British Army raised after 1947 being written.
17.	Insignia of Gurkha Units in India and Burma (Para-Military, Military Police, Frontier Force and War-raised units) up to 1948. March 2006. 75 Pages + Cover
18.	The Story of Gurkha Hill Racing. 2009. 5 Pages + Cover
19.	The Scottish Connection and Gurkha Pipe Bands. 2010. 23 Pages + Cover
20.	Battle Honours Awarded to Gurkha Regiments and Related Subjects March 1978. Revised editions July 1985, February 1987 and November 1996. 42 Pages + Cover
21.	Order of Battle of Gurkha Units 1940 – 1946 Showing the Formations and Theatres of War in Which They Served. June 1991. 23 Pages + cover
22.	The Gurkha Brigade in The Great War 1914 – 1920. A Brief Record of The Service of Each Unit and of The Formations and Theatres of War in Which They Served. July 1991. 19 Pages + Cover
23.	Gurkhas at Gallipoli May – December 1915. May 1992. 19 Pages + Cover

24.	Gurkha Battalions in Italy 1943 – 1945.
	32 Pages + Cover
25.	The Gurkhas in World War 2 - 4th Indian Division in North Africa 1942 – 43.
	5 Pages + Cover
26.	The 4th Indian Divisional Signals at Cassino 14 February – 27 March 1944.
	2009. 34 Pages + Cover
27.	The Gurkhas in World War 2 - Chindits.
	2009. 10 pages + Cover
28.	Gurkhas in the Burma Campaign 1941 – 1946. 1994.
	16 Pages + Cover
29.	The Gurkha Parachutist.
	2009. 15 Pages + Cover
30.	The Second Afghan War 1878-80. The Third Afghan War 1919.
	2009. 18 Pages + Cover
31.	The North West Frontier 1919 – 1947 – Two Frontier Actions.
	2009. 14 Pages + Cover
32.	Images of Delhi 1857.
	2007. 44 Pages + Cover
33.	Gurkhas in the Indian Mutiny 1857 – 1859.
	2007. 23 pages + cover
34.	The Royal Flying Corps and Royal Air Force in the North West Frontier 1915 – 1941.
	27 Pages + Cover
35.	North West Frontier, The Pathan Origins.
	10 Pages + Cover
36.	11th Gurkha Rifles 1918 – 1922.
	17 Pages + Cover

Available from

The Gurkha Museum
Peninsula Barracks
Romsey Road
Winchester SO23 8TS
England

ND - #0137 - 270225 - C0 - 297/210/10 - PB - 9781908487414 - Gloss Lamination